Volumes in this series:

Volume One: Genesis – Esther
Volume Two: Job – Song of Solomon
Volume Three: Isaiah – Malachi
Volume Four: Matthew – John
Volume Five: Acts – Galatians
Volume Six: Ephesians – Revelation

Wings Like Eagles

Reflections on Life in the Lord

Volume Two: Job – Song of Solomon

David King

Forward by Rickie Jenkins

© 2022 Spiritbuilding Publishers.

All rights reserved. Permission is hereby granted to use individual articles from this book in church bulletins, with the following attribution: "By David King, Wings Like Eagles, Vol. 2. Used by Permission."

Published by
Spiritbuilding Publishers
9700 Ferry Road, Waynesville, OH 45068
(800) 282-4901

WINGS LIKE EAGLES: Reflections on Life in the Lord (Volume 2)
by David King
ISBN 978-1-955285-53-7

Printed in the United States

Cover design by Adam Moore
Cover photo by Sesha Reddy Kovvuri on Unsplash
Author portrait by Joanna Roseborough

All scripture quotations, unless otherwise noted, are taken from the New King James Version. Copyright 1982 by Thomas Nelson, Inc. Used by Permission. All rights reserved.

Spiritbuilding
PUBLISHERS

spiritbuilding.com

He gives power to the weak,
And to those who have no might
He increases strength.
Even the youths shall faint and be weary,
And the young men shall utterly fall,
But those who wait on the LORD
Shall renew their strength;
They shall mount up with wings like eagles,
They shall run and not be weary,
They shall walk and not faint.

— *Isaiah 40:29-31*

Other Bible translations referenced in this volume:

Beck	*The Holy Bible: An American Translation* (William Beck)
CEV	Contemporary English Version (American Bible Society)
ESV	English Standard Version (Crossway)
GNT	*Good News Translation* (American Bible Society)
Message	*The Message* (Eugene Peterson)
Moffatt	*The Bible: A New Translation* (James Moffatt)
NASB	New American Standard Bible (Lockman Foundation)
NCV	New Century Version (Thomas Nelson Bibles)
NIV	New International Version (New York International Bible Society)
RSV	Revised Standard Version (National Council of Churches of Christ in the USA)
TCB	*The Complete Bible: An American Translation* (J. M. Powis Smith & Edgar J. Goodspeed)

*To my parents,
Elmo and Letha King,
whose gentle wisdom in the early
years was so crucial in shaping
my own view of the world.*

Contents

Forward *by Rickie Jenkins*	xi
Preface	xiii
Introduction	xv
Job	1
Psalms	29
Proverbs	213
Ecclesiastes	367
Song of Solomon	399
Scripture Index	401
Subject Index	411

Forward

I first met David King around 1975. I was a student at East Texas State University in Commerce, Texas, and he was preaching for a small congregation in nearby Wolfe City. I had begun to entertain the idea of preaching and was invited to speak at the church in Wolfe City. I don't remember a lot about that visit, but I do remember meeting David. My dad, Jesse Jenkins, had met David and was impressed with him. Dad is not easily impressed, so I thought David must be a talented Bible student.

David later left Wolfe City and I graduated from school with a degree in Vocational Agriculture Education. We each went our own way—David to his preaching, and me initially to teaching high school agriculture, then into preaching. For years we never spoke. Then I was invited to preach at Pleasant Valley in Wichita, Kansas, where David was an elder and preacher. In the first of my two opportunities to preach in meetings for that congregation, David was involved in secular work. On my second trip, David had returned to full-time gospel preaching. On each occasion, he and Melissa were so warm and welcoming. More than that, I enjoyed the opportunity to talk to David about the Lord's work and the Bible. I always thought David had a deeper bucket than I did; he had a mind that was able to think on a deeper level.

I knew somewhat of David's ability to write. I had seen a small sample of his work and was impressed. When David sent his first volume in this series (Genesis–Esther) to me, my appreciation for his writing was affirmed. His ability to take the Old Testament and make it come alive is so helpful. I was honored to write a recommendation for that work.

Now, it is a deep honor to recommend David's second volume. As we read these little vignettes of devotion, David takes what can be old and dusty and breathes new life into the word of God. He has a gift to take what we may overlook and give present day application to it. David's life has been dedicated to studying God's word. His passion is teaching it, and helping others understand who God is.

As we read these little missives, we can envision ourselves sitting down with David and sharing the stories. David writes like he is sitting across the table drinking a cup of coffee with us. He makes us feel welcome. David is warm and personable, and that character is reflected in his writing. David's love for God and His people is demonstrated by his thoughtful consideration of these Wisdom books. He tackles the task of making them relevant today.

That day I first met David I never imagined a lifelong friendship and mutual respect forming. I gave little thought to ever crossing paths again. But God's providential care brought us back together. I cherish him as a friend, and respect him as a Bible student. I want to follow his example in helping others see the truths of God in a fresh perspective.

One more thing: There are two women who must be acknowledged. David's mother, Letha King, has been a powerful influence in his life. Both David and his brother, Warren King, will be glad to tell you all about her. She is a godly lady. The second woman is David's loving and beautiful wife, Melissa. She has walked with him every step of the way. She has seen his highs and his lows. She has helped him grow into a man of God. She is worthy of great honor.

I ask you to join David on his journey through the Wisdom literature. I hope you are as enthralled in this shared experience as I have been. Great, my friend and brother!

—Rickie Jenkins

Preface

The history of the articles that comprise this series of books is documented in the Preface to Volume One; the reader is directed to that work for the background story behind this project. The following remarks are confined to personal reflections on my involvement with the Wisdom books of the Old Testament.

More than any other segment of the Bible, the Wisdom literature deals with the inner life of the individual. Each one of us is a complex bundle of emotions and passions, fears and joys, virtues and vices, and these books serve as a bright mirror that exposes all that raw material for our examination. If we want to better understand our inner motivations and struggles—and learn how to manage it all—a study of these five books is a good place to start.

That's why readers of this volume may notice a more autobiographical flavor to the articles. While my sufferings have not come close to those of Job, I can appreciate his experience with adversity. I have walked with David through the valley of the shadow of death, and have made his plea for God's forgiveness my own. With Asaph I have battled the demons of envy and doubt. I have quarried nuggets of wisdom from the deep mines of Proverbs, wisdom that has challenged my naive assumptions about life. Like Qoheleth, I have grappled with the contradictions that plague our brief sojourn under the sun. And, yes, I have enjoyed the erotic thrills of Solomon's marriage bed, as documented in his

Song. My journey through these majestic halls of self-reflection has transformed my life, as it will transform yours.

But the value of these books is not merely therapeutic. Underlying all this soul-searching is a quest to better understand the God who made us this way. This "fear of the Lord" is the key to living life well, and until we can see God's hand in all this complexity, we will always be flailing about in our effort to connect the pieces of the puzzle. Life is a beautiful tapestry, but it cannot be appreciated without ascending the heights and viewing it from God's perspective. In my study of the Wisdom literature, I have discovered a portrait of God and His creation that overwhelms the senses with its grandeur. By better understanding God, I have come to better understand myself. My hope is that the articles in this volume will aid others in their own voyage of self-discovery.

A final note on format: The Wisdom literature consists of Hebrew poetry, which utilizes a number of literary devices such as imagery, acrostics, word plays, and other elements that are often obscured in our English translations. One device that is captured in our modern versions is *parallelism*, the use of couplets to set synonymous or antithetical thoughts alongside each other. By breaking these couplets into separate lines, these translations draw attention to the author's intended contrast or comparison. However, in the interest of conserving space, quotations of Hebrew parallelisms in this volume remove the line breaks in favor of standard prose text. The reader is encouraged to read these passages in a personal Bible to better appreciate the beauty of the parallelisms.

Unless otherwise noted, all Scripture citations are from the New King James Version. The interpretations, as well as any mistakes, are my own.

Special thanks go to Rickie Jenkins for providing the Forward. Matthew Allen and Adam Moore also deserve gratitude for their contributions in bringing this volume to press.

Valley Center KS
November 2022

Introduction

From the dawn of time we humans have struggled to understand our place in the cosmos. What is man? Why are we here? How do we define a "good life"? Why do we experience suffering and injustice? What lies beyond death? Who is God, and how can we know Him? Or is knowledge in these areas even possible? These and related questions have occupied the deepest thinkers of our race.

The ancient Hebrews studied these questions, too. Their unique relationship with God gave them an advantage in this search, of course, but it did not entirely remove the limitations of their understanding. They wrestled with these issues just as we do, and their frustrations reflect our own.

Five books in the Old Testament document their meditations on these perplexing subjects. Following the Septuagint, our English Bible bundles these five books in what is popularly called the books of Poetry, or the Wisdom literature. Unlike the books that precede them, the Wisdom books contain little historical narrative; and unlike the works of the prophets that follow, they are light on authoritative "thus saith the Lord" pronouncements. Instead, the perspective that dominates these books is one of *personal experience*. These books give voice to the full range of emotions that are common to humanity: pain and pleasure, joy and sorrow, frustration and trust. If life is an adventure, the Wisdom books chronicle the experience in language to which we all can relate.

The story of *Job*, for example, uses a non-Israelite hero to explore the problem of human suffering. Throughout much of the book, the protagonists wrestle with the question of "Why?" When God finally makes His appearance, He reveals a more expansive view of His role in the cosmos, thus providing a deeper insight into life's purpose, a purpose that is less concerned with "Why?" than with "What now?"

Psalms is not a single composition, but a collection of Hebrew poems composed by many authors over several centuries. It is Israel's songbook, an anthology of praise in verse, giving expression to the deepest stirrings of the human heart. When we struggle to articulate our thoughts to God, the Psalms provide a fine source of inspiration.

Proverbs is a catalog of simple maxims addressing behaviors in every detail of daily life. Choices have consequences, and wisdom is knowing what choices produce what consequences, both good and bad. While the book exalts "the fear of the Lord" as the ideal foundation for life, its wisdom is often drawn from experience. Pay attention to what works and what doesn't, and make your decisions accordingly.

Ecclesiastes serves as an important counterweight to Proverbs. Whereas Proverbs is concerned with the rules that make for an ordered life, Ecclesiastes wrestles with the *exceptions* to the rules. Life doesn't always work out the way we think it should, and sometimes we're tempted to question if life has any purpose at all. Learning to live with these anomalies requires a frame of reference that secularism cannot provide.

The *Song of Solomon* is a poetic tribute to the beauty of romantic love. If marriage is the foundation of human society, it is appropriate that the Bible contains at least one book devoted entirely to that institution.

Studying the Wisdom literature of the Old Testament challenges our simplistic assumptions about how life works. Life is complicated and messy, and we must learn to live with its Gordian nature. But the quest is not hopeless, once we grasp the hidden foundation upon which a good life is built.

Fearing God for Nothing

It's easy to say that we fear God when life is going well. But what happens to that fear when the good times end and God is nowhere to be found?

"Does Job fear God for nothing? Have You not made a hedge around him, around his household, and around all that he has on every side? You have blessed the work of his hands, and his possessions have increased in the land. But now, stretch out Your hand and touch all that he has, and he will surely curse You to Your face!" (Job 1:9-11).

Job was the kind of man of whom God could be proud: blameless, upright, fearing God, shunning evil (1:8). But Satan smelled a phony. Nobody can be that goody-goody without some kind of payoff somewhere. He charged God with the evidence: "Have You not made a hedge around him?" Like a modern-day Calvinist, Satan believed that humans are too cold, too greedy, too selfish and depraved to serve God unconditionally. Satan was confident that as soon as Job lost his free ride, he would lose his shallow righteousness.

You know the rest of the story. God allowed Job's faith to be tested to the limits. He was hit with every possible tragedy a man could experience: the loss of his possessions, the loss of his family, the loss of his health. But through it all, Job held firm. "In all this Job did not sin nor charge God with wrong" (1:22). Satan's cynicism was discredited; Job *did* fear God for nothing. He remained loyal to God, even when he seemingly had no reason to do so.

For every Job, there are a million others who would fulfill Satan's prediction. As long as life is comfortable they have no problem being religious. But when troubles hit, God becomes a handy scapegoat. "If there is a God, why did He allow this to happen to me?" "I'll never set foot in that church building again while those hypocrites are there!" Such statements betray a mercenary spirit that serves God only if the pay is right.

Job's faith was not tied to his circumstances in life, so he answered his travails with a stoic response: "The Lord gave, and the Lord has taken away. Blessed be the name of the Lord" (1:21). The pain hurt, but it could not destroy his conviction that God was still in control. Though he had no idea why this tragedy befell him, or how it would play out, Job clung to the God he knew was always there. His love for God remained unconditional.

Carefully examine the motives underlying *your* religion. Is your fear of the Lord tied to the material blessings He bestows upon you? Or do you truly fear Him for nothing?

Happy New Year?

All of us have had one of those episodes in life when it seems that everything goes wrong, and we can see the suffering of Job with fresh eyes.

"Naked I came from my mother's womb, and naked shall I return there. The LORD gave, and the LORD has taken away; blessed be the name of the LORD" (Job. 1:21).

The Christmas decorations weren't even packed away yet when it began. The "happy new year" was starting out to be anything but.

On New Year's Day (Saturday), I felt the first signs of what turned out to be the flu. I went to work on Monday, but came home early and went to bed. A really miserable day.

I stayed home on Tuesday, curled up on the couch. I felt better as the day wore on, weakened but able to function. Which was a good thing, since we got hit with the Ice Storm of the Century that day. By the afternoon, the power was out.

Life in the country is usually pleasant, but when the electricity goes out in an all-electric home in a rural setting during an ice storm, life suddenly becomes very primitive. No heat, no running water, no working toilets, no cooking—and no idea when the power will come back on. You are truly at nature's mercy; and nature was showing no mercy this day.

Fortunately, our home has two fireplaces, so we started fires that kept the house from freezing. Several inches of rain had fallen, and the basement sump was filling rapidly. We have a small gasoline powered generator, but couldn't get it to start. So we fell back on the only remaining option: We bailed the sump by hand. Every hour or so for the next twenty-four hours, we bailed buckets of water to keep the basement from flooding. That makes for a long night.

Finally, on Wednesday afternoon, we got the generator going, which relieved us of the bailing operation. But we still had to feed the fireplaces every few hours. And despite the fires, it was cold. So bitterly cold.

On Thursday, I went in to work (despite having had no shower since Monday). Our director called everyone into a special meeting. There were layoffs, he announced. Fortunately I was spared, but the rest of the day was gloomy.

By the following Saturday, the power was still out, but the temperatures had moderated. We checked into a local motel for a night, then I flew to Colorado on a business trip, leaving Melissa in charge of keeping the fires and the generator going. Still no idea when the power would return.

Early Monday morning, I got an emergency phone call. Melissa's father had died in Texas. So I hastily arranged a flight back to Wichita and headed to the airport. Naturally, a traffic jam caused me to miss my flight. I found a seat on another flight, and got back into Wichita late that afternoon. We left for Texas on Tuesday morning, still without power.

So in the first two weeks of the new year, I had worked less than three days at the office. I had survived the flu, an ice storm, a dead home, a layoff, a canceled business trip, and a family funeral. Nothing "happy" about this new year, right?

Actually, there is a lot to be happy about. For all the inconveniences caused by the storm, our basic needs were never seriously threatened. The power eventually came back on. I still have a job. And we have a deeper appreciation for friends and neighbors who pitched in to help. Despite the rough start, we have every reason to believe this will be a happy new year.

After all, "happy" is a relative term, defined mostly by how we choose to look at life. Every new year is happy, when we enter it determined to find it so. "Blessed be the name of the Lord"—regardless of what else happens.

Why Suffering?

Living in a world of suffering and pain, we humans are consumed with the question of "why?" Perhaps we're asking the wrong question.

"Remember now, who ever perished being innocent? Or where were the upright ever cut off? Even as I have seen, those who plow iniquity and sow trouble reap the same" (Job 4:7-8).

"Who sinned, this man or his parents, that he was born blind?" (Jn. 9:1).

◆

Eliphaz tactfully reminded Job that innocent people do not suffer as Job had. Therefore, he must have done something to bring this tragedy upon himself.

The disciples of Jesus viewed suffering as Job's friends did: Somebody sinned, so somebody has to pay for the crime. Whodunit?!

The assumption that underlies both comments is that *all* suffering can be explained as the consequence of human rebellion. Good things happen to good people and bad things happen to bad people.

There is an element of truth in that assertion. The book of Proverbs, for example, is based on the principle that behaviors have consequences, so at least some of the bad things that come our way we bring upon ourselves by our poor decisions. When someone suffers, therefore, it's only natural that we try to identify the culprit who should get the blame.

But in both of these cases, that foundational premise was flawed. Job was a "blameless and upright" man who in no way deserved the tragedies that befell him (Job 1:1). And Jesus specifically absolved the blind man and his parents of any blame in his disability ("Neither this man nor his parents sinned," Jn. 9:3a).

Instead, Jesus challenged His disciples to look at suffering from a different perspective. This man was born blind, He said, so that "the works of God should be revealed in him" (Jn. 9:3b). By fixating on "Why?" the disciples were missing a question of far greater significance: "What now?"

In both of these episodes, God allowed the suffering to reveal a deeper purpose in life. Job needed to learn that his relationship with God was independent of his material success. The disciples of Jesus needed to view the blind man's misfortune as an opportunity for the love of God to be displayed through an act of kindness. In both cases, God's purpose was accomplished.

When we see terrible suffering in the world around us, or when it touches us personally, we must learn not to obsess over the "why?" but pay attention to the "what now?" How can my suffering help me develop a closer relationship with God? What can I do to help others who are suffering, and thereby show the work of God in a broken world? How can this bad be turned into a gateway for good?

Why does suffering exist at all? I'm not qualified to answer that question. But I *do* know what God wants me to do with it, and that is where I need to direct my energy.

I Am Mortal

The limitations of our human condition restrict our ability to enjoy life—especially if this life is all we have to look forward to.

"Can a mortal be more righteous than God? Can a man be more pure than his Maker? If He puts no trust in His servants, if He charges His angels with error, how much more those who dwell in houses of clay, whose foundation is in the dust?" (Job 4:17-19).

For this corruptible must put on incorruption, and this mortal must put on immortality (1 Cor. 15:53).

This "house of clay" in which I live is not long for this world. Subject to decay and constrained in knowledge, I am reminded of its limitations daily—especially when I compare my pitiful condition to an infinitely immortal God.

I am mortal. There is so much about life and God and the world—and even myself—that I do not understand. Ignorant and blind, I stumble through life frightened of the dangers that lurk about me. What lies in my future: Prosperity? Tragedy? Laughter? Terror? I do not know. All I can do is my meager best, knowing that fate may have a different and unexpected agenda for me.

I am mortal. Heroes in comic books may have superpowers, but I don't. Faced with threats that can destroy me or those I love, I am often powerless to overcome them. All I can do is watch in helpless grief as storms and diseases and wars ravage all that I hold dear. I scream for relief, but must live with the pain. Oh, God, how it hurts!

I am mortal. My spirit is weak and prone to sin. Even on my best days, I make mistakes that hurt others and embarrass myself. I have been created in the image of God, but that image is tarnished, dimmed by the stain of sin. I struggle to improve, but there is so much to learn, so many defects to patch up.

I am mortal. This earthly tabernacle in which I dwell is frail, susceptible to injury and illness. I am dust, and to dust I must return. Like all who have gone before me, my life will end in the grave; then all my dreams, all my labors, all my achievements, ALL of it, will in the end be as nothing.

And yet . . .

Through the death and resurrection of the Son of God, a day is coming when this mortal shall put on immortality, when all the imperfections and limitations and nightmares will be removed, and I shall stand before Him with boldness, basking in the light of His glory. On that day, I will realize that it was worth the struggle. It was all worth it.

Come, Lord Jesus!

The God Who Never Sleeps

We humans need sleep like we need food. God requires neither; and when we can't sleep, that fact should put our troubled minds at ease.

"Wearisome nights have been appointed to me. When I lie down, I say, 'When shall I arise, and the night be ended?' For I have had my fill of tossing till dawn" (Job 7:3-4).

He will not allow your foot to be moved; He who keeps you will not slumber. Behold, He who keeps Israel shall neither slumber nor sleep (Psa. 121:3-4).

Job's heart was consumed by grief over the loss of everything he held dear, and a terrible skin disease wracked his body with excruciating pain. These dual tragedies conspired to create one more problem that drove him to the brink of madness: He could not sleep. "I have had my fill of tossing till dawn."

Job's predicament should sound familiar. All of us know the frustration of being so exhausted by life's struggles that we cry out for sleep, but our mind is so consumed by anxious thoughts that sleep is impossible.

The human body cannot function without sleep. In the absence of a good night's sleep our judgment becomes impaired and our physical strength wanes. In extreme cases, psychosis can set in; we literally go crazy for lack of sleep.

But when the burdens of our waking life weigh heavy on our minds, sleep does not come easily. We toss and turn on our beds, our mind racing with troubled thoughts. A vicious cycle sets in—we desperately need the rest, but our worries prevent us from slipping into unconciousness. It's a miserable experience.

God does not have that problem. He does not sleep because He has no need to. He has no physical body that requires rest, no organic brain that must be rejuvenated. Consequently, there is no problem in His universe—or in my life—that He cannot handle with ease.

So whenever I lie awake at night fretting over some crisis in my life, I should turn all my problems over to God and let Him worry about them. All the affairs of my life rest in His capable hands. Even if I can't see the path forward in my circumstances, God can. I can trust Him to do what is best.

In the meantime . . . I can go back to sleep.

The Bible and Suicide

The Bible provides clues that help us understand the underlying problem that often motivates someone to take their own life.

"My soul chooses strangling and death rather than my body. I loathe my life . . ." (Job 7:15-16).

༺❦༻

According to a recent news report, the suicide rate among Americans has risen sharply over the past thirty years, especially among women and middle-aged people ("U.S. Suicide Rate Surges to a 30-Year High," *New York Times*, Apr. 22, 2016). Why do people choose to end their own life? And what does the Bible say about this?

Some insist that *all* suicide is a sin that condemns its victims to hell. Others go to the opposite extreme and argue that suicide is a perfectly rational life choice, and even advocate for physician-assisted suicide to make it a less traumatic experience.

There are three considerations we need to take into account when discussing suicide.

First, *how do we define it?* Sometimes people sacrifice their lives to save others. Think of the soldier who throws himself on a grenade to protect his buddies, or the man who gives up his seat in a lifeboat to allow a woman to survive a disaster. These people make a deliberate decision to end their lives, but it is for a higher purpose than themselves. The death of Samson falls in this category. He died in the destruction of the Philistine temple, but it was an act of war to deliver his people from affliction.

Second, *what is the mental state of the victim?* Some people are so overwhelmed by physical or mental disabilities that they cannot think rationally about what they are doing. It's not our place to judge someone who, for example, is coping with a horrible disease that has clouded their ability to reason.

In the remaining cases of suicide, we're dealing with otherwise healthy people *who have simply given up hope.* They see no value in their life, and view suicide as the only way out of their miserable existence.

We see this in several Bible characters who took their own lives. King Saul fell on his sword in a disastrous battle. Ahithophel, David's traitorous adviser, hanged himself. Zimri, an Israelite king, immolated himself in a civil war he was doomed to lose. Judas hanged himself after betraying Jesus. The details were different, but the common thread that links all these stories is *a life that was motivated entirely by selfish interests.* God played little or no role in their decision-making. Their suicide was simply the final act of self-centeredness in a life devoid of divine guidance.

It should not surprise us, therefore, to notice that the rising suicide rate among Americans tracks closely with a growing tide of secularism in the population. As people cast God out of their lives, they must fall back on their own resources to deal with the hard edges of life. But we were not designed to function as autonomous creatures. We *need* God in our lives, and when we shut Him out and the walls begin to fall in, it's easy to convince ourselves that we no longer have any reason for living.

In the midst of his deep pain, Job despaired of life, preferring death over his current condition. Yet he refused to act on that impulse. Life was God's prerogative, not his own, and he chose to leave that decision with God. Life may be hard, but in a relationship with God we can find strength to endure.

Happiness Can't Be Faked

Trying to paper over inward guilt with an outward smile is a fool's game, and sooner or later, the masquerade will collapse on us.

"If I say, 'I will forget my complaint, I will put off my sad face and wear a smile,' I am afraid of all my sufferings; I know that You will not hold me innocent" (Job 9:27-28).

In one day, Job had lost his children, his possessions, and his health. When his friends came to "comfort" him, he learned that he had lost them, too. The book of Job is the story of one man's struggle to cope with horrifying loss.

But how to cope? In this passage, Job considered, then quickly dismissed, one strategy: Just ignore the pain and put on a happy face. Maybe if he *pretended* to be happy, the suffering would not hurt so bad.

But that approach was unworkable for one obvious reason: "I know that You [God] will not hold me innocent." In Job's theology, all suffering was the result of sin. For Job to have been hit so hard, he must have done something terribly wrong. So Job was consumed with guilt, even though he had no idea what his crime was. That's why he couldn't just "put on a happy face." The guilt of his mysterious sin was consuming him on the inside; it was impossible to fake happiness.

In the end, Job learned that his theology was flawed. Not all suffering is caused by sin, and he had committed no sin to bring such terrible losses upon himself. So his guilt evaporated under the warm glow of divine approval, and he eventually learned to be happy again.

But Job's observation that happiness cannot be faked is still valid. His words haunt me, for they describe with chilling accuracy modern man's approach to finding happiness in the midst of self-inflicted pain. People today try to do what Job knew he could not: Wear a smile on the outside, while consumed with guilt on the inside. Unlike Job, however, they continue the charade long after it's obvious it won't work.

The human psyche was designed to respond to a strong internal regulator: *guilt*. This knowledge of good and evil serves a useful purpose in guiding our lives. The guilt, or the fear of guilt, motivates us to avoid wrong behavior and adopt good behavior. As we learn to make good choices in our life, we reap the reward of happiness. Even when bad things happen to us, as long as we maintain a clean conscience, we can retain a strong sense of inner peace, a genuine happiness that suffering can't touch.

But modern psychology has declared that guilt no longer has a place in our culture. By this new definition, guilt is merely a relic of ancient superstitions, and with adequate education and therapy, can be eliminated altogether. People should be free to live their lives as they please, and feel no remorse for their behavior. Or, to express it in the words of Job, they should be able to "wear a smile," without regard to the moral propriety of their conduct.

This effort to eradicate guilt from human experience is based on a destructive denial of human nature. Behaviors have consequences, and we instinctively know it. We see demonstrations of that truth every day in society around us, yet we chose to ignore it. We have become a nation of depressed clowns, wearing painted smiles for the public, but inwardly consumed with the knowledge that we are headed for a judgment that will not hold us innocent.

After all, in our hearts we know that happiness can't be faked.

The Hope of the Hypocrite

No one wants to be thought a hypocrite, but there's one simple test to determine if we are—if we have the courage to apply it.

"Though He slay me, yet will I trust Him. Even so, I will defend my own ways before Him. He also shall be my salvation, for a hypocrite could not come before Him" (Job 13:15-16).

"For what is the hope of the hypocrite, though he may gain much, if God takes away his life? Will God hear his cry when trouble comes upon him?" (Job 27:8-9).

Before we dig into these verses, let's take a moment to define our subject. A *hypocrite* is a person who is consciously putting on an act to deceive others, with full knowledge that he is not living up to his own standard. A hypocrite is not to be confused with someone who is genuinely striving to do the right thing, but stumbles here or there in the execution. There is a difference between a sinner who grieves over his own failings, and a hypocrite who knows he is living a lie and tries to pretend otherwise.

Throughout the book of Job, his friends accused him of being not just a sinner, but a hypocrite. Why else would God cause such horrible tragedies to rain down upon a man? Only a hypocrite would deserve that kind of karma. In their view, Job had done a good job of hiding his crimes, but now it was time to come clean and get right with God!

Of course, Job's friends could not read his heart, and their accusations were without merit. In both of these passages, Job contrasted his own condition with that of the hypocrite. The hypocrite has no grounds for coming into the presence of God. He has no hope, whatever profit he may gain from his duplicity. He is a phony, a fake, a pretender who has no claim on God's mercy—and he knows it.

Job's argument here is, *that's not me.* Job had a deep and abiding desire to see God, to honor his Creator in everything he did (see 19:25-27; 23:10-12). He did not claim perfection; indeed, he acknowledged his utter dependence on God's grace: "Though I were righteous, I could not answer Him; I would beg mercy of my Judge" (9:15). Even in adversity, Job refused to renounce his dependence on God. "Though He slay me, yet will I trust Him."

Job's words provide a template for evaluating our own character. Take a close look at how you process adversity in your life. Do you cry out in prolonged prayer to God, seeking to better understand your own weaknesses and begging mercy from the only One who can give it? Or do you respond with bitterness and anger, blaming and lashing out at others around you? Is your hope in God, or in the perfect little world you've created for yourself through your scheming?

Perhaps you've wrestled with the question: Am I a hypocrite, or am I a sinner genuinely trying to grow and improve? How you respond to hardship is a good indicator of your real character.

The Sins of My Youth

The energy and ignorance of youth is usually accompanied by painful mistakes, remembered in later years with regret. That can be a good thing.

"You write bitter things against me, and make me inherit the iniquities of my youth" (Job 13:26).

Do not remember the sins of my youth, nor my transgressions; according to Your mercy remember me, for Your goodness' sake, O Lord (Psa. 25:7).

We remember Job and David as heroes of faith whose lives we should emulate. But they did not see their own lives that way. In their later years, both looked back with regret on what they called "the sins of my youth," misdeeds from their younger days that they knew deserved the judgment of a holy God. That both men would make the identical confession points to an experience that is shared by all who live full lives.

All of us come into this world devoid of wisdom, and must somehow learn how to live life successfully. That knowledge can be gained by two ways: preferably by listening to the counsel of our elders; or, more likely, by *not* listening and making our own mistakes. As one sage summarized it, "Good judgment comes from experience, and experience comes from bad judgment"—much of which is encountered in our younger, dumber days. If we live long enough and maintain a modicum of integrity, like Job and David we will eventually gain a heart of wisdom, paid for with the scars of past sins.

This is not to disparage youth. Many of the heroes of the Bible were young people who, perhaps with some idealistic naivete, put their elders to shame by their fearless faith. One old apostle certainly saw value in the contributions of young people: "I have written to you, young men, because you are strong, and the word of God abides in you, and you have overcome the wicked one" (1 Jn. 2:14). The world would be impoverished without the reckless enthusiasm of young people.

But the achievements of the young often come at a price, and it is not until later in life that we recognize the foolishness of the words and deeds committed in earlier years. We may be older and wiser people now, but the memory of those youthful blunders will always remind us of our frailties. All we can do is seek comfort in forgiveness, and try to pass our hard-earned wisdom on to the next generation.

That is why, apart from a few cranks who never learned from their mistakes, older people tend to be more patient and less judgmental. A frequent complaint of young preachers is that their older colleagues seem to "go soft" on sin in their later years. That may account for some cases, but the more likely explanation is that the old-timers have gained greater humility about the reality of the fallen human condition. None of us are perfect, and older people have had a lifetime of hard experience to appreciate the implications of that simple truth. When Jesus gave his critics permission to stone an adulteress—but only on the condition that they were without sin—they all walked away, one by one, "beginning with the oldest even to the last" (Jn. 8:9). The older fellows, having a keener sense of their failings, were the first to get the point of Jesus' challenge.

The sins of our youth may be painful, but they can be stepping stones to a deeper wisdom—if we are humble enough to learn from them.

Miserable Comforters

Comforting the afflicted is part of our life of faith. But there is a right and wrong way to do it. Job's friends demonstrate the wrong way.

Then Job answered and said: "I have heard many such things; miserable comforters are you all!" (Job 16:1-2).

Following the devastating tragedies that befell Job, his three friends, Eliphaz, Bildad, and Zophar, came "to mourn with him, and to comfort him" (2:11). For seven days they sat with Job in silence, too overwhelmed with sorrow to speak (2:13). Once Job started opening up (ch. 3), the friends began to offer their condolences (ch. 4 onward). The bulk of the rest of the book is a dialog between Job and his friends about his misfortunes.

Job's friends would have done better to stay silent. Their "condolences" consisted of unfounded speculations about something in Job's private life that must have brought on this horrible turn of events. By chapter sixteen, Job had enough of their lecturing. They were "miserable comforters" whose counsel only added to his misery.

The story of how Job's friends dealt with his hardship serves as an object lesson in how *not* to comfort the afflicted. Despite our good intentions, we can say the wrong thing that will not only *not* impart comfort, but intensify the sufferer's pain. Staying silent and letting our friend struggle alone is not an option; but we must educate ourselves on the right and wrong way to go about this.

Job's friends made three mistakes that rendered them miserable comforters.

First, *they spoke from a faulty understanding of what was going on in Job's life.* They had no insight into the cosmic causes of Job's suffering. They could not peer into his heart to know the truth about the crimes they were accusing Job of having committed. Instead of approaching Job with compassion, they came at him with judgment. That condescending attitude only intensified Job's anguish.

Second, *instead of giving comfort, they presumed to fix a problem.* True, some suffering is the result of foolish behaviors, and sometimes people need to learn a lesson from their poor decision-making. But as counselors, we must be very careful about taking on the role of critics when helping someone cope with problems in their life. Some problems can't be fixed, and we're only insulting the pain of the sufferer when we make that our primary goal. People in grief first need comfort, not repair advice.

Finally, Job's friends were *motivated more by theology than by sympathy.* Their remarks were grounded in a broad (and incorrect) view of God and justice that blinded them to the reality of what was happening in this poor man's life. There is much about this world and how it functions that we simply don't understand. Sometimes the best we can do is admit our own ignorance and focus on easing the pain of those who are struggling. We should leave the deep thinking alone, and concentrate on being a friend to the one who needs our compassion.

In the end, Job's friends served only as tools of Satan to intensify Job's suffering, not heal it. When we take on the role of comforting the afflicted (and we should!), we must take care to do it well. If our hearts are filled with the compassion of Jesus, we will find the right words that will bring comfort to the tortured soul.

How to End Pornography

The scourge of pornography will continue to wreak havoc in our society until one key demographic decides to put an end to it.

"I have made a covenant with my eyes; why then should I look upon a young woman?" (Job 31:1).

Do not lust after her beauty in your heart, nor let her allure you with her eyelids (Prov. 6:25).

"Whoever looks at a woman to lust for her has already committed adultery with her in his heart" (Matt. 5:28).

Pornography is as old as the human race. Lurid sexual images and graffiti have been found on the walls of Pompeii, buried by volcanic ash in AD 79. Archaeologists have unearthed statuettes featuring exaggerated genitalia from cultures thousands of years old. Using images to get a sexual thrill has been around a long time.

But in the last couple of decades, the rise of the internet and smartphones has created an explosion of pornographic material unparalleled in history. According to one researcher, the porn industry is now a $100 billion business, "using more bandwidth than Facebook or Amazon" (Terry Schilling, "Science Says Porn Is a Huge Problem. Lawmakers Must Stop Ignoring It," *Newsweek*, Nov. 16, 2020). Pornographic content is more violent, more degrading, and more twisted than ever, leading to addiction, sexual dysfunction, marital breakups, and criminal behavior. We are now facing what the author labeled "a national emergency."

What can we do about it? There is growing pressure to enact legal sanctions to regulate it, or at least limit its exposure to children. That's helpful, but passing laws and handing out prison sentences is a stop-gap measure that really doesn't address the root of the problem. Just as Prohibition had unintended consequences in trying to solve an earlier generation's struggles with alcohol, any legal solution will not permanently solve today's pornography problem.

So what can be done? Job, Solomon, and Jesus all point to the same remedy: *self-discipline.* The pornography problem must be addressed one human heart at a time. Only by educating men, especially young men, to harness their thoughts and habits can this scourge be curtailed. Parents must train their sons to have a wholesome respect for women. Preachers must give practical guidance on how to control our thoughts. Elders must provide counseling to men struggling with their passions. If men in huge numbers simply refuse to watch this garbage, it will wither away for lack of customers.

But what if millions of men choose not to control their lusts and remain addicted to porn? Then society, including these men and their families, will pay a ghastly price. And God in heaven will weep over their destruction.

Men, this is a challenge we must win. Our civilization's survival depends on it.

Waiting for Justice

The desire for justice is strong among us, but is often expressed in destructive ways. Sometimes justice requires that we wait on God to act.

"Although you say you do not see Him, yet justice is before Him, and you must wait for Him" (Job 35:14).

❧

When quoting from the book of Job, we must be careful to note the speaker whom we are quoting. The three friends of Job—Eliphaz, Bildad, and Zophar—believed (incorrectly) that Job's suffering was due to some hidden sin in his life. Consequently, their speeches throughout the book are riddled with misleading generalizations and outright falsehoods.

But that's not to say there is nothing of value in their speeches. Buried in this verse, spoken by a fourth friend, Elihu, is a gem worthy of our consideration.

Other versions render Elihu's words slightly differently, for example, "your case is before him and you must wait for him" (NIV). Either way, this verse captures a key truth that lies at the heart of the Bible's message, namely, justice belongs to God, and He will administer it on *His* timetable, not ours. In Job's case, if he believed he was being treated unfairly, he had to wait for God to make it right.

Whatever assumptions lay behind Elihu's advice, his basic thought is sound, if hard to accept. All of us encounter circumstances in our lives in which we believe we have been wronged, and feel a burning desire for something to be done to correct the injustice. Unfortunately, justice doesn't always come when we think it should. Sometimes it doesn't come at all, at least not in our lifetimes. It's easy to conclude that since justice is such a fickle fact of life, then there must not be a God, for if there was, surely He would step in and fix the problem.

Some take this a step further and conclude that since God is either impotent or nonexistent, then justice is left up to us. This is what fuels the endless cycle of conflict that still plagues much of the world today. People believe they have been abused, so they take action to even the score, which triggers more retaliation, *ad infinitum*. Nobody wins in such a scenario.

Elihu points to a preferred alternative: If justice seems far away or even unattainable, then we must wait for God to act in His own good time. Sometimes the wheels of justice turn very slowly, and it's difficult to see any hope of a resolution. But it's there, and it will eventually come.

In some cases, we'll go to our graves without ever seeing justice done, but that doesn't mean God's promise has failed. "Surely there is a hereafter," Solomon reminds us (Prov. 23:18), a final judgment when all of this world's wrongs will be addressed. It's hard to appreciate that fact when the present pain is so deep, so raw. But this is where the character of our faith meets its true test: Do we *really* believe there is a God, and that He will someday judge the world in righteousness—or do we not?

Elihu's premise in his advice may have been flawed, but he stumbled upon a important truth that all of us should take to heart. Whatever injustices we feel life has dished out to us, we must train ourselves to take the long view, and trust that God will eventually do what is right—if not in this life, for certain in the life to come.

Deity

Trying to understand the nature of God is inherently difficult. Nevertheless, there are some clues that point us to one important characteristic.

"Behold, God is great, and we do not know Him" (Job 36:26).

Then God said, "Let us make man in Our image, according to Our likeness;" . . . So God created man in His own image; in the image of God He created him; male and female He created them (Gen. 1:26-27).

One of the great controversies that racked the church in the early centuries of its existence was the question of the nature of God, particularly as it related to the person of Jesus Christ. Early church councils debated these questions exhaustively, with excommunication facing the losers. Today, orthodox Christianity has settled on a view of deity that recognizes three persons in the godhead—Father, Son, and Holy Spirit—popularly known as "the Trinity." This trinitarian view of God is denied by Unitarians, Jehovah's Witnesses, Jews, Muslims, and others who insist that God is a single entity.

I seldom preach or teach on the Trinity, chiefly because I do not consider myself qualified to explain it. John Wesley put the problem well: "Bring me a worm that can comprehend a man, and then I will show you a man that can comprehend the triune God." There is much about God that we mortals simply cannot know, and it is presumptuous to pretend that we have all the answers. So in coming to this question, a large dose of humility is in order.

Nevertheless, there is sufficient evidence in the Scriptures to support the proposition that God is more than a single, isolated being, but rather possesses some characteristics of a community.

First, God frequently speaks of Himself as a plurality. This is apparent in the early chapters of Genesis: "Then God said, 'Let **Us** make man in Our image, according to Our likeness'" (Gen. 1:26). "Then the Lord God said, 'Behold, the man has become like one of **Us**, to know good and evil'" (3:22). "And the Lord said, '. . . Come, let **Us** go down and there confuse their language, that they may not understand one another's speech" (11:7). Some argue that this is God talking to His angels. But these are deliberative statements, and we know that God takes counsel from no one (Isa. 40:14). In some sense, the God who made these decisions was a "we."

Second, unlike any other prophet, the human Jesus was accorded treatment as God. He was worshiped by men, an honor due only to God (Jn. 9:38). He claimed a pre-existence with God that no human could ever claim (Jn. 17:5). He was even called "God" (Jn. 1:1; Jn. 20:28; Tit. 2:13; Heb. 1:8).

Finally, reflect on the statement that "God is love" (1 Jn. 4:8, 16). Love, by definition, requires a *relationship*, an "other" upon whom expressions of love can be bestowed. If God is a single mind, whom did He love prior to creation? But if "one God" is comprised of three perfectly aligned personalities—like a single cube having three dimensions—the dynamics of love take on a whole new meaning.

Whatever the details, Elihu summarized our position elegantly: "God is great, and we do not know Him." We will never fully comprehend the nature of God, but we *can* appreciate His awesome power and majesty, and commit our lives to knowing and doing His will.

God's Questions

Like Job, we have a lot of questions we'd like to ask God about how He runs His universe. But God has some questions for us, too.

"Now prepare yourself like a man; I will question you, and you shall answer Me" (Job 38:3).

Throughout much of the book of Job, the patriarch challenged God with questions about His perplexing role in the patriarch's life. For example:

- "Why have You set me as Your target?" (7:20).
- "How can a man be righteous before God?" (9:2).
- "Why do You hide Your face, and regard me as Your enemy?" (13:24).
- "When He punishes, how shall I answer Him?" (31:14).

In Job's mind, God owed him an explanation as to why all these tragedies had befallen him. If he could only have an opportunity to talk to God face to face, he would take full advantage of it. "I would present my case before Him, and fill my mouth with arguments" (23:4).

So when God finally made His appearance in chapter 38, Job was in for a rude awakening. God turned the tables and began quizzing Job about how He [God] created and maintains even the most ordinary details of His universe. The showdown humbled Job, who realized that he had no grounds to challenge God's wisdom.

Living in a broken world, we, too, have many questions for God. But this questioning works both ways. In the Bible, notice how often God questions us:

- To Adam: "Where are you?" (Gen. 3:9)
- To Cain: "Where is your brother?" (Gen. 4:9)
- To the kingdom of Judah: "What have I done to you? And how have I wearied you?" (Mic. 6:3)
- To Judas: "Are you betraying the Son of Man with a kiss?" (Lk. 22:48)

Every one of these questions could be directed to each one of us personally. God has been extraordinarily generous with us, providing us with an abundance of material prosperity and spiritual guidance. Yet we respond with such crass indifference, messing up our lives and blaming God for the carnage. We treat God like an assistant or an ATM machine—nice to have around when we need Him, but otherwise out of sight. Do we really think He doesn't notice?

If we are befuddled by how God runs His universe, know that He is just as disappointed at how we respond to His presence in our lives. We owe Him better than this—a lot better.

Someday it will be our turn to face a grilling before God's throne. We'd best start preparing our answers now.

The God Who Laughs

On those days when it seems that evil is winning and the righteous are doomed, it helps to know how God views the situation.

The kings of the earth set themselves, and the rulers take counsel together, against the LORD and against His Anointed, saying, "Let us break their bonds in pieces and cast away their cords from us." He who sits in the heavens shall laugh; the LORD shall hold them in derision (Psa. 2:2-4).

The Lord laughs at him, for He sees that his day is coming (Psa. 37:13).

༺༻

Our fallen world operates on the principle of the strong oppressing the weak. Those who have the power can impose their will on everyone else without consequence. They know it and delight in it, daring God to do anything about it.

For those who suffer under the thumb of these despots, the outlook is grim. Tyrants are merchants of misery, indifferent to the tears of those they oppress. They mock the cries of their victims. There's nothing funny about life under an autocratic ruler.

The book of Psalms counsels us to take a cosmic perspective on the problem. For all their bluster, the powerful are mere poseurs who do not know the fate that awaits them. The Lord doesn't just despise their presumptuousness—He laughs at it. At a time and place of His choosing, He will gently puff on their little house of cards, and all their strutting will come to a wretched end. Like a cat toying with a doomed mouse, God will win and they will lose.

History provides abundant evidence of this pattern. Pharaoh, Nebuchadnezzar, Antiochus Epiphanes, the Roman governor Pontius Pilate and Caiaphas the high priest—all these believed themselves to be beyond God's grasp. They crushed the weak without mercy, confident in their power. Yet in every case, God prevailed over their schemes. Their swagger was no match for God's dominance. He laughed as He brought them down.

The greatest example of this principle can be seen in the cross. At the very moment the devil thought he had won his cosmic war by having Jesus slain, God raised His Son from the dead. God knew what He was doing all along, and the joke was on Satan.

Seeing this larger picture of reality should give us the strength to endure evil days. When injustice abounds and the powerful oppress the weak, remember what is happening in heaven. God is chuckling at the pretensions of the mighty and preparing for their demise. He will win, they will lose. And it will make a big difference whose side we have been on throughout the struggle.

Believe that, and you can smile in even the darkest night.

What Others Say

Whether we admit it or not, the opinions of others can have an impact on us, for better or worse—unless we are prepared to deal with it.

Many are they who say of me, "There is no help for him in God" (Psa. 3:2).

There are many who say, "Who will show us any good?" Lord, lift up the light of Your countenance upon us (Psa. 4:6).

In these early Psalms of David, we catch a glimpse of some of the problems that made his life difficult. Among these issues was the discouraging language spoken by those around him. In some cases, the language was ridicule pointed directly at David: "There is no help for him in God"; that is, they viewed David as a scoundrel whom God had cast off. In other cases, the language had no specific target, but was merely a general expression of despair: "Who will show us any good?" All is lost, why bother, the game is rigged, we're doomed, and on and on.

Whatever the details, the language David was hearing was overwhelmingly *pessimistic*. It's hard to keep your spirits up when surrounded by a horde of Debbie Downers. We humans are social creatures who derive much of our value and purpose from our interactions with those around us. But when the message we hear from others is nothing but doom and gloom, that spirit rubs off on us, and the fatalism soon becomes our own.

The problem is the sheer *volume* of the negativity. We can ignore the occasional snide remark, but when the pessimism becomes a torrent rushing in from every direction, from everyone around us, the natural response is to question our own thinking. Maybe I'm out of touch, unaware of the real situation? If so many around me share the same outlook, maybe I'm the one out of sync with reality?

When we encounter that kind of crushing social pressure, we must remind ourselves of two important facts.

First, the cacophony of noise that passes for public opinion usually serves only to obscure the truth, not illuminate it. When Jesus asked His disciples, "Who do men say that I am?" the answers were all over the map (Matt. 16:13-14). The wide range of opinions were so divergent that they were of no value in trying to ascertain Jesus' true identity. All it proved was that the majority had no clue what was going on. The apostles were wise to trust their own experiences with the Savior and accept Him as the Christ, the Son of the Living God (v. 15-16). The majority may be loud, but they are very often wrong.

Second, the voice of the masses is always, always, *always* drowned out by the voice of the Lord—but only if our ears are tuned to hear Him. Later in David's career, at a very low point when everything that could go wrong had gone wrong, and even David's own men "spoke of stoning him," David retreated to the one place where he could find encouragement: He "strengthened himself in the Lord his God" (1 Sam. 30:6). No matter how bleak our circumstances may seem, or how bitter the words that are heaped upon us, if we cling tightly to the promises of God, we can endure the storms that assail us. "Faith comes from hearing, and hearing from the word of God" (Rom. 10:17).

What others say cannot shake our courage, if we have trained ourselves to value the opinion of God above all else.

Anger Management 101

The art of channeling our anger to constructive rather than destructive ends is not easy to master. But it can be learned, if we apply ourselves to it.

Be angry, and do not sin. Meditate within your heart on your bed, and be still. Offer the sacrifices of righteousness, and put your trust in the Lord (Psa. 4:4-5).

"Be angry, and do not sin"; do not let the sun go down on your wrath, nor give place to the devil (Eph. 4:26-27).

Contrary to popular belief, the Bible does not condemn anger. Anger is a perfectly normal human emotion that has a legitimate role in our lives. Under the right circumstances, anger can even be a positive motivator. Parents training children, for example, are quite familiar with this normal reaction to wrong-doing. Much of the progress that is accomplished by those who fight for social or moral issues is driven by a righteous indignation that seeks to oppose evil and defend good. Moses was often angry trying to keep the Israelites faithful to the Lord (Ex. 16:20; Num. 16:15); Jesus was angry at the hypocrisy of His enemies (Mk. 3:5); anger is even attributed to God (Ex. 4:14; Josh. 23:16).

What the Bible *does* condemn is inappropriate expressions of anger. When we allow our anger to flare out in an uncontrolled display of rage, either verbal or physical, we have crossed the line into sin. In those passages where the Bible condemns anger, the context often makes it clear that this out-of-control anger is the issue (for example, "outbursts of wrath," 2 Cor. 12:20; Gal. 5:20).

So as our opening texts describe, we should recognize that anger has its place ("be angry"), but we must take care to keep it under control ("do not sin"). That is the challenge that confronts us.

How do we manage our anger? How can we accept the reality of anger in our emotional toolkit, yet prevent it from doing harm?

The first task, of course, is to *learn to control your anger*, to resist the urge to react instantly. Look again at our opening passage in Psalm 4. The injunction to "be angry and do not sin" is followed by the command to "be still." When you feel anger boiling up inside, assume that anything you do at that moment probably will be wrong. Just be still and allow yourself time to think about the situation and determine a more measured response ("meditate on your bed"). You're more likely to make a wise decision if you give yourself the space to craft one.

As part of the thinking process, *target the issue, not the person*. In many cases it is not the person with whom you are angry as much as it is impersonal events over which you have little control. Lashing out at others when things go wrong is pointless and destructive. Even when people are the source of your frustration, look at the situation as a problem to solve, not an enemy to destroy.

Finally, *deal with the anger, then move on*. Paul's advice to "do not let the sun go down on your wrath" is not intended as a literal deadline, but a reminder that allowing unresolved anger to fester in your soul will turn you into a bitter, miserable person. At some point, you just have to let it go. Where possible, take action to resolve the issue. Sometimes your only recourse may be to forgive someone unconditionally in your heart, and let a matter drop. It's not ideal, but it's better than letting a simmering anger poison your spirit.

Managing anger is like dealing with any other temptation: We must educate ourselves on how it works, and learn practical strategies on how to deal with it.

I Am Weak

Though we remember them as examples of strength, most of our Bible heroes experienced times of weakness, desperate for God's help.

Have mercy on me, O LORD, for I am weak; O LORD, heal me, for my bones are troubled (Psa. 6:2).

As with most Bible heroes, we like to think of David as a tower of strength, a fearless champion for God who conquered his foes and stood firm in the storms that assailed him. But if we study his life in detail, we learn that this image is a caricature of the real David. Whatever his achievements, this Psalm provides a peek into the tumultuous inner life that David lived.

David wrote this Psalm at some low point in his career. The pressures of life were closing in on him and he was nearing the breaking point. His soul was "greatly troubled" (v. 3), and he was overwhelmed with despondency: "I am weary with my groaning . . . my eye wastes away because of grief" (v. 6-7). He even questioned if God cared anymore; had God turned against him (v. 1)? Whatever the circumstances he was experiencing at this time, David's plea for God's mercy reflected a state of spiritual exhaustion. "I am weak" is the cry of a man who is hanging on by his fingernails.

David's honesty about the fragility of his faith should inspire us to be honest about our own struggles. In our eagerness to live our lives as Christians, we set ourselves up for failure by expecting our faith journey to be a steady upward progression. But that's not how it plays out. Instead, life is often a wild ride full of peaks and valleys. Our little bubble can be punctured by some rude shocks along the way, and our faith will take some serious hits. When those days come, all of David's language will become our own: weariness, grief, groaning, trouble, weeping. Like David, we will fall to our knees and cry out to God, "I am weak!"—because we are.

On those days when nothing seems to be going right, and you struggle for answers to questions that make no sense, remember these words of David. There is nothing happening in your life that other people of faith have not encountered also. This struggle is part of the package that comes with being a believer.

David was weak, but he knew where to turn for help: "O Lord, heal me!" We must learn to do the same, and hold fast to the God whose patient love will guide us through the darkness.

Boomerang Justice

When wickedness seems to triumph, we might question God's justice. But there is a greater principle in play that will take a while to see.

Behold, the wicked brings forth iniquity; yes, he conceives trouble and brings forth falsehood. He made a pit and dug it out, and has fallen into the ditch which he made. His trouble shall return upon his own head, and his violent dealing shall come down on his own crown (Psa. 7:14-16).

David, the author of this Psalm, knew a thing or two about injustice. He spent much of his young adulthood on the run, the target of King Saul's maniacal jealousy. In his own heart and conduct he sought to do the right thing; but his integrity was often answered by scorn, betrayal, rejection, persecution. A lesser man would have blamed God and turned to bitterness. But not David. Despite all the cruelties that life threw at him, David clung to a stubborn confidence that God would somehow work it all out. That confidence was eventually rewarded as, one by one, David's enemies got their comeuppance and David was vindicated.

Through all his travails, David learned a valuable lesson about how justice and injustice play out in human affairs. In general, those who traffic in iniquity reap what they sow. The trouble they scheme for others often returns upon their own heads in ways they cannot anticipate. In may take a while to play out, but evil eventually boomerangs back upon its perpetrators.

The Wisdom literature often highlights this principle of divine retribution. The metaphor that David uses here of the wicked falling into the pit they have dug to entrap their enemies comes up again and again (see Psa. 57:6; Prov. 26:27; Eccl. 10:8). History provides numerous examples of this principle. Think of the brothers of Joseph who gloated over their successful elimination of their rival, only to suffer twenty years of guilt and remorse for their evil deed; or wicked Haman, who was hung on the gallows he had prepared for his enemy Mordecai. Evil carries within itself the seeds of its own destruction.

We learn two important lessons from David's experience. First, we must look to God to save us from our enemies: "O LORD my God, in You I put my trust; save me from all those who persecute me" (v. 1). We have the Lord's promise that He will do so: "Vengeance is Mine, I will repay" (Rom. 12:19)—often using instruments and stratagems that we never would have anticipated. Even if we do not see justice served immediately in this life, for sure He *will* settle the score in the next. God does not need our help to set the world right.

This principle should also serve as a warning when we are tempted to return harm upon another. Even if we feel we are justified in administering a reprisal, the end result will likely harm us more than our intended victim. "Love does no harm to a neighbor" (Rom. 13:10) must be our guiding motive, even if our neighbor does not deserve our kindness.

True justice is not ours to give, nor to demand. It belongs to God, and we must trust Him to administer it in His own time. Our job is to reflect His love and generosity to all without qualification.

Moon, Man, and God

Our ability to admire God's handiwork in space far surpasses anything the ancients could have imagined. More than ever, we are in awe of God.

When I consider Your heavens, the work of Your fingers, the moon and the stars, which You have ordained, what is man that You are mindful of him, and the son of man that You visit him? (Psa. 8:3-4).

On Christmas Eve in 1968, astronaut Bill Anders took a dramatic photo of the earth rising over the lunar horizon as Apollo 8 orbited the moon, the first manned mission to another heavenly body. In a broadcast to a worldwide audience back on earth, Anders and his two crewmates took turns reading verses from the creation account in Genesis 1, concluding with this farewell greeting: "And from the crew of Apollo 8, we close with good night, good luck, a Merry Christmas, and God bless all of you—all of you on the good Earth."

Atheists pitched a fit, of course. But the astronauts were on solid ground. Over the next several years other astronauts witnessed the same breathtaking view, and even walked on the moon. Among the astronaut community, the experience of seeing the earth from space strengthened their faith in God. Some examples:

- "I had an enormous feeling that there had to be a power greater than any of us—that there was a God, that there was indeed a beginning" (Frank Borman, Anders' crewmate on Apollo 8).

- "I felt the power of God as I'd never felt it before" (James Irwin, Apollo 15).
- "To look out at this kind of creation and not believe in God is to me impossible" (John Glenn, Friendship 7 and STS-95).
- "I can tell you I felt a sense of awe out there looking at the Earth that I never had before, and it's easy to relate that to a spiritual kind of thing" (Bryan O'Connor, STS-61-B and STS-40; O'Connor later ran the space shuttle program for NASA).
- The first food consumed on the moon was a communion wafer and wine, taken by Buzz Aldrin shortly before Neil Armstrong took his first step off the LEM. He later explained, "I could think of no better way to acknowledge the Apollo 11 experience than by giving thanks to God."

Ironically, the man who took the historic photograph, Bill Anders, remained skeptical of a divine presence. But among the early astronaut corps, he was in the minority. Their experience in space reinforced their belief in God.

We do not have to leave earth to taste a glimpse of what these men experienced. God created this entire universe—only a fraction of which we can see at night—as a signpost to knowing Him. Like David, gazing upon that vast expanse should humble us in the presence of the Almighty.

Every Christmas Eve, the words of Apollo 8 remain as fitting as ever: "Good night, good luck, a Merry Christmas, and God bless all of you—all of you on the good Earth."

A Final Accounting

Once people become convinced that they will not have to answer for their behavior, they lose a major incentive to behave responsibly.

Why do the wicked renounce God? He has said in his heart, "You will not require an account" (Psa. 10:13).

In this one short verse, the Bible goes straight to the heart of why so much evil exists in this world. Once men convince themselves that they will not have to give an account for their behavior, there no longer exists any meaningful check on wickedness.

Throughout history, virtually every human society has shared some kind of belief in an afterlife, the quality of which is somehow linked to how individuals live in this life. The details of this belief—and the conduct it inspires—may vary from religion to religion; but the net result is always the same: People's lives are deeply influenced by their belief in a final judgment.

The idea of a final judgment is a central message in the Bible. In the Old Testament, for example: "Fear God and keep His commandments, for this is man's all. For God will bring every work into judgment, including every secret thing, whether good or evil" (Eccl. 12:13-14). And in the New Testament: "[God] has appointed a day in which He will judge the world in righteousness by the Man whom He has ordained. He has given assurance of this to all by raising Him from the dead" (Ac. 17:31). In the Judeo-Christian tradition, human behavior is regulated by a strong conviction that every word and deed is accountable to God, and our eternal destiny hinges on that accounting.

But when that conviction of a final accounting is weakened or eliminated, the corresponding incentive to regulate behavior is damaged along with it. The results can be devastating.

One of the reasons communism was such a dismal failure is because it was founded on an official platform of atheism—no God, no afterlife, no final judgment. The government alone held absolute power over the conduct of its citizens. But while the citizens may have yielded to that authoritarian control, they could see the misuses of power wielded by those in control. The result was a society infested with resentment, cynicism, and despair—not a healthy foundation for a happy and prosperous nation.

In our own nation, the religious traditions that once permeated society are crumbling, being supplanted by various flavors of atheism, mysticism, and personal feel-goodism. Even many mainline Christian denominations, which once embraced the Biblical message of a final judgment, now minimize that message in favor of a vague, ill-defined belief that somehow "everybody's going to heaven." The notion of a final judgment is disappearing from the public consciousness. Consequently, our society is struggling with an epidemic of behavioral-based problems: poverty, divorce, homosexuality, drugs, crime, and so forth. People believe in their hearts that they will never be held responsible for their conduct, so they become irresponsible. It's that simple.

It's not the government's job to turn this problem around. It's the work of God's people to patiently teach the truth about the final judgment, one person at a time.

If the Foundations Are Destroyed

Societal collapse may alarm us, but we should take comfort in the knowledge that God has not been dethroned. He will have the last word.

If the foundations are destroyed, what can the righteous do? (Psa. 11:3).

With the recent Supreme Court decision removing barriers to same-sex marriage, those who respect God and His word have yet another reason to be disheartened. The moral foundation of our nation is crumbling before our eyes, and we seem powerless to stem the tide of ethical anarchy that is overwhelming our culture. How should we respond?

Actually, this development is nothing new. Other nations in history have passed through the same kind of moral freefall that we are experiencing, and God's people in those generations struggled with the same question: "What can the righteous do?" This Psalm speaks directly to our fears.

Our first task is to remind ourselves that regardless of how degenerate our society may become, "The Lord is in His holy temple" (v. 4). No President, Supreme Court, Congress, nor any other ruling power can take God's place in His universe. It really doesn't matter what men in their arrogance may decree; God still rules and someday He will have the last word. Fixing our heart on that bedrock truth will go a long way toward providing us peace of mind.

As the ultimate authority, God is not indifferent to what goes on in this world. "His eyes behold" everything that happens, whether good or bad (v. 4), and He is keeping score. We can be confident that no one will get away with anything.

For those who flout God's law, this will not end well. "The wicked . . . His soul hates" (v. 5), and someday "upon the wicked He will rain coals; fire and brimstone and a burning wind shall be the portion of their cup" (v. 6). In this life they can presume to abrogate power to themselves and force their will upon others. But in the end, God will render the final verdict. (Notice that this is God's doing, not ours. We cannot—must not—take it upon ourselves personally to dish out punishment upon the wicked. Judgment is God's prerogative, and we must leave it in His capable hands.)

So what happens to His people, who have to suffer through the depravity of this world? God does not forget us, but neither will He pamper us: "The Lord tests the righteous" (v. 5). That is, He leaves us exposed to the hard edges of life. He wants us to face these setbacks head on—not to beat us down, but to make our faith stronger.

Here is the conclusion: "The Lord is righteous, He loves righteousness; His countenance beholds the upright" (v. 7). When the proud and haughty strut about, waving their legal victories in our faces, it's hard to see any good coming from it. But we have to understand that there is a much bigger program unfolding, the details of which we cannot see. It's all playing out under the watchful eye of a God who truly has our best interests at heart. We have to trust Him to know what is best.

In the meantime, our job is to keep the faith, love our enemies, and teach our children the truth about moral standards. We cannot impose God's will upon the rest of society; but we can live it in our own lives and prepare the next generation to do the same. Our options may be limited, but God's are not, and someday He will set right everything that is now so twisted. Believe it!

The Lord Tests the Righteous

When life is brutal, we must learn to view the hardship as God sees it—not as a punishment, but as a test. It's God's way of strengthening us.

The Lord tests the righteous (Psa. 11:5).

David was well acquainted with injustice in his life. He knew the frustration of seeing wicked people prosper at the expense of the righteous. Some days it seemed that the whole fabric of the universe was turned inside out, and evil was triumphant over good everywhere. He felt helpless in the face of all the depravity. "If the foundations are destroyed, what can the righteous do?" (v. 3).

But his experience with injustice taught David an important lesson: God doesn't *pamper* the righteous; He *tests* them. The suffering serves as a trial to purge the dross from our lives and make us stronger and more humble.

The hardships the Israelites endured in their wilderness journey served that same purpose. God allowed them to suffer, "that He might humble you and that He might test you, to do you good in the end" (Deut. 8:16). It was hard to appreciate in the midst of the pain, but they *needed* the adversity to toughen them up. Now it was David's turn to be tested.

God tests us, too. We strive to be good, not because it pays well, but because it's the right thing to do. Unfortunately, the world is a broken, ugly mess that does not care nor respect what we do—and in some cases will actively seek to oppose our efforts to live right. When the storm hits, we must remind ourselves that it's not because God is indifferent to our predicament; indeed, He cares very much. But it is precisely *because* He cares that He brings trials into our life. The suffering is His tool for making us stronger, better people.

That's why we should not pray that problems and hardships be removed from our lives. Instead, we should pray for God's strength to endure them—to pass the test and emerge stronger on the other side.

On those days when it seems that nothing is going right, everything seems to be against you, and God is nowhere to be found, just remember—you're being tested. "The Lord's throne is in heaven; His eyes behold" (v. 4), and someday He'll bring all this chaos to a satisfactory conclusion.

In the meantime, stay the course, be patient, pray for strength—and trust God to do what is right in His own time.

God Under Attack

The growing influence of atheism in our culture poses a threat, but Christianity is more than capable of responding—if we know how.

The fool has said in his heart, "There is no God" (Psa. 14:1; 53:1).

൙ൟ

In recent years, a number of popular books have been published that directly attack the idea of God. These include *The God Delusion* (Richard Dawkins, 2006), *Letter to a Christian Nation* (Sam Harris, 2008), and *God: The Failed Hypothesis* (Victor Stenger, 2008). These books have remained high on the best-seller lists, indicating a growing interest in atheism as a viable alternative to religion. One reviewer applauded that atheists are finally "coming out of the closet."

The days are long gone when we could approach the society around us with the assumption that most everyone believed in God, and our job was merely to convince them of the details that God has revealed in His word. Today, there is a decent chance that those with whom we come in contact do not believe in God. Or if they do, their "God" is some kind of weird, impersonal "force" rather than a personal deity of the Judeo-Christian variety. We must deal with the fact that our nation is rapidly turning into a post-Christian society.

These latest attacks on religion and belief are merely repackaging the same arguments that skeptics have been hurling at believers for centuries: If there is a God, why is there so much evil in the world?; religion (belief in God) causes far more suffering than it relieves; the advances of scientific knowledge have removed the need for God; so forth and so on. Mixed with a hearty dose of humor, ridicule, and scientific prose, the latest presentations of these arguments tap into the current widespread dissatisfaction with contemporary Christianity, and introduce a new generation to the possibility of another viewpoint.

But the new face on these old arguments cannot hide the deficiencies that have always doomed them. Even the *New York Times* reviewer who reviewed Dawkins' book conceded that "Darwinian processes can take you from simple to complex, but they can't take you from Nothing to Something" (Jim Holt, "Beyond Belief," *New York Times*, Oct. 22, 2006). In other words, after all the rhetorical twisting and posturing, atheists cannot explain where this universe and everything in it came from. To the believer, it's a no-brainer. To the atheist, it remains the ultimate mystery, a mystery that ironically must be accepted by *faith*.

Despite the ferocity of this latest assault on God, the battle is not lost. On the contrary, this development provides us with an opportunity to do what true Christianity does best, that is, to offer people a solution to the spiritual void in their inner lives. Despite the claims of the academic elites who write these popular tomes, human beings are spiritual creatures, and if God is taken from them, they will find or create something to replace Him. Genuine Christianity will always be in the game. It is our job to make sure that people see and appreciate the distinct advantages of true faith.

He is a fool who argues that there is no God. But he is a wise man who provides compelling evidence *by his life and conduct* that there is a God. Philosophical arguments for God have a role in this debate, but the best argument is a life that reflects His goodness.

If You Do Not Believe in God

Atheists accuse believers of clinging to an irrational belief system. But believers are not the only ones who carry a burden of proof.

The fool has said in his heart, "There is no God" (Psa. 14:1; 53:1).

◆

Listen to the God-deniers, however, and that label is turned around. Those who believe in God are considered ignorant dupes who rely on superstition and myth rather than reason and logic. Science, we are told, has so utterly discredited the idea of an all-powerful deity that only a fool would continue to cling to that belief. So believers today are on the defensive.

But we shouldn't be. Consider the logical consequences of believing there is no God, and it becomes clear that believers are not the ones with an intellectual problem.

First, if you do not believe that God exists, you must offer a reasonable alternative explanation as to *where everything came from*. In scientific language, this is known as "cosmogony," the study of the origin of the universe. The usual explanation is that determining the "first cause" of the universe lies outside the scope of natural science, so the question must remain unanswered.

That's a cop-out. The overwhelming evidence points to the universe having a beginning. (Some argue for a steady-state model, in which the universe has always existed. But that only further complicates the puzzle.) The skeptic is forced to take the position that this vast universe in which we live just popped into being out of absolute nothing. One moment, nothing existed—no matter, no thought, no design, no God; and the next moment, POOF!—there was a rapidly expanding universe, fully operational with a complete set of physical laws to guide it. Somehow, the skeptic has to explain how that transition took place.

Second, if you do not believe that God exists, you must explain the virtue of *morality*. I'm not talking about *how* morality came to be; I'm asking *why* it should exist at all. Flowery language about behaving "for the greater good of humanity" sounds appealing, but it does not answer the question of why "the greater good" should even matter at all. If there is no God, no judgment, no afterlife, no standard of right or wrong, then it doesn't matter how I behave, or who gets hurt by my behavior. How I live my life is my business, nobody else's; and there are no consequences to my behavior that matter one way or the other. "Morality" is merely a human construct that I can choose to honor or ignore at my whim. The only thing that really matters in the end is whether or not I can achieve some state of happiness before I die. Everyone else is on their own. The end result, of course, is the law of jungle, a mad rush to grab and hold while I can.

Let's sum up the evidence. Is it more reasonable to believe that an infinite Mind has always existed and created everything, or that Nothing gave birth to everything? Does it make more sense to believe that morality is merely the random product of human evolution, or that morality is in our social DNA, a fundamental element of our humanity that we neglect to our peril?

If you do not believe God exists, that's your business. But please don't ridicule believers as being stooges of blind faith. They aren't the ones with an irrational belief system.

Truth in the Heart

A man cannot be truthful in life if he is not first truthful with himself. That is often the hardest challenge of all.

Lord, who may abide in Your tabernacle? Who may dwell in Your holy hill? He who walks uprightly, and works righteousness, and speaks the truth in his heart (Psa. 15:1-2).

Honesty is an essential ingredient in our relationships with others, but even more so in one's relationship with himself. God requires that we continually examine ourselves in our faith journey (2 Cor. 13:5); but what good is a self-examination if the one taking the test cheats on the exam? The most fundamental requirement in approaching God, therefore, is a willingness to be brutally honest with ourselves about who we are.

Consider the parable of the prodigal son (Lk. 15:11-24). Here was a young man who made a series of foolish mistakes that cost him dearly. As long as he blamed his problems on his father, the weather, society at large, or "life is tough," his predicament would not improve. The first step on his road to recovery came when he took a long look at his situation and said to himself, "I have sinned" (v. 18). No excuses or intellectual feints; just cold, hard truth. His restoration was comparatively easy after that.

Or consider King David, "a man after God's own heart," who went on a detour of passion that took him far afield from his normal path. It took a stern lecture from a friend to wake him up to the awfulness of what he had done. The adultery and murder were bad enough, but the real damage was what David was doing to his soul. "You desire truth in the inward parts," he later confessed to God (Psa. 51:6), and that inner honesty was what David had lost and needed to regain. As long as he refused to face up to what he had done, correction and reconciliation was impossible.

This principle is not limited to juvenile delinquents and murderers. The need for self-improvement—and the willingness to admit it—is an ongoing struggle for all of us. "If we say that we have no sin, we deceive ourselves, and the truth is not in us" (1 Jn. 1:8). We must continually submit every aspect of our behavior, our words, and even our innermost thoughts and motives, to a rigorous review. There will never be a time in our life when we cannot find *something* that needs upgrading. Why pretend otherwise?

The biggest obstacle to speaking the truth in our hearts is stubborn pride. Like the Pharisee of old, we are eager to justify ourselves (Lk. 10:29; 16:15); that is, to obfuscate the facts and declare ourselves "not guilty." But that kind of dishonesty is a cruel trick we play on ourselves. God knows the real truth, even if we will not admit it, and someday we will be forced to face it, whether we like it or not.

The worst lie a man can tell is the lie he tells himself when he says he has no need of correction. Real growth cannot begin until he "speaks the truth in his heart," especially concerning his imperfections.

Another God

> Everyone of us has something in our life that we hold most dear. If that something is other than God, we have a problem with idolatry.

Their sorrows shall be multiplied who hasten after another god; their drink offerings of blood I will not offer, nor take up their names on my lips (Psa. 16:4).

The first rule in Israel's relationship with God was simple: "You shall have no other gods before Me" (Ex. 20:3). God's exclusive claim was not mere jealousy; it was a statement of fact: He existed, while the other gods were figments of human imagination. By replacing the true God with false substitutes in their affections, Israel was trading reality for a fantasy, truth for a lie.

Yet throughout her history, Israel balked at that restriction, flirting with a host of other gods they encountered among their neighbors. Baal, Asherah, Chemosh, Molech—mirages every one—captured Israel's affections, taking them down dark paths. But these adventures never turned out well. David warned that "their sorrows shall be multiplied who hasten after another god," and Israel learned that lesson the hard way, again and again.

We shake our heads in bewilderment; why would God's people dabble in such foolishness? But before we wag an accusing finger at them, we need to take a close look at our own lives. We may reject the pagan gods of old, but we have gods of our own that are just as seductive—and just as destructive—as their ancient counterparts.

Material prosperity is the deadliest false god. We knock ourselves out to acquire more money, more gadgets, more and bigger and better homes, cars, clothes, and investment portfolios. By chasing these physical things—which we cannot take with us when we go—we have replaced God with a counterfeit.

Careers and work necessarily consume a good chunk of our lives. But when they become the end-all of our existence, then we have surrendered our lives to another god. And when the day comes that we must give it up—sooner than we think—what will replace it?

Hobbies and recreation are perfectly legitimate fun, but they can easily crowd out activities that are more important. If we catch ourselves sacrificing more important functions (church, Bible study, family, prayer, charitable work) for our pastimes, it's a good bet those pastimes have become our personal god. But in the end, what do they really gain us?

Curiously, even *relationships* can become idolatrous. What else can we call it when a boyfriend or girlfriend becomes so important to us that we would just die—literally!—if we lost them? Spouses, children, and grandchildren are all delightful, but if we elevate them to a position of ultimate meaning in our lives, we are setting ourselves up for a terrible fall.

It is not a question of whether or not we believe that God exists; it's a question of what *role* He plays in our life. Try this mind-game on yourself: If your entire life were to be taken from you, one piece at a time, and you could choose what you had to give up, one piece at a time, *what is the very last thing you would cling to?* If you answer that question honestly, you will have identified your god. If the true God does not instantly come to mind, you have a false god running your life.

And somewhere down the road, that misplaced affection will cost you dearly.

Lines in Pleasant Places

Like a fortuitous allotment in a land drawing, our relationship with God puts us in a good place, no matter what happens around us.

O Lord, You are the portion of my inheritance and my cup; You maintain my lot. The lines have fallen to me in pleasant places; yes, I have a good inheritance (Psa. 16:5-6).

When Israel conquered the land of Canaan, the territory was apportioned to the people first by tribe, then by family (Num. 26:55; 33:54). The primary means of apportioning these plots of ground was by casting lots. This random process ensured a fair and impartial distribution of the land among all parties involved. Once the apportionment was completed, the boundary lines marked each family's plot of ground and were considered sacred, never to be violated.

David used this imagery of a random allotment to illustrate how circumstances in his life had turned out to his benefit. The "inheritance" that David is speaking of here, however, refers not to a spread of land, but to his relationship with God. Just as the Levites received no land in the dividing of Canaan but had God as their inheritance, so David viewed his relationship with God as his heritage. In reviewing all that God had done for him, he declared that "the lines have fallen to me in pleasant places; yes, I have a good inheritance." Like a lucky draw in the real estate lottery, David realized that he had been blessed in his life.

But David's cheerful message here seems problematic. Unless he wrote this Psalm very early in his life, his description of this "good inheritance" seems a little out of sync with the facts. Consider all the hardships that he encountered at the hands of King Saul, or the tragic consequences of his sin with Bathsheba, and the family disasters that followed thereafter. Throughout his life, David was well acquainted with grief; so how could he write something so positive? Wasn't he being a little unrealistic?

Unlike many of us, David viewed his life through an intensely *spiritual* framework. He considered the daily circumstances of his existence, whether good or bad, to be merely fleeting images—experienced momentarily, then quickly receding in the rear-view mirror. What gave his life real meaning was not these passing moments, but the knowledge that his life was in the hands of an all-powerful, all-knowing, and ever-present God. It was the *permanence* of that relationship that gave David a firm place to plant his feet, whatever tempest might be swirling around him at any given moment. When the storms of persecution and heartache crashed upon him, David saw his relationship with God as an unshakable inheritance. Even during his worst days, David knew that ultimately the lines had fallen to him in pleasant places, and life was good.

Remember that David lived in an age when God's plan for humanity was still shrouded in mystery. The hope of eternal life was there, but only dimly. Today, with the work of God's Son completed, we have even more reason to view God's blessings as a glorious inheritance. The lines have fallen to us in pleasant places, too—but only if we are mentally prepared to see them.

When life becomes difficult, look beyond the pain of the moment and ponder all that God has done for you. You have a good inheritance; enjoy it!

Science and Religion

> The conflict between science and religion
> need not be so antagonistic, if each side would
> take the time to understand the other.

The heavens declare the glory of God; and the firmament shows His handiwork (Psa. 19:1).

Since the creation of the world His invisible attributes are clearly seen, being understood by the things that are made, even His eternal power and Godhead, so that they are without excuse (Rom. 1:20).

Talk to people of faith about science, and you're likely to get a disdainful response. Talk to people of science about religion, and the reaction will no doubt be equally contemptuous. For a long time, science and religion have been antagonists in a bitter struggle for the hearts and minds of society. This hostility need not be, if both parties would take the trouble to understand one another.

For starters, both parties in this struggle need to be honest about their deficiencies. Religion, especially the Judeo-Christian variety, has provided a stabilizing influence through the ages, but there have been enough counterfeits and frauds to give the entire venture an ugly reputation. There's plenty of good and bad to go around (See Ross Douthat, *Bad Religion: How We Became a Nation of Heretics*, 2012).

Likewise, science has made notable contributions to human flourishing, but it has plenty to be embarrassed about, too. All the human foibles that corrupt religion are present

57

here as well: prejudice, confirmation bias, jealousy, dogmatism, deceit, and so forth (See Thomas Kuhn, *The Structure of Scientific Revolutions*, 2nd ed., 1970).

In other words, whatever our philosophical predispositions on this question, we all have need of a great deal of humility.

Since the early days of the Enlightenment, scientists such as Galileo, Newton, Kepler, Faraday, and others, grounded their discoveries in their faith. They believed that the God of the Bible left His fingerprints on His physical creation, and that motivated them to understand how His laws of nature worked.

Over the course of the nineteenth and twentieth centuries, that synergy between science and religion collapsed as the philosophy of materialism gradually pushed religion to the margins. However, scientific advances over the last several decades promise to restore the connection between theistic faith and science. Stephen Meyer's recent book, *Return of the God Hypothesis* (2021), highlights three independent streams of evidence that together build a compelling case for an intelligent designer: from *astronomy*, evidence that the universe had a beginning; from *physics*, evidence that the universe has been finely tuned for life; and from *biology*, evidence that life is the product of a remarkable information system encoded in DNA. Science and religion are not as far apart as we've led to believe. Indeed, as Paul says, God's "invisible attributes are clearly seen" through what has been made. We could even argue that the best way to come to God (religion) is to study what He has made (science).

Science and religion, each properly understood, need not be in conflict. Our challenge is to approach both fields of inquiry with an open mind, evaluating all the evidence from the Book of God and the Book of nature to learn the truth about ourselves and our world—and where it all came from.

Learning from the Night Sky

Gazing up at the night sky can make us feel small. But it can also deepen our faith, as we consider the One who made and sustains it all.

The heavens declare the glory of God; and the firmament shows His handiwork (Psa. 19:1).

The heavens declare His righteousness, and all the peoples see His glory (Psa. 97:6).

Lift up your eyes on high, and see who has created these things, who brings out their host by number; He calls them all by name, by the greatness of His might and the strength of His power; not one is missing (Isa. 40:26).

༺⚜༻

My favorite form of exercise is an early morning walk. Depending on the season, these walks often begin in darkness, well before dawn. If the skies are clear and it's a moonless night, I am greeted by a dazzling display of stars overhead. The Big Dipper and the Little Dipper, with its handle suspended from the North Star, dominate the northern sky. Orion's Belt looms overhead. Thousands of other points of light sparkle like tiny diamonds flung across the canopy of heaven. It's an awesome sight.

The night sky is magnificent to behold, but its wonder is magnified by the knowledge we have gained over the last century, as astronomers have peered deeper into the vastness of space. We have learned that our galaxy is only one among countless others, containing trillions of stars, stretching out at distances our minds struggle to comprehend. We do not have the words to describe the scope of what we are seeing.

To the Biblical writers, the wonders of the night sky force our minds to grapple with three unavoidable truths.

First, the heavens reinforce our appreciation for *the role of law in nature*. The cosmos is not a chaotic jumble, but a "handiwork," a complex system of physical laws characterized by orderliness and regularity. Structure and order in the physical realm suggest structure and order in the ethical realm as well, as we seek to find some purpose for our existence on this grand stage. There is meaning in this infinite arrangement, and it is worth our trouble to search for that meaning with all our might.

The scope and precision of this design in turn argues for *the existence of a divine Being*. When we stumble across an ancient complex of structures in a remote jungle, we correctly intuit that it was the creation of an intelligent agent. How much stronger is the evidence for a Master Designer and Builder when we study the vastness of space and all the heavenly bodies that inhabit it? It takes far more blind faith to believe that all this "just happened" than to believe in a wise and powerful God who designed and created it.

Finally, the heavens help us understand *the dignity of man*. It was David's awe at the beauty of the night sky that helped him appreciate the specialness of humanity (Psa. 8:3-8). We humans are part of this enormous creation, and the fact that, of all the life forms we know, we alone have the capacity to study it, to explore it, and to discover its secrets elevates us to a special place. Yes, we are a tiny blip in the universe; but we are uniquely privileged to ponder the reason why it should be so. That truth gives our lives a perspective that ought to inspire us to do our best.

When Job complained about God's apparent lack of concern for his miserable life, God gave him a primer on a variety of physical phenomena: geology, oceanography, meteorology, biology . . . and astronomy. He asked Job, "Do you know the ordinances of the heavens? Can you set their dominion over the earth?" (Job 38:31-33). No, we don't and can't. But we *can* know the One who created them all.

Sins of Ignorance

How do we—and God—deal with sins that we commit unawares? This is a very real problem for the honest believer, and the Bible addresses it.

Who can understand his errors? Cleanse me from secret faults. Keep back Your servant also from presumptuous sins; let them not have dominion over me. Then I shall be blameless, and I shall be innocent of great transgression (Psa. 19:12-13).

David's plea to God here recognizes two categories of sin: Sins that we commit *presumptuously*—that is, with full knowledge of our transgression; and *secret* faults—that is, sins of which we are unaware. Our interest here is in this latter category of transgressions.

These "secret faults" may arise out of an immature knowledge of God's law on some point, especially in a new believer; or we might say or do something in complete innocence, not realizing the harmful impact our conduct may have on others. Either way, these are transgressions committed by someone who, on the whole, is sincerely trying to do the right thing, but blindly making mistakes in the effort. We call these *sins of ignorance*.

Unfortunately, there is a great deal of ignorance about sins of ignorance and how God deals with them in the life of the believer. Let's review some basic facts about these sins.

Sins of ignorance are still sins. Some have argued that God does not hold people accountable for sins committed ignorantly. Moses wrote that if an Israelite violated God's law but "does not know it, yet he is guilty and shall bear his iniquity" (Lev. 5:17). Clearly, ignorance of the law is no excuse. And like all sin, sins of ignorance must be forgiven.

Sins of ignorance do not necessarily indicate a bad heart. I once heard a preacher argue that every sin a person commits, either presumptuously or in ignorance, is the result of an evil heart. That is Biblically inaccurate. It is entirely possible, especially in the lives of new believers, for someone with a good and honest heart to nevertheless commit a sin simply because they don't yet realize that some behavior is wrong. Consider, for example, the people of northern Israel who came to Jerusalem at the invitation of Hezekiah to worship God. Because they had had little exposure to the Law of Moses, their worship was "contrary to what was written" in a few particulars. Yet they had "prepared their hearts to seek God," and God forgave them (2 Chron. 30:18-20). They were honestly mistaken, but wanted to do the right thing. God can work with people like that.

Sins of ignorance need not be specifically identified in order to be forgiven. At the annual Day of Atonement, the high priest went into the temple's Most Holy Place to offer a sacrifice "for the people's sins committed in ignorance" (Heb. 9:7). Throughout the year, the Israelites offered other sacrifices for sins of which they were aware. But for all the other sins they had committed unawares, there was one annual "generic" sacrifice. It is entirely appropriate for a child of God to pray, "cleanse me from secret faults" (Psa. 19:12), without giving a detailed list of what those faults are.

Finally, *sins of ignorance are not the same as willful ignorance.* God's provisions for dealing with sins of ignorance do not apply to the person who, through laziness or defiance, chooses simply not to know. God expects us to "grow in the grace and knowledge" of our Lord (2 Pet. 3:18). Over time, our sins of ignorance will become fewer and smaller. If we fail to maintain this growth, expecting God to cover the bill, we abuse His grace. And *that* is the greatest sin of all.

Pure Heart, Clean Hands

What God asks of us is not complicated.
Two simple ingredients make all the difference
in defining our relationship with Him.

Who may ascend into the hill of the LORD? Or who may stand in His holy place? He who has clean hands and a pure heart . . . (Psa. 24:3-4).

Cleanse your hands, you sinners; and purify your hearts, you double-minded (Jas. 4:8).

The definition of a righteous life has never changed throughout the ages. Both David in the Old Testament and James in the New Testament reduce everything to two simple character traits: *a pure heart* and *clean hands*.

True religion always begins with a pure heart. To our modern Western minds, the heart is the seat of our emotions, that part of our inner topography that "feels" some emotional response to our outer circumstances. But in Biblical lexicology, the heart lies much deeper in the inner self. It is the engine of all our decision-making, the foundational starting point of all our words, actions, and thoughts. "Everything you do flows from it" (Prov. 4:23, NIV).

That's why James directs the injunction to "purify your hearts" to the *double-minded* person, the one who goes through life with two minds—one serving God, the other serving his own selfish interests. His thinking is a jumbled confusion of half-committed intentions and weak passions. The "pure in heart" does not suffer this spiritual schizophrenia. His thoughts are carefully calibrated toward one goal in life—to serve God. Everything he does is measured against that objective. He is not a religious freak; he just has a single straightforward purpose in life. And it starts in his heart.

This pure heart will be accompanied by clean hands. Our hands are the primary instruments by which our bodies interact with the world around us. With our hands we build civilization; we bind the wounds of the sick; we write notes of encouragement to the weak; we lift the burdens of the oppressed. But with our hands we also stab our neighbor in the back, or take what is not rightfully ours. Or we can simply sit on our hands and do nothing. Whatever we do with our hands, God is taking notes, and someday we will have to give an account for what we have done with them.

Clean hands and a pure heart always go together. A virtuous life doesn't just happen; it is the result of a deliberate exercise of the will, a heart that is concentrated with laser focus on doing the right thing, even when it hurts. Likewise, we cannot pass off irresponsible behavior with the cliché, "at least my heart is in the right place." If your life is a reckless mess, it's because your heart led you there. Cosmetic adjustments on the outside won't fix that mess; a wholesale transformation of the heart must be performed deep down inside. *What is it that I really want in life? Who is it that I am really serving?* Until we confront those questions in a serious self-examination, our lives will always be disjointed and directionless.

A pure heart is not perfect, but it knows the ultimate destination for which it is striving, and is constantly adjusting it's trajectory to get there. And our hands will follow where the heart is leading.

What God requires of us is not impossible nor unreasonable. All He asks is that we give our lives, both heart and body, to Him. Such a life is liberating, refreshing, and rich with meaning and purpose. It is the only life worth living.

To Trust God

Trusting God is much more than an empty slogan. It demands a complete reordering of our approach to life, putting God at the center.

O my God, I trust in You; let me not be ashamed (Psa. 25:2).
Though He slay me, yet will I trust Him (Job 13:15).

"Trust God" has become a tired cliché in our modern religious culture. If we are uncertain about a course of action, we fall back on "trust God" as the default response. It sounds spiritual, but it usually reduces God to a good luck charm, not much more.

In the Biblical tradition, trusting God involves much more than merely invoking His name to get His blessing. Rather, it requires four responses in our life:

First, *we must trust His word.* God has gone to a great deal of trouble to provide us a body of instruction that can be of enormous benefit in navigating our path through life. His word can save us from confusion and stumbling, if we take it seriously. The problem comes when His guidance contradicts our feelings, or when His instructions seem counter-intuitive (for example, "Love your enemies." Really??). But if we truly trust God, then we must honor His word, regardless of how challenging that message may be.

Second, *we must trust His providence.* Instead of allowing our minds to become consumed with anxiety when things seem to be going sideways, we must turn all our worries over to God's capable hands. Even when it looks like everything is spiraling out of control, we have to remind ourselves that God knows what is best, and sometimes "what is best" won't make sense to us. Disappointments, setbacks, loss—God can use all this detritus to accomplish ends we cannot see. But we must deal with them without becoming bitter.

Third, *we must trust His promises.* There are tangible benefits that we can generally expect from following God's directions: long life, healthy relationships, prosperity, and so forth. These are nice to have, but not guaranteed. There are other promises, however, that stand on surer ground, and are much more useful: peace of mind, a sense of divine forgiveness, and the expectation of eternal life on the other side of death. These promises make life worth living, if we can cling to them regardless of our current circumstances.

Finally, *we must trust the outcome.* Job's trust was severely tested by the trials that befell him, yet he refused to surrender his conviction that God knew what he was doing. He trusted that someday God would make everything right again. "Though He slay me" was not a clever rhetorical flourish; it was a grim reality that Job could not understand, but was willing to accept as part of a broader plan he could not see.

Do you trust God? Apply these four tests to your life, and you'll know if you really do trust Him—or if you are just using Him to get what you want.

Wait on the Lord

When life appears to be one long torture session, our only option is to wait for the Lord to bring it to a conclusion. He will do so—when He is ready.

Wait on the LORD; be of good courage, and He shall strengthen your heart; wait, I say, on the LORD! (Psa. 27:14).

Rest in the LORD, and wait patiently for Him; do not fret because of him who prospers in his way, because of the man who brings wicked schemes to pass (Psa. 37:7).

I wait for the LORD, my soul waits, and in His word I do hope (Psa. 130:5).

৩০৫

David knew a thing or two about waiting on the Lord. Several times in his life he found himself in a bind from which he could not extricate himself, and the path forward was dark and foreboding. He knew he had been chosen by God, but God provided no details about how this story would play out. All he could do was . . . wait.

The concept of "waiting on the Lord" is found over a dozen times in the Psalms, usually in the context of dealing with hardship. Like David, we need to develop an appreciation for this godly discipline in our lives.

Americans in general are not a patient people. We demand prompt service in every area of life, and if we don't get it, we take our business elsewhere. But there are some problems in life over which we have no control, and all our complaining about how unfair it is won't change the outcome. What do we do then?

In its simplest definition, waiting for the Lord means that we look to God to deal with our problems in His own way and on His own schedule. In our individualistic culture, we are conditioned to think that it's up to us to think, plan, and work our way out of whatever troubles we encounter in life. But sooner or later we find that there are some obstacles we cannot overcome on our own effort. There are enemies whose cruelties seem never to end. When we've exhausted all our resources and come to the end of our strength, we have no other recourse: We must look to God to deal with it as He chooses. And He *will* deal with it—but on His timetable, not ours.

Waiting for the Lord involves viewing our life through the lens of eternity. Our life is but a vapor, a shadow, a flower that blooms for a short while, then is gone. Once we develop that mindset, we can better appreciate the fact that all the issues we encounter in this life are really not that important. Sooner than we expect, our life—and all the troubles that accompany it—will be over, and we will be ushered into eternity. What will we have gained from all the worry and anxiety that we expended during our brief sojourn here in this life?

Friend, your life is too short to waste it fretting about your problems. Do the best you can with what you have, and wait on the Lord to do His part. He understands your predicament, and He will strengthen your heart to endure it.

Rise of the "Don'ts"

The decline of faith in our culture is nothing new. It has happened before, and history provides an outline of how this trend will eventually play out.

Because they do not regard the works of the LORD, nor the operation of His hands, He shall destroy them and not build them up (Psa. 28:5).

Therefore I said, "Surely these are poor. They are foolish; for they do not know the way of the LORD" (Jer. 5:4).

For many years, George Barna has been conducting surveys to gauge the spiritual status of American culture. In the most recent survey (2021), Barna discovered what he called "the most rapid and radical cultural upheaval our nation has ever experienced" (David Closson, "New Barna Research Reveals Extent of America's Loss of Faith," *FRC.org*, June 22, 2021). The shift is especially pronounced among millennials. This latest survey does not bode well for orthodox Christianity over the next half-century.

Barna calls this emerging class of Americans the "Don'ts." They either don't believe in God, or don't know, or don't care. Whatever the specifics of their individual beliefs, the net effect of this intellectual emptiness is a widespread societal drift away from God and His word. People will not live up to an ideal if they are not convinced of its validity.

This development may alarm us, but none of it is new to God. The Old Testament is the history of an earlier people who had every opportunity to recognize God's role in their lives, yet who again and again drifted into complacency or outright defiance. Their digressions never ended well for them. Their story serves as a template for all of human history: The closer a nation draws to God and His principles of moral conduct, the more likely they are to experience peace and prosperity; the farther away they drift from God, the more likely they are to encounter societal decay and collapse.

Our nation's evolution into spiritual indifference is not exempt from this cause-and-effect principle. Eventually the day will come when "He shall destroy them," not in a fit of pique over being ignored, but as a natural consequence of their apathy. God's instructions for our life are not arbitrary; they fit what we were designed to be, and when we flout those instructions we set ourselves up for a dramatic fall. The collapse of moral integrity we are witnessing around us is the inevitable outcome of a population that has jettisoned God.

Lest we become disheartened by these developments, let's remember the other side of Israel's story. No matter how dark the times, God always had a remnant who remained loyal to Him, and that remnant usually served as the foundation for a renaissance of faith on the other side of catastrophe. God still has His remnant today, and somewhere beyond the present gloom He will rebuild civilization anew.

Let us not be discouraged, but let us hold fast to our faith and look to God's final victory.

My Rock and My Fortress

When life conspires to beat us down, we have access to a strength that will enable us to stand firm, if we will take advantage of it.

Bow down Your ear to me, deliver me speedily; be my rock of refuge, a fortress of defense to save me. For You are my rock and my fortress; therefore, for Your name's sake, lead me and guide me (Psa. 31:2-3).

൭൦ഏ

In ancient times, the ideal refuge from marauding armies was a strong fortress built on a high mountain. Attackers could not use siege engines against its walls, and its elevated position limited the amount of damage that could be done by lobbing stones into it. Stocked with ample supplies of food and water, a mountain fortress was impregnable, and its inhabitants safe from harm.

In David's mind, this image of a strong mountain fortress was the ideal metaphor to describe his relationship with God. He often used the expression "my rock and my fortress" to describe the role that God played in his life (see also 18:2 and 71:3). A study of this Psalm will help us see in God that same refuge.

David wrote this Psalm in a time of extreme affliction: "I am in trouble; my eye wastes away with grief, yes, my soul and my body!" (v. 9). This affliction came from two directions. First, he was targeted by personal enemies who sought to destroy him: "I hear the slander of many; . . . they take counsel together against me, they scheme to take away my life" (v. 13, see v. 4, 15). Even his friends turned against him

(v. 11). It's hard to be optimistic when it seems that the whole world is out to get you.

But trying to evade the schemes of his enemies was complicated by a second problem: the frustration of having to deal with his own mistakes and failures: "My strength fails because of my iniquity, and my bones waste away" (v. 10). Between the attacks of his enemies and the burden of his own guilt, David felt like "a broken vessel" (v. 12), worthless and despised.

All of us at one time or another can relate to David's despair. We may try to hide the pain behind a false front of cheerfulness, but in our hearts we struggle to find anything to cheer about. Life seems destined to destroy us.

David found refuge from his depression in God. Three times in this Psalm, he says that his trust was in God (v. 1, 6, 14). He could not trust others; he could not trust his own abilities. But in God he found a source of strength that enabled him to face the challenges that threatened him.

David's trust in God was not merely an act of mental concentration. His confidence influenced the way he lived. "You are my rock and my fortress; therefore, for Your name's sake, *lead me and guide me*" (v. 3). David cast himself upon God's mercy, not only as a shield from harm, but as a source of guidance. By staying close to God, David found the counsel he needed to make better decisions in dealing with the challenges that confronted him. We cannot expect God to help us, if we reserve the right to ignore His instructions when we find them inconvenient.

The message of this Psalm is simple: Life can be tough, but it need not be miserable: "I will be glad and rejoice in Your mercy" (v. 7). If we flee to God as our rock and our fortress we, too, can take on life with assurance. "Be of good courage, and He shall strengthen your heart" (v. 24).

Confess Your Sins

Making progress in overcoming our weaknesses requires that we own up to them. That's why confessing our sins is so important.

I acknowledged my sin to You, and my iniquity I have not hidden. I said, "I will confess my transgressions to the Lord," and You forgave the iniquity of my sin (Psa. 32:5).

Confess your trespasses to one another, and pray for one another, that you may be healed. The effective, fervent prayer of a righteous man avails much (Jas. 5:16).

Our society long ago dismissed the concept of sin as a relic of a more unsophisticated age. Today, rather than confess our sins, we redefine them as "failing to meet our potential"; or we blame others for the mess we made; or we minimize the seriousness of the error; or we stubbornly deny that we did anything wrong at all—anything other than just owning up to our mistakes.

Why it is so important that we confess our sins? From a practical standpoint, it's the only way we can make any progress in improving our character. If we cannot admit that we have a problem, the problem will never be fixed. That's why the unwillingness to confess our sins usually has a detrimental effect on our psychological well-being. The unresolved guilt and shame remains bottled up inside, leading to a decline in mental health.

Consider the two parties to whom confession should be made. The first is *God* ("confess . . . to the Lord"). Telling God that we have sinned seems so abstract and pointless. After all, God already knows everything we've done, right? Furthermore, He does not respond to our confession in any visible, tangible way, so what's the point?

David's experience in Psalms 32 reveals the value of this private act of honesty. Prior to his confession, while he "kept silent" about his sin (v. 3), he felt the sharp pangs of guilt: "groaning all the day long" (v. 3); his "vitality was turned into . . . drought" (v. 4). But once he acknowledged his wrong to God, he felt the cathartic relief of forgiveness (v. 5).

The second party to whom we should confess our sins is *other believers* ("confess . . . to one another"). When we are transparent with others, we accomplish two things: First, we make ourselves accountable for our actions. The feedback, encouragement, and counsel that others provide us can be immensely helpful in overcoming our weaknesses. Furthermore, if our sins involve pain that we have inflicted upon others, then a genuine apology can go a long way toward providing the reconciliation—James uses the word "healing"—that we desire. Strong relationships are built upon this kind of honest humility.

When we refuse to confess our sins—either to God or to one another—we are displaying a symptom of a deeper and more serious sin: *pride*. By keeping our sins bottled up, hidden, out of sight, we're being dishonest, not just with God and others, but with ourselves.

It requires a generous dose of humility to admit that we've made a serious error. But once we have mustered the courage to make that admission, we are then in a better position to address the issues that led to the sin. We're better people for it—and that's a good thing.

Confession of sin is not just a generic acknowledgment that "I am a sinner." That's important, but confession also involves being as specific about our wrongdoing as possible. Once we build that habit into our character, we'll start to make significant progress in our growth as children of God.

Harnessing the Mind

Unlike animals, we have the ability to make moral choices in our lives. But making good choices first requires a willingness to accept God's guidance.

I will instruct you and teach you in the way you should go; I will guide you with My eye. Do not be like the horse or like the mule, which have no understanding, which must be harnessed with bit and bridle, else they will not come near you (Psa. 32:9).

One of the great inventions in the history of technology is the *harness*, a contraption placed on an animal's head that enables its owner to control the animal. With the advent of the harness, wild and untamed animals have become domesticated partners in the building of civilization.

Humans are animals, too, but with one important difference: We can reason abstractly about our purpose in life, and make ethical choices based on that reasoning. This awareness of right and wrong forces us to struggle with temptations that do not concern the lower animals. Passions such as lust, envy, pride, greed, hate, laziness, and so on, scream to be unleashed in our lives. Let these passions run loose, and humans can be just as wild as any animal—and far more destructive.

We need restraints on our behavior. But where do those restraints come from? At one level, that's the role of society. Little children, for example, must be restricted by their parents from behaviors that will harm themselves. Adult sociopaths must be confined behind prison bars to limit the damage they can inflict upon the rest of us. When people live like animals, they will be treated like animals. Without these shackles, we all suffer.

But there is another kind of restraint. The very thing that makes us different from the animals also provides an alternative to external chains. The "harness" that best serves humanity is the one we impose upon ourselves: *self*-restraint. Control imposed from within frees us from bondage to our passions and enables us to better serve others and self.

But where does this self-discipline originate? In this Psalm, God points to its origin: "I will instruct and teach you in the way you should go." Unlike the animals, who must be trained by a crude system of rewards, punishments, and/or physical restraints, human behavior can be shaped by instruction. The same mental apparatus that allows us to *reason* abstractly can be *taught* abstractly. To state the matter simply, human behavior is tamed by educating the mind that controls it. And God's word is the ideal source of that instruction.

But why should we listen to God? The world offers a plethora of philosophies, ideologies, and dogmas to fill this mental vacuum. Why not choose one of these alternatives that is more to my liking? Because much of this intellectual material is worthless, even harmful, in some cases promoting behavior that can harm ourselves and others. Of course, we won't learn of these harmful consequences until after we've drunk the Kool-Aid. Only then will we discover that we built our mental framework on a foundation of quicksand.

So we are caught in a circular loop. Our minds are deeply influenced by our intellectual surroundings; but those surroundings are shaped by the choices we make—the friends we hang out with, the media we watch and listen to, the books we read, the educational institutions we immerse ourselves in, the worldview we adopt, and so forth. Amid this cacophony of noise, God calls out to us, desiring to instruct us in the way we should go. But we must make a conscious effort to open our hearts to His guidance.

Or we can choose to do our own thing and be treated like a stubborn mule. Choose wisely.

The Secret to a Happy Life

A good life is not the product of happenstance. It is the result of a long series of choices guided by commitment to a simple moral code.

Come, you children, listen to me; I will teach you the fear of the Lord. Who is the man who desires life, and loves many days, that he may see good? Keep your tongue from evil, and your lips from speaking deceit. Depart from evil and do good; seek peace and pursue it (Psa. 34:11-14).

According to the preface of this Psalm, it was written by David during that lonely period when he was fleeing from Saul, when he had few friends upon whom he could depend. With these words, David reminded himself that regardless of how others treated him, "the fear of the Lord" still compelled him to maintain a certain lifestyle. His current circumstances did not offer much evidence of it, but he was confident that such a life would ultimately result in the greatest good.

David's guidance remains good advice for those today who desire to live their lives to the best possible effect. It is such an excellent summary, that Peter quotes it verbatim in writing to people who, like David, were suffering persecution (1 Pet. 3:10-12). We can think of this passage, therefore, as the recipe for a long and happy life in the midst of a crazy and imperfect world.

David reduces this good life to four simple rules:

Keep your tongue from evil. James wrote that one who has mastered his tongue is a "perfect" man, who has learned the art of self-discipline (Jas. 3:2). There are so many temptations to misusing our tongues—cursing, gossip, reviling, slander, anger, blasphemy, boasting, and so on—that this battle will occupy our attention throughout our lives. David singles out one misuse of the tongue for special warning: *deceit,* or lying. Above all, we must strive to be truthful in all our dealings with others. Nothing will damage our character more deeply than a habit of being untrustworthy. The person who keeps his word and tells the truth, even when it hurts, will go far in life.

Depart from evil. Beyond the use of the tongue, there are many other moral failings that we must learn to avoid. The fact that we have free will does not mean that all choices are equally valid or good. Some behaviors are prohibited specifically, and we must respect the boundaries God has erected: Do not steal. Do not commit fornication. Do not physically harm others. Do not mistreat your own body. Other offenses are of a more general nature, and must be learned through experience. "Love does no harm to a neighbor" is a good yardstick to apply when trying to determine the correct course of action (Rom. 13:10).

Do good. It is not enough merely to avoid evil; any Pharisee can do that. We must also be devoted to a life of *active* goodwill. Share your possessions with those who are in need. Encourage the weak. Pray for all men, even your enemies. Nothing will help you more effectively manage your own troubles than getting involved in helping others with theirs.

Seek peace and pursue it. In a world being ripped apart by conflict, this is the trait that can have the greatest impact. As much as possible, we must strive to promote harmony in all our relations with others. Of course, David knew from his own troubles that this isn't always possible. But in the end, peacemakers will leave a positive mark on the world.

David eventually lived to see his faith in this moral code vindicated. We will see it, too, but only if we diligently train ourselves to live by its direction.

The Afflictions of the Righteous

God promises to deliver his people. But how can we reconcile that promise with the harsh reality of pain in the lives of even the best of people?

Many are the afflictions of the righteous, but the Lord delivers him out of them all (Psa. 34:19).

The Lord will deliver me from every evil work and preserve me for His heavenly kingdom (2 Tim. 4:18).

David knew a thing or two about affliction. According to the preface that leads Psalm 34, he wrote these words during an especially difficult time in his life. He was hounded by enemies among his own people, and scorned by the Philistines in whose company he sought refuge. Life couldn't get any more ugly for him.

Yet even in the midst of all his troubles, David was confident that someday God would deliver him. Did God live up to David's expectations? Well, sorta. David did eventually outlast his enemies and become a very successful king over all Israel. But that improvement in his circumstances merely traded one set of problems for another. His personal life was an unholy mess involving scandal, estrangement, even treason. Several of his children met violent ends, and one led an armed rebellion that nearly cost David his throne. Again and again, he felt the bitter heartache of tragedy and loss. Where was God in all of this?

The story of David's life illustrates one of the great enigmas of divine providence: If the righteous endure affliction throughout their lives—in some cases, "many" afflictions—

how can the Bible speak in such lofty terms of God "delivering" them? With stories like those of David or Job or the exiles in Babylon, that promise seems like a cruel joke. Even the Bible speaks of God's people as being "sheep for the slaughter" (Rom. 8:36). Where's the deliverance in *that*?

There are two answers to this dilemma. First, for all their hardships, the righteous generally do enjoy a reduced level of suffering compared to the wicked. Life is not perfect for any of us, but the wicked almost always have a harder time of it.

Second, this dilemma arises out of a narrow perspective on life. Yes, the righteous often suffer in this life, sometimes cruelly so. *But this life is not all there is.* When the righteous man dies from a horrible disease or accident or persecution, his demise does not invalidate God's protection. Rather, his death is merely the leaving of one form of existence for something much better. The few difficult years spent here on this earth cannot compare to the eternity of peace that lies beyond—a deliverance that was promised by God all along.

Like David, Paul also endured many afflictions in his life. At the end, as he faced certain execution at the hands of his captors, he could have railed at God for failing to deliver him. But he didn't. Instead, his impending departure filled him with an eager anticipation of the reward that lay beyond in that "heavenly kingdom." "The Lord will deliver me" was no idle promise to Paul; it was a hope that guided every moment of his life, right up to the very end.

When we face adversity in our life, we can find comfort in God's promise to deliver us. But we must be careful to place that promise in the much larger context of God's plans, not ours. Whatever good things we may experience here, the real deliverance will not come until after the transition to our eternal home.

Do Not Fret

It's hard to be optimistic when the wicked seem to have the upper hand. But optimism is not only possible, God demands it. One psalm tells us how.

Do not fret because of evildoers . . . Trust in the Lord and do good. . . . Rest in the Lord, and wait patiently for Him; do not fret because of him who prospers in his way, because of the man who brings wicked schemes to pass. Cease from anger, and forsake wrath; do not fret—it only causes harm (Psa. 37:1, 3, 7, 8).

Psalm 37 is my go-to text when anxious thoughts start to creep into my mind. In an age when it seems that evil is corrupting every corner of society and good people are targeted for persecution, the words of this Psalm are more powerful than ever. We all need to dig deeper into this Psalm and learn encouragement from its message.

First, notice that the psalm does not minimize the gravity of what confronts us. David freely acknowledges the success of the wicked in pushing their evil agenda. They scheme (v. 7), plot (v. 12), defraud (v. 21), and attack incessantly (v. 14, 32). They achieve positions of extraordinary power that enable them to impose their evil agenda upon others (v. 35). It's hard to be optimistic when facing such an implacable foe.

But optimism is not only possible, God insists upon it. This psalm offers a simple three-pronged approach for maintaining a positive attitude in a negative world.

First, there is something we must learn to avoid: *"Do not fret"* (v. 1, 7, 8). Other versions read, "don't be upset," or "do not be agitated," or simply "don't worry." In other words, we need to calm down and get a grip. The natural inclination when we are mistreated is to strike back, to somehow put the wicked in his place. But that never works. In fact, "it only causes harm" (v. 8). What have we accomplished if we allow a wicked person to drag us down to his level?

Instead, we must train ourselves to *"trust the Lord"* (v. 3, 5, 40). When surrounded by evil, it's easy to get discouraged and assume that all is lost. But if our mind is focused on God, we realize that what we are witnessing is only a temporary blip in a much larger pattern of history. David assures us that the wicked "shall soon be cut down like the grass" (v. 2). "In a little while" the wicked will be no more (v. 10, 20, 28, 34, 36, 38). However ominous his threats, it is only bluster and bluff. "The Lord laughs at him, for He sees that his day is coming" (v. 13). If God is laughing at the pompous posturing of the wicked, can't we at least smile? We must look at the larger canvas and realize that God is still in control, and the wicked will someday get his due.

Finally, we must *"wait on the Lord"* (v. 7, 9, 34). This is not a passive sitting on our hands expecting God to do something; rather, it is an active lifestyle of godliness. That means we "do good" (v. 3, 27), "show mercy and give" (v. 21, 26), and "speak wisdom and . . . justice" (v. 30). Our lives must be a reflection of the One whose glory we honor, even when it appears that nothing comes of it.

What will be the outcome of such a strategy? "The future of that man is peace" (v. 37). Someday we'll be able to look back on the hard times and realize that God knew what He was doing all along.

But that insight only comes to those who calmly trust and wait.

The Meek

"The meek shall inherit the earth" doesn't make much sense, until we take the trouble to learn who "the meek" are. The answer may surprise us.

But the meek shall inherit the earth, and shall delight themselves in the abundance of peace (Psa. 37:11).

Blessed are the meek, for they shall inherit the earth (Matt. 5:5).

❧

The Biblical concept of meekness is difficult to capture in English. The various translations struggle with the word, variously rendering it as *gentle, humble, lowly,* or *poor*—none of which adequately capture the rich nuance of the idea. The ambiguity of the term is further complicated by the promise attached to it: "Inherit the earth." Huh?

As is often the case, the context in which this verse is found illuminates its meaning. Psalm 37 is David's look back over his life from the vantage point of old age (v. 25). His life experiences taught him one lesson above all else: Whatever the momentary triumphs of the wicked, in the end they will lose, and the righteous will be rewarded. No matter how rigged the game seems to be in the moment, eventually the truth will win out and justice will be served.

This general theme is summarized in v. 9: "Evildoers shall be cut off; but those who wait on the Lord, they shall inherit the earth." The language here provides a clue to the identity of the "meek"—they are those who "wait on the Lord" (see also v. 34). In short, *the meek are those who have learned the value of patience.* When evil and injustice swirl around them, they do not get upset or angry (v. 1, 7, 8). They remain poised, calm, deliberate, focused, confident that God is in control and will eventually balance the books. They know that someday the wheels of justice will catch up, and God will see to it that the wicked get what is coming to them.

In the meantime, the righteous have an outlook on life that prepares them to engage it successfully. No drama, no anxiety, no panic—just a steady walk in the light of God's truth, confident in the outcome. "The future of that man is peace" (v. 37), both in this life and the next. Moreover, it is the righteous—those who "meekly" endured the madness of the wicked during the height of his folly—who are positioned to rebuild society after the wicked crash and burn.

When Jesus borrowed from this Psalm in one of His Beatitudes, He was drawing on a rich Hebrew tradition of faith. The meek are those who have figured out that life is not the train wreck it appears to be. They hold to a confidence that someday God will sort out all the chaos and make everything right again. Armed with that knowledge, they are prepared to enjoy life to the fullest, despite the mischief that surrounds around them. When the dust settles, the meek are best positioned to rebuild from the ruins.

Look at your own response to the turmoils of life. Does "meekness" describe your approach? If not, you have some serious reconstructive surgery to perform on your faith. Start by reading Psalm 37 several times.

The Arc of the Moral Universe

> History may appear to be a jumble of chaotic indifference, but there is an invisible Hand guiding events inexorably toward a just conclusion.

I have been young, and now am old; yet I have not seen the righteous forsaken, nor his descendants begging bread. . . . For the Lord loves justice, and does not forsake His saints; they are preserved forever, but the descendants of the wicked shall be cut off" (Psa. 37:25, 28).

෴

The Bible teaches the concept of a final judgment, a grand tribunal where every evil will be fully recompensed. All perpetrators will be punished, all victims will be vindicated, and the scales of justice finally will be balanced.

But justice is not necessarily limited to the afterlife. David's words in this Psalm, written near the end of a long life experiencing both good and evil, reflect an understanding of justice that plays out even as history unfolds before our eyes. We may not have to wait until the final judgment to see the wicked man get his due; there is a good chance we will witness it here in this life.

In the mid-19th century a Unitarian minister named Theodore Parker predicted the demise of slavery by appealing to what he saw as an historical template. In his words, "The arc of the moral universe is long, but it bends toward justice." It took a bloody civil war, but Parker's prediction eventually came to pass, and justice was served upon that evil institution. A century later, Martin Luther King, Jr., often quoted Parker's words to revive the hopes of those who longed to see the end of forced segregation. Once again, the moral arc slowly but inexorably bent toward justice.

Study the vast sweep of history and you'll see the wisdom of this truth play out again and again. Without exception, every great empire that established itself upon violence and oppression eventually came to an ugly end. The Old Testament prophets spoke confidently of the downfalls of Assyria, Babylon, Persia, and Greece—in some cases before these empires even existed. Tyrants who boasted of their power and invincibility died like everyone else, and the monuments they erected to their own vanity were soon torn down. The early church suffered at the hands of mighty Rome, yet over time the movement proved to have greater staying power than its persecutors. Again and again, the moral arc of history has tended toward the vindication of the innocent and the repudiation of the guilty.

In a day when it seems that the forces of evil are crushing everything that is right and good—and, ironically, even misappropriating Parker's maxim to justify their own wicked schemes—it is important that we keep this principle firmly fixed in our minds. Somewhere down history's road, the ungodly will be judged and the blameless will be exonerated. It may not happen in our lifetime, and it could involve a violent upheaval to set everything right again, but it *will* happen. The arc of the moral universe will not be denied.

"The Lord loves justice," and history bears the imprint of that eternal truth. No matter how grim our current circumstances may appear, the child of God can take comfort in the knowledge that they are only temporary, and that justice will someday prevail. History is in the hands of a just God; He will make sure of it.

To Inherit the Earth

A final reward in the afterlife is our ultimate hope, but there is a sense in which our righteousness is rewarded in this life, if we patiently wait for it.

*For evildoers shall be cut off; but those who wait on the LORD, they **shall inherit the earth**. . . . But the meek **shall inherit the earth**, and shall delight themselves in the abundance of peace. . . . For those blessed by Him **shall inherit the earth**, but those cursed by Him shall be cut off. . . . The righteous **shall inherit the land**, and dwell in it forever (Psa. 37:9, 11, 22, 29).*

Written by King David in his old age (v. 25), this Psalm reflects on a pattern of events that he had seen unfold again and again throughout his life: Evil men make life miserable for others (v. 1, 21, 32), while people of faith quietly go about doing good, even when it is not reciprocated (v. 27, 28, 30). Eventually the wicked get what is coming to them (v. 9, 10, 13, 15, 17, 20, 28, 34, 38), while the righteous "wait patiently" for God to balance the books (v. 7, 9, 34).

David repeatedly assures the righteous that in this cosmic calibration of right-and-wrong, they "shall inherit the earth." Jesus underscores this promise by quoting it verbatim in one of His Beatitudes (Matt. 5:5). It is tempting to read this promise as referring to a final reward in the afterlife. Although a final judgment of the righteous and the wicked awaits us all, this chapter seems to be describing a pattern of history that we can witness *now*. The reward involves "the earth . . . the land," not heaven. Notice also that David uses the past tense to describe his own experience with this phenomenon ("I have seen," v. 35), and assures us that we can see it, too (v. 34). Clearly, there is a sense in which the righteous can experience some degree of recompense in this life. What does it mean to "inherit the land"?

We can quickly eliminate for consideration any hope of a formal land grant ("forty acres and a mule") in the here and now. Not only do we rarely ever see that kind of payoff transpire for the righteous, it smacks of a carnal health-and-wealth approach to serving God.

Some have used this language to support their concept of life on a rejuvenated earth following the Second Coming. Not only does this violate David's description of an ongoing phenomenon, it flies in the face of other texts that describe this heavens and earth passing away (Rev. 21:1; 2 Pet. 3:10).

The best way to read this promise is to see it as *a prevailing trend in history*. Evil people prosper for a while, and good people suffer at their hands, but that imbalance never lasts long. The wicked fade away, and the righteous—who quietly kept on doing good during the dark days—resume their rightful place as the salt of the earth. For every Genghis Khan, Hitler, or Stalin who makes life miserable for their victims, there are millions of good people whose decency and hard work keep this world moving forward, long after the tyrants are gone. The earth belongs to these people, not their oppressors, and God will make sure that order is maintained. Even in the midst of their troubles, the righteous can take solace in the knowledge that "all things are yours" (1 Cor. 3:21). They see a reality that others cannot see.

If you are troubled by the success of evil people in our society who seem to be gaining the upper hand, spend more time reading Psalm 37. Someday the forces of evil will overplay their hand, and the meek shall be restored to their rightful place as the keepers of God's good earth. "When the wicked are cut off, you shall see it" (v. 34). In the meantime, our job is to "rest in the Lord, and wait patiently for Him" (v. 7).

My End

> Believers are not obsessed with death, but neither do they fear it. A healthy appreciation for the brevity of life is essential to living life well.

LORD, make me to know my end, and what is the measure of my days, that I may know how frail I am. Indeed, You have made my days as handbreadths, and my age is as nothing before You; certainly every man at his best state is but vapor (Psa 39:4-5).

༄༅

Intellectually, everyone of us knows that our life has an end. Someday we will die. But emotionally, we prefer not to think about it. In fact, we try to *avoid* thinking about it.

David took a different approach. He was not concerned about the manner of his death, but the timing—"the measure of my days." He recognized that he needed to be reminded of how truly brief his time on this earth really was.

David used two metaphors to highlight the brevity of his life: a series of handbreadths quickly marking off the whole; and a vapor that appears for a moment then disappears, leaving no trace of its existence. David knew that in the vast sweep of human history, his time on this earth was vanishingly small.

David did not shy away from the reality of his impermanence. In fact, he welcomed God's help in developing a deeper awareness of it: "Make me to know my end." David knew that only by appreciating the frailty of his life could he develop the wisdom to use his limited time well. In contrast to those who fill their days with busyness to avoid thinking about their demise, David saw his approaching death as an incentive to accomplish something worthwhile. His time here was brief, but he was determined make it count.

David's perspective on life and death was not a morbid obsession that kept him in a melancholy funk. Rather, it inspired him to look beyond death to an eternal life in the presence of God Himself: "And now, Lord, what do I wait for? My hope is in You" (v. 7). That mindset of eternal life gave David confidence that his fleeting time on this earth was worth something; it was merely a prelude to something far greater in the hereafter.

My life may be short, but it is not without meaning. By taking a longer view—a *much* longer view—I can know that my life and death are only the start of a magnificent journey that has no end. I have every reason to embrace that journey with eager anticipation.

To the Sick

Sickness is an inevitable part of the human condition. Whether it wears us down or makes us stronger depends on how we respond to it.

The LORD will strengthen him on his bed of illness; You will sustain him on his sickbed. . . . As for me, You uphold me in my integrity, and set me before Your face forever (Psa. 41:3, 12).

༄

This psalm was written by David at some unknown point in his life when he was bedridden with a serious illness. Anyone who has gone through such an ordeal can relate to David's message here.

First, David's physical discomfort taught him the humility to recognize his dependence on God. It opened his eyes to what was truly important in life, and how little attention he had been paying to it: "Lord, be merciful to me; heal my soul, for I have sinned against You" (v. 4). Nothing helps us get our priorities in order like a close brush with death. So in an ironic way, physical distress can provide a spiritual benefit.

But a personal hardship like this can sometimes provide an opening for another problem to raise its ugly head. David's enemies saw his illness as an opportunity to gloat. "An evil disease clings to him," they bragged, "and now that he lies down, he will rise up no more" (v. 8). It's hard to be positive when you're hurting and people are rubbing the pain in your face.

At a time when large numbers of our population are stricken with a terrible virus [Covid-19], we see the same two responses play out. Some are turning to God for mercy and comfort; the physical ailment is drawing them closer to God. Others are using the occasion as an opportunity to take cheap shots at their rivals. Human nature hasn't changed much in three thousand years, has it?

David refused to let his circumstances get him down, confident of God's care for the righteous: "The Lord will deliver him in time of trouble. The Lord will preserve him and keep him alive, and he will be blessed on the earth" (v. 1-2). Notice that David did not say that God would *shield him from trouble*; rather, He would *deliver him in time of trouble*. The Lord will provide a measure of strength even on our sickbed, followed by full deliverance in the hereafter, when God will "set me before Your face forever" (v. 12).

Sickness and slander. Disease and persecution. Both are inevitable in the lives of those who choose to embrace a life of integrity. We can take comfort in knowing that they are only temporary troubles on a path that will someday bring us to perfect peace.

Whatever afflictions comes in this life, let us cling to the Lord and His promise of what lies beyond.

Where Is God?

No question haunts the human race more.
Yet a major lesson of the Bible is that God is
never unaware or indifferent to our suffering.

I will say to God my Rock, "Why have You forgotten me? Why do I go mourning because of the oppression of the enemy?" As with a breaking of my bones, my enemies reproach me, while they say to me all day long, "Where is your God?" (Psa. 42:9-10).

This psalm of the Sons of Korah addresses so eloquently one of the great mysteries of life with which we all struggle. If God is so powerful and merciful, why doesn't He intervene when my life goes off the rails? Where is God when everything is going wrong and I am helpless to deliver myself?

It's a question with a long history in the story of humanity. Even the best of people have suffered horribly, without a hint of explanation from the God whom they served. Consider some examples:

Job was a good man who lost everything in a rapid succession of catastrophes: his possessions, his children, his health, his friends. Throughout much of the book that tells his story, his anguished cry was some form of "Where is God?"

As a teenager, Joseph was sold into slavery in Egypt, where the few good turns of fortune he experienced were followed by terrible setbacks. For years this went on, with no promise of deliverance and no explanation. Where was God?

David served his master King Saul with loyalty and distinction—and was rewarded with exile in the wilderness of

Judah, a man without a country or a future. For someone who already had been anointed to be the next king of Israel, the downward spiral of circumstances in his life had to wear on his faith. Where was God?

Even Jesus, the Son of God, following a lifetime of devotion to His Father's will, was entrapped by His enemies, betrayed by His disciples, and nailed to a cross by a crooked politician. He, too, felt the sting of abandonment: "Why have You forsaken Me?" (Matt. 27:46). To that cry, the heavens remained silent. Once again, *where was God?*

Are we beginning to see a pattern here? Even the best of people suffer terribly in this life, in circumstances that make no sense to those stuck in the middle of them. But the inexplicable nature of the suffering doesn't mean God is indifferent or uninvolved. He has a much bigger canvas He is painting that we can't see. And suffering is often a necessary part of that portrait.

When the walls start closing in on your life and God is nowhere to be found, think of Job, Joseph, David, Jesus, and countless other heroes of faith who, despite the agony and heartache that hounded them throughout their lives—and even in the face of death itself—refused to give up hope. We can look back and see the hand of God in their lives in a way they couldn't. God was always there, fulfilling a purpose they couldn't understand.

Now it's our turn to ask, "Where is God?" . . . and to trust that He knows exactly what He's doing.

God Knows

> The first requirement in living a moral life is to recognize that our thoughts are an open book before God. We can't hide anything from Him.

Would not God search this out? For He knows the secrets of the heart (Psa. 44:21).

"You are those who justify yourselves before men, but God knows your hearts" (Lk. 16:15).

For if our heart condemns us, God is greater than our heart, and knows all things (1 Jn. 3:20).

Search me, O God, and know my heart; try me . . . (Psa. 139:23).

❦

There are many arguments for the existence of God, but one of the least appreciated is the role of *the conscience* in the human psyche. We have an innate awareness of the rightness and wrongness of our behavior, and that inner small voice incessantly drives us to live up to a higher standard.

But the scope of that judgment is not limited to our external behavior. It likewise regulates even how we *think*. Even if we manage to keep our outward conduct within socially acceptable boundaries, evil thoughts in the heart will still trouble us. The Bible presses that point by emphasizing that God judges not just what we *do*, but also what we *think*. He can read our minds like an open book, and the knowledge that He is doing so 24/7 is a powerful incentive to keeping our minds—and therefore our conduct—clean.

This simple truth has serious implications for our lives. We can hide lust in our heart; but *God knows* the illicit passion we are nurturing. We can hide hate for a brother in our heart; but *God knows* the venom we are storing up. We can hide an inordinate desire for wealth and possessions in our heart; but *God knows* the selfishness that dominates our life.

When we feast our eyes on pornography, or rehearse over and over our evil intentions toward someone who has wronged us, or spend every waking moment thinking how we can increase our material wealth, we are not merely living in a fantasy world. We are preparing ourselves to act out those fantasies; we are setting ourselves up for a life of sin. We may not be acting out those thoughts yet, but deep in our hearts, that's who we really are.

Knowing that our innermost thoughts are wide open before God can be scary, if we are in the habit of harboring sin in our hearts. But the awareness that God is reading our minds can also be a source of great comfort. David invited God to "search me and know my heart," not because he believed he was sinless, but because he realized that was where the real battle was being fought, and God's scrutiny would help keep him honest. What better incentive is there to maintain clean books than to invite an audit at any time?

The atheist may claim to live a moral life, but where it really counts—in his heart—he has nothing to monitor his morality. In his view, there is no God to examine his heart. He has no auditor, so his heart really is a sealed record, open to no one. He is free to entertain every hateful, lustful, greedy thought . . . as long as he doesn't act on them.

Of course, that's the problem, isn't it? Sooner or later, a heart that feeds on unrestrained thoughts will produce a harvest of unrestrained behavior. The only way to keep our thinking under control is to constantly remind ourselves of the obvious: *God knows*.

Be Still and Know That I Am God

It's easy to become overwhelmed by all the suffering that dominates our world. But one simple truth can provide strength to endure.

God is our refuge and strength, a very present help in trouble. Therefore we will not fear, even though the earth be removed, and though the mountains be carried into the midst of the sea. . . . Be still, and know that I am God; I will be exalted among the nations, I will be exalted in the earth! The Lord of hosts is with us; the God of Jacob is our refuge (Psa. 46:1-2, 10-11).

A monster hurricane hits a major metropolitan area, inflicting billions of dollars in damage and leaving thousands homeless.

An unprecedented market meltdown wipes out billions of dollars in net worth and threatens to drag down the entire economy—including *my* retirement investments.

Another election cycle exposes the ugly side of politics, with vicious charges and counter-charges stirring up passions and driving a wedge deeper into an electorate that is already at war with itself.

Then add your own personal problems to the list—health issues, stacks of unpaid bills, family crises, an endless parade of maintenance headaches on the house and cars, hassles at work . . . and on and on and on.

And remember, this is what life is like for the freest, most prosperous people on earth. Imagine what it must be like for everyone else.

The 46th Psalm was written for times such as these. Its prescription for dealing with the uncertainties and anxieties of life is simple: "Be still, and know that I am God." It's a lesson that we need to be reminded of again and again.

This world and everything in it is the creation of God. While we may not understand all the details of why He runs it the way He does, we can have confidence that He has a purpose behind it all. We are playing out our roles in a vast master plan, one that has a well-defined end. God knows what He is doing, even if we don't. We can trust Him to bring everything to a just and fitting conclusion.

But it's hard to develop that trust when all our attention is riveted on the threats in front of us. Natural disasters seem to argue that God has lost control of His creation. Man-made catastrophes—wars, economic chaos, cultural collapse—overwhelm us with their power to destroy everything that is dear to us. God is so abstract, so distant; our problems are so real and immediate. How can we not be terrified by the evils that surround us?

It comes down to the mental model of the universe that we choose to adopt: Do we base our thinking on the premise that God is in control and everything will turn out well in the end? Or do we view the world as some kind of cosmic runaway freight train that is careening out of control, with disaster as the only foreseeable outcome?

The Psalmist advises the former outlook. "Be still"—stay calm, don't panic, keep a clear head—and "know that I am God"—fix your faith on God and His plan. Trust Him to work everything out in His own time.

"God is our refuge and strength"—but only if we choose to make Him so. Otherwise, we're on our own. And *that* scenario is truly frightening.

The Secret to a Tranquil Life

In a crazy world, maintaining a calm and stable life is a challenge. It can be done, but only if we grasp the simple foundation that makes it possible.

Be still and know that I am God (Psa. 46:10).

Every human heart longs for peace and tranquility. Unfortunately, the chaos of our messy world does not leave much room for it. A tranquil life can be found, but it requires a deliberate strategy. In this verse, God offers a simple three-step approach.

Step One: *Be still.* The greatest obstacle to a peaceful life is a frazzled lifestyle. When we max out every waking hour with work, family, housekeeping, recreation, hobbies, and socializing, we are left with precious little time to decompress. The result is usually burn-out—physical and mental exhaustion. We must learn how to "be still," to periodically disconnect from this world and reconnect with another. Even Jesus, in the midst of His world-changing ministry, understood the need to "come aside by yourselves to a deserted place and rest a while" (Mk. 6:31). We should heed His advice. Dial back the commitments. Schedule quality "down" time. Find a quiet place where the world does not intrude, and immerse ourselves in the solitude.

Step Two: *Know.* To "know" something is to open our minds to a truth outside ourselves. This is not "MY truth," a convenient fiction that we create for ourselves. Our feelings and wishes are as unstable as the world around us and provide a poor foundation. That's why our lives are such a frenetic mess to start with. Rather, this truth is an external reality which we do not control and cannot change. There is a source of strength outside of ourselves, but we must align our thinking with its nature. We must open our hearts and minds to *know* it.

Step Three: *That I am God.* There is much in the Bible that we need to know, but the one central truth that buttresses all the others is the knowledge that God exists and that He is everything He claims to be. God's existence gives purpose to ours. He alone brings order out of confusion and meaning out of chaos. He is the Rock in the midst of the storm. Because of who He is and what He does, "God is our refuge and our strength, a very present help in trouble" (v. 1). To know that truth is to find a peace that calms the anxious soul.

Friend, if you feel that your life is spiraling out of control, ponder the message of this simple verse. Peace and tranquility are possible, but only if you let God take over.

Be still and know that He is God.

To the Rich and Poor

Economic inequality has plagued humanity since the beginning of time. One day it will be remedied—but not on our terms.

Hear this, all peoples; Give ear, all inhabitants of the world, both low and high, rich and poor together (Psa. 49: 1-2).

ಲ್ಲಿ

Jesus once said it is easier for a camel to go through the eye of a needle than for a rich man to enter heaven (Matt. 19:24). Jesus was addressing the corrupting effect that prosperity has on spirituality. Wealthy people rarely care about spiritual values, and non-wealthy people often suffer—directly or indirectly—from those skewed values.

The 49th Psalm was written to address this problem. It is a message for both rich and poor alike (v. 2). For the rich man, it is a warning to view his wealth in light of eternity; for the poor man, it is a promise of justice in another life.

The Psalm deals with those who "trust in their wealth, and boast in the multitude of their riches" (v. 6). Their wealth provides them with every comfort, and they need nothing else. "Their inner thought is that their houses will continue forever, and their dwelling places to all generations" (v. 11). Feeding this attitude of self-sufficient superiority is the praise of sycophants who flatter and fawn (v. 18).

The rich know how to use their wealth to get what they want, often at the expense of others. Consequently, their power is often feared by their potential victims (v. 5, 16).

But for all his wealth and power, there are some things the rich man cannot do. First, his money cannot save the lives of those he loves. "None of them can by any means redeem his brother, nor give to God a ransom for him . . . that he should continue to live eternally, and not see the Pit [lit., *sheol*, the realm of the dead]" (v. 7-9). When the time comes for a beloved family member or close friend to die, his money is powerless to prevent it. He can drive a hard bargain with others; he cannot bargain with God.

Furthermore, the rich man cannot even save himself. Throughout his life he can use his money to get his way with others, but a day will come when not only will his money be of no use to him, he will have to give it up. On the day of his death, the rich man becomes exactly like everyone else in this world. "He sees that wise men die; likewise the fool and the senseless person perish, and leave their wealth to others" (v. 10). "When he dies he shall carry nothing away; his glory shall not descend after him" (v. 11). "Like sheep, they are laid in the grave; death shall feed on them . . . and their beauty shall be consumed in the grave" (v. 14). Death is the ultimate equalizer, reducing the rich and powerful to the same level as the lowliest pauper.

And what of the poor man? If he has kept his faith in God, death shall be a reward for his patience. "God will redeem my soul from the power of the grave, for He shall receive me" (v. 15).

Despite our best efforts to rectify it, economic injustice is a fact of life that we will never entirely eliminate. But God's message to the wise is reassuring: Someday, the scales will be balanced, and on that day money will not matter.

Why Should I Fear?

When surrounded on every side by evil and oppression, it's easy to become overwhelmed by fear. God invites us to take a broader view.

Why should I fear in the days of evil, when the iniquity at my heels surrounds me? . . . God will redeem my soul from the power of the grave, for He shall receive me (Psa. 49:5, 15).

There are any number of hardships in this world that can make our lives miserable: accidents, illnesses, natural disasters, economic reversals, and so forth. But in this Psalm the author is concerned with one above all the rest: The injustices inflicted on us by other people, especially those "who trust in their wealth" (v. 6). When we find ourselves on the receiving end of this kind of tyranny, the days of our lives can be truly evil.

The rich oppress the poor. The powerful crush the weak. Good and decent people who are trying to do the right thing are exploited by scoundrels who have no conscience. Ideally, governments exist to hold these outrages in check and punish those who do evil (Rom. 13:1-4). But governments themselves are often corrupted by evil—in some cases even feeding off the injustice. The godly man becomes an easy target.

When these abuses become deeply embedded in a society, how can we respond? What recourse do we have when we have no power to resist?

Our default reaction is *fear*. We fret over the damage our oppressors can inflict upon us in our helpless condition. Our hearts are filled with a dread of what's coming next.

But the Psalmist invites us to take a closer look at what's coming next. We should consider the future from a more distant frame of reference. As for our oppressors, "death shall feed on them" (v. 14); and as for myself, "God will redeem my soul . . . He shall receive me" (v. 15). Even if my oppressors kill me, in the end I have nothing to be afraid of. God will one day repair everything that is crooked. The injustices of this world are fleeting, a temporary aberration that will soon be righted.

Indeed, "why should I fear in the days of evil?" My life is in the capable hands of a God who sees everything and takes very careful notes. He *will* fix this. Believe that, and you can face anything with calm assurance.

Their Houses Will Last Forever

Endless home improvement projects prompt a question: Why are people spending so much effort on something they will soon leave behind?

Their inner thought is that their houses will last forever, their dwelling places to all generations; they call their lands after their own names. Nevertheless man, though in honor, does not remain; he is like the beasts that perish (Psa. 49:11-12).

Melissa and I recently went to the grand opening of a new home center here in town. Despite the fact that our community already has several large stores (and many smaller ones) catering to the needs of home owners, apparently there is a market for yet another, even bigger than all the rest. This new store was jammed with hundreds of customers gawking at the thousands of products available to make their homes better, bigger, stronger, safer, more beautiful, more efficient, or more durable.

This Psalm was written to the vast throngs of humanity who fear the power and influence of the rich (v. 5-6, 16). There are several ways to identify someone as a rich man, but the author points to just one: "The glory of his house is increased" (v. 16). In ancient times, just as today, the primary status symbol of one's wealth was a large house designed to "last forever" (v. 11a). These exotic structures were often surrounded by vast land holdings bearing the owner's name (v. 11b). The rich man's domicile sent a powerful message to all who passed by: "I am rich! I am important! I have arrived!"

The message in this Psalm is that the rich man's devotion to his house and land betrays a distorted view of life. The rich "trust in their wealth and boast in the multitude of their riches" (v. 6), but their wealth proves to be a false god. Their money cannot prolong life (v. 7-9), and in the end they will die like everyone else "and leave their wealth to others" (v. 10). Whatever mansions they may have constructed for themselves in this life shall soon be left behind. The only home that will truly be forever is their grave, "far from their dwelling" (v. 14). In view of the transitory nature of life, their obsession with their houses labels them as fools (v. 13).

It's easy to convince ourselves that we are not rich, we don't live in a mansion, so none of this applies to us. Really? How much of our time and money do we spend on our houses? How many of our home improvement projects are really necessary, as opposed to projects designed to feed our vanity? How different are we, really, from the rich man in this Psalm?

None of what is written here should be construed as an argument for laziness or neglect. Like every other gift with which the Lord has blessed us, we should maintain and care for our homes. But there reaches a point where the amount of resources we spend on a place to live exceeds the limits of practical wisdom. Our homes can become our gods, consuming resources that should be directed toward more enduring purposes.

Many years after this Psalm was written, Paul summarized its message in these words: "For we brought nothing into this world, and it is certain we can carry nothing out. And having food and clothing, with these we shall be content" (1 Tim. 6:7-8). He doesn't even mention housing. Every time I make another trip to the home center, I can't help but wonder: Am I really content with food and clothing? Or am I foolishly attempting to build a house that will last forever?

Born in Sin?

The doctrine of original sin, embraced by much of Christendom, provides a plausible explanation for humanity's sin problem. But is it Biblical?

Behold, I was brought forth in iniquity, and in sin my mother conceived me (Psa. 51:5).

Truly, this only I have found: that God made man upright, but they have sought out many schemes (Eccl. 7:29).

The doctrine of original sin holds that all of Adam's descendants are tainted by the guilt of his sin; that we are by nature born sinners, hopelessly lost the moment we are conceived. The doctrine was articulated by Augustine in the fifth century, then refined by Calvin in the sixteenth. Today, the doctrine of original sin is a bedrock component of modern Christian theology, both Catholic and Protestant.

It's not hard to build an argument for the doctrine of original sin. The sorry history of mankind, with all the wickedness and evil that permeates our miserable existence, screams that *something* about us is terribly broken. The universality of sin is a common theme in the Scriptures ("All have sinned," Rom. 3:23; "There is not a just man on earth who does not sin," Eccl. 7:20; and so on). Indeed, sin seems to be baked into our very nature.

In Psalm 51, David's frustration at his own shortcomings seems to affirm this hereditary origin of sin. If David was "conceived in sin," surely that settles the matter.

But similar language elsewhere challenges that interpretation. For example, David also said, "I was cast upon You from birth. From my mother's womb You have been My God" (Psa. 22:10). Does anyone believe that David was conscious of God's presence while a fetus in his mother's womb? I doubt it. David was using poetic language to describe a relationship with God that extended as far back as he could remember ("from my mother's womb"). Similar language is used in Psalm 58:3—"The wicked are estranged from the womb; they go astray as soon as they are born, speaking lies." Here, too, the message is not that newborns are chronic liars, but that people fall under sin's clutches very early in their life.

Another Bible author provides a more straightforward description of man's condition: "God made man upright"—that is, we are born pure and untainted by sin—"but they have sought out many schemes." In other words, we are born into a world that is hopelessly corrupted by sin, and that influence starts its work on us right away. Beginning with our parents, then extending to our relatives, neighbors, friends, schoolmates, co-workers and the broader culture at large, we are exposed to a torrent of temptations that we are ill-equipped to resist. We are born pure, but we are also born ignorant, and the combination of ignorance, physical appetites, and faulty role models dooms us to failure. The evil that early infects our life is pervasive and inevitable—but it is *not* congenital.

To say that we are "born in sin" reinforces a mindset that keeps many people captive to sin's power: "I can't help it . . . I was born that way . . . I'm not responsible." A correct reading of the Bible destroys that excuse. "Death spread to all men, *because all sinned*" (Rom. 5:12), not because they were born that way. Whatever the influences that lead us down this dark path, ultimately we are responsible for our own misdeeds. We cannot blame it on our ancestry.

The Joy of Salvation

If our relationship with God does not fill our hearts with joy, something is broken and needs to be fixed. The problem is on our end, not God's.

"Restore to me the joy of Your salvation" (Psa. 51:12).

In the aftermath of his sin with Bathsheba, David was so overcome with remorse over what he had done that he poured out his heart to God in a composition that we know as Psalm 51. The dominant theme in this prayer of penitence is David's sharp sense of loss of fellowship with God. Many people were hurt by what David did, but he never mentions that. Rather, his greatest pain was the knowledge that his rebellion had severed his relationship with God.

As part of the healing of that relationship, David pleads for a restoration of "the joy of Your salvation." As long as he was with God, his spirit was buoyed by an inner happiness that could not be touched by the hardships of life. Now alienated from God, David was vulnerable, and he felt it keenly. Oh, to have that joy back again, to feel the warmth of God's arms enfolding and comforting him!

This life can be a cruel affair, but especially so to those who try to navigate it without God. The salvation that God has provided us is not some theological abstraction, but a very real and personal change in how we approach life and its problems. In this relationship, we have guidance and counsel to help us make wise decisions; we have promises of an infinitely brighter future to give us encouragement; we have the reassurance that God loves us deeply, and is willing to forgive our stumbles; and we have the knowledge that no matter how crazy and insane this world gets, God is still in control, and everything will turn out well in the end. You can't get this kind of therapy from a bottle or billable hours on a couch.

That's why, in the New Testament accounts of people being saved, we read again and again of the emotional catharsis that accompanied the salvation of those who responded to the gospel of Christ.

- The preaching of Philip brought "great joy" to the city of Samaria (Ac. 8:8).
- The Ethiopian eunuch "went on his way rejoicing" following his baptism (Ac. 8:39).
- The Philippian jailer—who only a few hours earlier was so distraught that he was on the verge of suicide—heard and responded to a message that brought joy to his house (Ac. 16:34).
- Peter wrote of the "joy inexpressible" that Christians possess, even in times of hardship (1 Pet. 1:6-8).
- This inner joy is a common refrain in the writings of Paul, who knew from his own experience the pain of being alienated from God (Rom. 5:2; Rom. 12:12; Phil. 4:4; 1 Thess. 5:16).

If your life seems empty and meaningless, or you struggle with feelings of despair, take a hard look at your relationship with God. Something is broken, and needs to be healed. Like David, perhaps you need to reassess where God fits into your scheme of things. A great joy awaits you, but only if you are willing to surrender to God to find it.

Oh, To Fly Away!

Life in this world wouldn't be so bad, if it weren't for the people we have to share it with. David knew that feeling well, and knew how to cope.

Oh, that I had wings like a dove! I would fly away and be at rest. Indeed, I would wander far off, and remain in the wilderness. I would hasten my escape from the windy storm and tempest (Psa. 55:6-8).

Have you ever been so frustrated dealing with people that you wished you could just get away from everybody? If so, then Psalm 55 was written for you.

Like so many of the Psalms, this composition deals with the pain of persecution inflicted by the writer's enemies—and David had many. "The wicked . . . bring down trouble upon me, and in wrath they hate me" (v. 2-3). What was particularly painful in this instance was the betrayal of a close friend who had turned on him: "It is not an enemy who reproaches me; then I could bear it. . . . But it was you, a man my equal, my companion and my acquaintance. We took sweet counsel together, and walked to the house of God in the throng" (v. 12-13). The treachery of this friend had been especially hard to take: "The words of his mouth were smoother than butter, but war was in his heart; his words were softer than oil, yet they were drawn swords" (v. 21). David not only had to deal with enemies, now he had been stabbed in the back by a friend.

We do not know the circumstances that prompted the writing of this Psalm. The most likely candidate would be the treachery of Ahithophel, who betrayed David during the rebellion of Absalom. But there were several other occasions when David got burned by people who had been close to him. Whatever the circumstances to which he is referring, the effect was the same. The anguish of having to deal with enemies from every direction, even from those closest to him, was more than David could bear. He was ready to give up on the human race altogether. He wanted to "fly away and be at rest" (v. 6-8).

Of course, David knew that wasn't an option. Instead, he would continue to do what he had always done: "I will call upon God, and the Lord shall save me. Evening and morning and at noon, I will pray, and cry aloud, and He shall hear my voice" (v. 16-17). He was confident that eventually, the scales of justice would balance out, and his tormentors would get their due: "He has redeemed my soul in peace from the battle that was against me, for there were many against me. God will hear and afflict them" (v. 18-19). Trusting in others can be risky and disappointing, but God will never disappoint: "I will trust in You" (v. 23).

David never gave up by turning his back on humanity. He remained active and engaged, serving and helping others all the days of his life. He knew that he had to stay in the game, no matter how difficult. The bitter disappointments inflicted by a few could not overcome his devotion to a higher cause. His confidence was in God, not men, and it was that faith that enabled him to stay steady through the storms.

David's example should inspire us to do the same. Dealing with people in this world can be painful, especially when those we count as friends turn on us. But David knew the frustration is bearable if we make the Lord, not man, the foundation of our faith: "Cast your burden on the Lord, and He shall sustain you; He shall never permit the righteous to be moved" (v. 23).

When People Disappoint Us

Few experiences hurt worse than the betrayal of a friend. The pain can be a growth opportunity, if we know how to process it wisely.

For it is not an enemy who reproaches me; then I could bear it. Nor is it one who hates me who has exalted himself against me; then I could hide from him. But it was you, a man my equal, my companion and my acquaintance. We took sweet counsel together, and walked to the house of God in the throng (Psa. 55:12-14).

༄༅

This psalm was written by David, probably during the rebellion of his son Absalom (2 Sam. 15-18). However, the companion whose betrayal David bemoans in these verses is not Absalom, but his trusted counselor, Ahithophel, who inexplicably switched sides in the rebellion and gave Absalom advice on how to defeat his father.

This is not the only story in the Bible of relationships broken by betrayal. Jesus was killed by the treachery of one of His closest companions, Judas. In a Roman prison, Paul was stung by the conduct of his co-worker Demas, who deserted him, "having loved this present world."

The common theme in these stories is the tragedy of broken friendships. There are few things in life more painful than experiencing the disintegration of a relationship built up over years of shared communion. Whatever the details of the breakup, the knowledge that something has changed and the relationship is no longer what it once was, can be a bitter pill to swallow.

As we pick through the detritus of such an experience, what can we do to cope with the loss?

First, wisdom counsels that we should ask ourselves how many times we have disappointed our friends by something we have said or done. This self-reflection does not justify the wrongs inflicted upon us, of course, but it does help us keep things in perspective. None of us is perfect, and in some cases we may have to share at least some responsibility for a break-up. We expect others to be forgiving of our mistakes, to not judge us harshly. We must be willing, therefore, to be charitable toward those who we believe have betrayed us. If there is any hope of reconciliation somewhere in the future, it will be nurtured by planting seeds of kindness now.

Second, we must concentrate on the relationships that remain. If we are not careful, we can let our disappointment infect our other friendships to the point that they are threatened as well. We can allow bitterness and cynicism to poison our attitude toward people in general, and begin treating everyone with suspicion and aloofness. Over time, this will serve only to undermine whatever friendships we have left.

Finally, this experience should be a cause to re-examine the foundation of our faith. Whom do we really serve: God or men? If our faith is deeply shaken by what people have done, then perhaps we need to take a closer look at our relationship with God. Our love for Him must transcend whatever others may do.

When people disappoint us, it can be a terrible blow. But like all of life's hard knocks, it can also be an opportunity to learn and grow, if we are willing to process the experience wisely.

When We Cry

The tears that we cry are a record of the emotional trauma we experience in life. It helps to know that God is not indifferent to our sorrow.

You number my wanderings; put my tears into Your bottle; are they not in Your book? (Psa. 56:8).

Reading the story of King David can be a depressing experience. For all the glory and prestige that we normally associate with his name, the reality is that David's life was consumed by grief. Let's take a quick tour.

Early in his career, when pressure from King Saul forced him into exile, David had to bid farewell to his dear friend Jonathan. "They wept together, but David more so" (1 Sam. 20:41).

Near the end of his exile, while David and his men were away on a campaign, Amalekite raiders overran the village in which they lived and carried off their families. David and his men "wept until they had no more power to weep" (1 Sam. 30:4).

After recovering from that disaster, David heard that Saul and Jonathan had been killed in a battle against the Philistines. David and his followers "mourned and wept and fasted" over this terrible loss (2 Sam. 1:11-12).

In the civil war that followed the death of Saul, the assassination of Abner robbed David of the only man who could help him bring peace to a divided nation. At Abner's funeral David "lifted up his voice and wept" at the loss of this "great man in Israel" (2 Sam. 3:32, 38).

All these occasions of grief were inflicted upon David by the actions of others. But his greatest pain came from the suffering he brought upon himself. Following his affair with Bathsheba and the murder of her husband, the child born from this illicit relationship was stricken with a fatal illness. David "fasted and wept for the child," begging God to spare him. His anguish was so intense that his servants hesitated to inform him when the child died, for fear that he would harm himself (2 Sam. 12:16-21).

The climax came when his own son, Absalom, was killed while leading a rebellion against his father. David saw in his son's conduct a mirror image of his own sins, and the young man's death plunged him into a grief so loud and deep that his army could not celebrate their victory over the rebels (2 Sam. 18:33–19:4).

I have had occasions to weep in my life, but never as often and as intensely as David. How he bore up under all the agonizing experiences of his life provides a lesson in how we can do the same.

David saw God as more than an abstract object of worship. His statement, "You number my wanderings; [and] put my tears into Your bottle" reflects David's confidence in God as a friend who took a personal interest in his pain. It was as though God stored each tear in a special bottle with David's name on it, and kept a ledger that recorded the time and occasion it was shed. David was sure that some day God would redeem every one of those tears with blessings that would more than make up for the heartbreak.

When life beats us down and we cry until we have no more tears to cry, remember the story of David. God is storing up your tears, too, in a bottle with your name on it. Some day, He will open that bottle and personally "wipe away every tear from their eyes" (Rev. 21:4). Fix your hope on that day, and you will find strength to endure.

God Is for Me!

God's wrath can be motivating. But a far greater motivation is found when we see Him as a loyal friend who is always with us through thick or thin.

When I cry out to You, then my enemies will turn back; this I know, because God is for me (Psa. 56:9).
If God is for us, who can be against us? (Rom. 8:31).

According to the preface of this psalm, David composed this work during his self-exile among the Philistines in Gath (1 Sam. 21:10-15). A quick review of that history provides the context for several of David's comments in this psalm.

"There are many who fight against me" (v. 2). His chief antagonist, of course, was King Saul, who had become insanely jealous of David's accomplishments, and sought to kill him. His agents lurked everywhere, and assassination was a constant threat.

"You number my wanderings" (v. 8a). In desperation, David fled Israel for Gath, a chief city of the Philistines. Naturally, the Philistines didn't trust him so David had to run from them, too. His life became that of a vagabond. He eventually ended up in a cave in the wilderness of Judea. He no longer had a home.

"Put my tears into Your bottle" (v. 8b). Before fleeing to Gath, David met one last time with his best friend, Jonathan. It was an emotional parting. Both men wept, "but David more so" (1 Sam. 20:41). David was separated from everything he loved—his wife, his best friend, his nation. His losses were becoming unbearable.

This was a low point in David's life. Despite his best efforts to be a good person, it seemed that everything was falling apart. What else could go wrong?

In the midst of this gloom, David found a single ray of light that enabled him to keep going forward: his unwavering conviction that "God is for me" (v. 9). David was convinced that God truly cared for him, and although He would not shield him from the vagaries of life, He still loved him, and in the end would save him. He believed that somehow God would work everything out for the better.

Centuries later, Paul picked up David's refrain and turned it into a challenge: "If God is for us, who can be against us?" (Rom. 8:31). In God's capable hands, we have nothing to fear. In the end, He will make everything right, no matter how dark the present.

God is for me! If we could grasp the significance of that simple fact, it would provide all the strength we need to persevere in life. Few of us have somebody trying to physically kill us. But maybe we have critics whose hurtful words and unkind actions make our lives miserable. So what? *God is for me!*

Perhaps we have encountered tragedies that sow seeds of doubt and fear in our heart—illness, the death of a loved one, financial setbacks, accidents. Yeah, it hurts, but Someone else feels your pain, too, and will someday make up for it. *God is for me!*

For some of us, the deepest wounds are those we inflict upon ourselves. We make terrible mistakes, and fall far short of the ideals for which we strive. But even there, His grace is sufficient to forgive the worst sins, and to empower us to keep trying. *God is for me!*

When you find yourself lost and confused, grieving over the unfairness of it all, seek comfort where David found his: *God is for me!*

The Power of Prayer

We often fret over how—or even whether—God answers our prayers. In doing so, we may overlook some tangible benefits that prayer provides.

Hear my cry, O God; attend to my prayer. From the end of the earth I will cry to You, when my heart is overwhelmed; lead me to the rock that is higher than I. For You have been a shelter for me, a strong tower from the enemy (Psa. 61:1-3).

○○○

In our studies on prayer, we often focus our attention on questions relating to how God responds to our prayers: Does He answer them or not? If so, how? If not, why not? If we believe in the providential care of God for His people, these are legitimate topics of study.

However, by concentrating so much of our attention on *how* God chooses to answer our prayers, we may be depriving ourselves of more immediate rewards that prayer can provide, regardless of how God responds. The simple act of expressing our inner thoughts to God imparts some tangible psychological and emotional benefits all by itself.

We see evidence for this principle in this Psalm. David looked to God as "a strong tower" to shelter him during a period of hardship when his heart was "overwhelmed" by troubles. In pouring out his heart to God in prayer, David was obviously seeking divine deliverance. But notice that David viewed God as his shelter *even before God had an opportunity to respond to David's prayer*. In other words, the very act of praying was itself a source of strength.

This principle has profound implications for our prayer life. First, consider that *it's hard to sin against God while I am in the act of praying to Him.* Jesus' night of prayer in the Garden of Gethsemane was critical to Him staying strong and finishing His mission the following day. When I struggle with a strong temptation to sell out my convictions, talking to God about the battle that is raging in my heart will reinforce my will to stay strong and do the right thing. Prayer is a powerful weapon against the schemes of Satan.

Second, *it's hard to get discouraged in the face of adversity when I am praying.* After experiencing a prolonged period of failure in my life, it is easy to fall into a mode of thinking "why even try?" I'm tired of the struggle, and search in vain for the tiniest scrap of good news to bring joy into my miserable life. Talking to God about my struggles—and recounting the blessings I have received from His generous hand—will help restore a sense of perspective in my thinking and remind me that life is not nearly as desperate as it appears. Prayer can bring a small but significant jolt of positive emotion into my life.

Finally, *it's hard to hold a grudge against someone who has wronged me at the same time I am praying for him.* Jesus tells us to pray for those who spitefully use us (Matt. 5:44). Even if my prayers regarding my tormentor involve some imprecatory element, the fact that I am praying to God in behalf of my enemy will soften my feelings toward him. I will gradually come to view him as an object of pity, not revenge. I can even reach a point where I can ask God to be merciful to my enemy for his crimes committed in ignorance (Lk. 23:34).

How God chooses to answer our prayers is His business, and we should let Him deal with that. In the meantime, if we are struggling with temptations, burdened with discouragement, or seething with bitterness, we should know that relief is just a prayer away. Talk it out with God, and experience the relief of a burden being lifted from your shoulders.

Only God

When evil takes the field and we have nowhere else to turn, there is one recourse that is available to us—if we will open our eyes to see Him.

My soul, wait silently for God alone, for my expectation is from Him. He only is my rock and my salvation; He is my defense; I shall not be moved (Psa. 62:5-6).

This psalm, like so many that David wrote, gives advice on how to cope with the slings and arrows of enemies who "delight in lies" (v. 4). The simple answer, David says, is to look to God as our source of strength. Not just "a" source, but the *only* source. If we really want to deal successfully with the intimidation of the wicked, we must learn how to find refuge in God alone.

But that concept is so abstract. How do we find refuge in a Being whom we cannot see?

David offers two clues to explain how this works. First, we should "pour out [our] heart before Him" (v. 8). When we come before God in fervent prayer, expressing all our pain, all our frustration, all our fears, we gradually build a confidence that He is listening and cares.

Second, notice his statement that "God has spoken" (v. 11). We cannot see God, but He has spoken to us in His Word. In that source of instruction we find advice on how to navigate the twisted paths of life; we discover words of encouragement, comfort, and hope; we encounter examples that will inspire us. God has not left us to figure this out on our own. We should drink deeply of this fount of wisdom.

So will this strategy make all our problems go away? No, probably not. That's why David provides one more piece of advice: "Wait silently" (v. 1, 5). If we are truly seeking refuge in God alone, then there is nothing more to do but wait for Him to act.

Of course, that could take a lifetime. Since God does not operate on our timetable, we often take shortcuts to solve the problem ourselves. David warns against some of these shortcuts in verses 9-10. Let's look at them:

Some seek the companionship of "men of low degree" (v. 9a). That is, they find comfort in the company of their peers, people who are struggling with all the same problems as they are. Misery loves company—but it's still miserable.

Others seek the approval of "men of high degree" (v. 9b). They look up to presidents, preachers, even celebrities, to protect them. They hang on every word, and swallow every empty promise, hoping the coattails will save them.

Some become so frustrated with the inequities of life that they take matters into their own hands; they resort to "oppression" and "robbery" to find satisfaction (v. 10a). If they feel they have been wrongfully treated, they will find a way to strike back. Their refuge is their own ability to force their will upon others.

Finally, some look to "riches" as the answer to all their troubles (v. 10b). Money can buy anything, including happiness, revenge, or whatever else they need—or so they think. So they dedicate their lives to their possessions, hoping to find protection in their little empires.

But all these alternatives, David argues, are poor defenses against the schemes of the wicked. All are vulnerable to weaknesses that will expose us to further disappointment. Only God can provide a refuge that we can fully trust. He will not make our problems go away; but He *will* give us the strength to endure them.

To See God's Glory

"The glory of God" sounds hollow to those who are going through hard times. But even they can see God's glory—if they know how to look for it.

I have looked for You in the sanctuary, to see Your power and Your glory (Psa. 63:2).

Jesus said to her, "Did I not say to you that if you would believe you would see the glory of God?" (Jn. 11:40).

There will come a day when all humanity—every single person who has ever lived—will see the glory of God. All doubts will be removed, all questions will be answered, all longings will be satisfied, all pain will be healed. The struggles of this life will be over, and those who have sought God in this life will finally rest in His tender embrace.

But that day has not yet arrived. Instead, we must live with trouble and tears, wondering at the unfairness that life throws at us again and again. God's glory seems so remote, so enigmatic. How can we trust a God whom we cannot see? How can we discern His glory, when everything around us reeks of ugliness?

These two passages provide clues that show us the way. First, notice that in his time of trouble David sought God's power and glory "in the sanctuary." It's unlikely that David is speaking of the tabernacle at Shiloh, which was an unimpressive structure—and not accessible to him during his wilderness exile anyway. "The sanctuary" in the book of Psalms is often a metaphor for a deep spiritual connection with God, chiefly through the avenue of prayer and reflection.

Meditation in a formal place of worship can serve that purpose—but so can staring at a brilliant night sky full of stars. The physical location is not as important as the concentration of thought on God and His role in our life. That exercise awakens an awareness of who He really is. David may have been in a dark place in his life, but those circumstances could not prevent him from visualizing the glory of God.

Martha grieved for her brother Lazarus, who had just died. Jesus promised her that she would see the glory of God "if you would believe" (v. 40). He then raised her brother from the dead, a dramatic miracle that set all Jerusalem in an uproar (v. 45-54). Jesus was not making the miracle dependent on Martha's faith. Rather, He was encouraging her to see this sign for what it really was: God using a human tragedy to accomplish a greater purpose. Only after the whole affair was over could Martha and the disciples finally recognize, through the eye of faith, what God was doing.

Both of these episodes illustrate how we can see the glory of God today. We behold His glory when we open our hearts to understand the grandeur of His creation and His provisions for our life. We see the glory of God when we witness the kindness of others who bring healing and comfort to the afflicted. The world may be an ugly place, but the glory of God shines as a beacon in the darkness to those whose eyes are open to see it.

When life treats us cruelly, we must train our hearts to look past the pain of the moment to the larger objective God is working out in this world. "Our light affliction, which is but for a moment, is working for us a far more exceeding and eternal weight of glory, while we do not look at the things which are seen, but at the things which are not seen" (2 Cor. 4:17-18). Lift up your eyes to that final consummation, and your troubles will become more manageable.

A Home for the Lonely

The collapse of the institution of the family in our society has created an epidemic of loneliness. God's people must provide the solution.

God sets the solitary in families; He brings out those who are bound into prosperity; but the rebellious dwell in a dry land (Psa. 68:6).

⚜

Another version renders the first line of this verse, "God makes a home for the lonely" (NASB). The context is describing God's compassion for the weak. For those who are lonely, His special gift is the *family*, a refuge where fears and masks are set aside, and unconditional love is bestowed on everyone.

The truth of this Psalm was demonstrated literally in the Garden of Eden, when God saw that "it is not good that man should be alone." So He gave Adam a special companion with whom he could spend the rest of his life (Gen. 2:18). Elsewhere in the Bible, this special relationship between a husband and wife is held up as the purest form of human companionship (Prov. 5:18-19; Prov. 31:10f; Eccl. 9:9). The children who bless this arrangement are described as an additional source of happiness (Psa. 127:3-5; Psa. 128:2-4). In a sin-cursed world, of course, nothing is perfect and every family must deal with its share of bumps and bruises. But history has shown that there is no alternative that surpasses the family as a source of emotional strength.

However, this is the ideal, and life sometimes falls short of the ideal. Spouses and parents die young, or poor decisions are made that tear families apart and leave the innocent abandoned and hurting. But even then, other families can step in to make up for some of the loss. Part of Job's righteousness was his willingness to share his home with those whose families were broken (Job 31:17-18).

In the New Testament, when the Lord chose language to describe the special relationship among those who embraced the new religion of Christ, He used the family as the model. That's why we are called "brothers" in the "family" of God (1 Pet. 3:8; Eph. 2:19). Even if someone is denied the joy of a biological family, they can still enjoy the love and affection of a whole group of surrogate fathers, mothers, brothers, and sisters (1 Tim. 5:1-2).

There are three simple but powerful lessons that we can learn from this study.

First, we must work hard to make our homes the best possible examples of what God intended they be: little beacons of happiness that show the world God's solution to loneliness. This is especially critical for the sake of our children, who will be entrusted with carrying on the tradition in later generations.

Second, we must share this happiness with those who do not experience it. We must open our homes to others, and let them experience the emotional healing that comes from being part of a family.

Finally, we must defend this arrangement without apology or timidity against the attacks of those who seek to destroy it. The traditional family is being vilified as outmoded, even dangerous, and sinister forces are at work to replace it with alternative definitions of "family." Their efforts will eventually fail, but they will do a lot of damage to society in the meantime.

God has made a home for the lonely in families. We can find companionship there, if we will honor the institution as He intended.

Why Families Are Collapsing

The disintegration of the family in American culture is wreaking havoc on our social fabric. The causes are not hard to identify.

God sets the solitary in families (Psa. 68:6).

"Honor your father and mother," which is the first commandment with promise: "that it may be well with you and you may live long on the earth" (Eph. 6:2-3).

ಎಲ

Columnist David Brooks recently penned an article entitled, "What's Ripping American Families Apart?" (*New York Times*, July 29, 2021). The article is behind a paywall, but commentator Dennis Prager provided a summary of its contents, including selections from reader comments on the original article.* The article and the comments that followed paint an appalling picture. Brooks noted that at least 27% of adult Americans are estranged from other family members, revealing an epidemic of intergenerational alienation.[1] The effect of this breakdown is reflected in the comments of readers who not only see no problem with it, but actively encourage it, often on grounds of political differences.

Prager suggests four contributing factors behind this tsunami of family dysfunction:

- *Narcissism*. A generation of young Americans have been brought up to view themselves as the center of the universe. Anything that offends their sense of self-importance, including imperfect parents, must therefore be evil.

- *Radical secularism.* God has disappeared from the worldview of millions of people—and with Him, any concept of a higher, nobler purpose in life. The sexual revolution has destroyed respect for traditional concepts of marriage and family.
- *Naivete about life.* Americans, especially young people, are convinced that life should always be pleasant and fun. When it's not, somebody must be blamed for the adversity. Parents are the usual suspects.
- *Incompetent psychotherapists.* Troubled young people are getting awful advice from counselors who actually encourage the tearing down of the family structure.

The institution of the family, consisting of father, mother, children, and extended relations, is God's formula for a stable society. No family is perfect, of course—that's why humility and forgiveness are so important in family relations. But ditching the family altogether produces a life of emptiness and cheerlessness. We weren't designed to live life without this kind of social structure, and our culture is beginning to learn that lesson the hard way.

Whatever its flaws, God gave you your family for your good. Appreciate them and let them know you love them. Someday you'll be glad you did.

---

* The Prager summary is available at https://dennisprager.com/column/whats-ripping-american-families-apart-responses-from-the-bizarre-world-of-new-york-times-readers/.

Thanksgiving

The traditional Thanksgiving holiday should remind us not only of what we have to be thankful for, but of how shriveled our gratitude really is.

I will praise the name of God with a song, and will magnify Him with thanksgiving (Psa. 69:30).

Be anxious for nothing, but in everything by prayer and supplication, with thanksgiving, let your requests be made known to God (Phil. 4:6).

Every Thanksgiving season our thoughts turn to visits with family, turkey dinner, Thursday afternoon football, and early Christmas sales at the stores. Perhaps we should spend a moment to reflect on another aspect of the holiday that deserves attention: the spirit of thankfulness that it is intended to cultivate.

Thanksgiving is a uniquely North American tradition (Canada has its own version, celebrated on the second Monday of October). In the U.S., the origins of the holiday can be traced to the first harvest by the Pilgrims at the first Plymouth settlement in 1621. In the early decades of the republic, various Presidents issued single Thanksgiving proclamations, but there was not an annual Thanksgiving holiday. Abraham Lincoln was the first President to declare Thanksgiving as a Federal holiday. The current date of the fourth Thursday in November was set by Congress in 1941.

In reviewing the history of this holiday, the one theme that dominates the story is the profound gratitude the early observers had for God's blessings. George Washington, for example, encouraged his fellow Americans to devote that special day "to the service of that great and glorious Being, who is the beneficent Author of all the good that was, that is, or that will be—That we may then all unite in rendering unto him our sincere and humble thanks—for his kind care and protection of the People of this Country." If America was not a Christian nation, at least its leaders acknowledged the role of God in its founding and success.

Today, of course, the holiday remains but the historical foundation is largely lost. The rise of secularism has removed much of the spiritual character from the occasion, and only the name remains to remind us of its real meaning.

However, at the risk of being misunderstood, let me suggest that the designation of a single day of thanksgiving may itself be a sign of an ungrateful spirit. Shouldn't we be thankful to God *every* day of the year? What does it say about our gratitude if we have to designate a special day to remind ourselves of it?

Genuine thankfulness is much more than an annual ritual. It is a deeply embedded way of thinking that influences every word, every behavior, every decision, every day. A truly thankful heart never takes for granted *any* gift, however small. It always honors God as the source of all things. It is ever willing to repay by sharing its good fortune with others. It is not easily discouraged by setbacks or losses, choosing instead to focus on all the good things that yet remain.

This Thanksgiving Day, enjoy all the traditions that make the day so special. But remember that God does not bless us only one day a year. Neither should our giving of thanks be constrained by the calendar.

Comparing Ourselves to Others

Many of our emotional and psychological troubles can be traced to a single cause: the constant need to compare ourselves to others.

I was envious of the boastful, when I saw the prosperity of the wicked. For there are no pangs in their death, but their strength is firm. They are not in trouble as other men, nor are they plagued like other men (Psa. 73:3-5).

"*The Pharisee stood and prayed thus with himself, 'God, I thank You that I am not like other men—extortioners, unjust, adulterers, or even as this tax collector'" (Lk. 18:11).*

The moment we are born into this world, we enter into a contest with billions of other people. The comparisons are endless: Who is the smartest? Who is the most beautiful? Who is the richest? Who is the strongest? Who is the wisest? Who is the most popular? The competition is relentless, and we are constantly reminded of how we stack up against others in all these categories.

Faced with this endless pressure to measure up, the impact on our self-image gravitates toward one of two extremes: Either we will see ourselves losing most of these face-offs, which will discourage and embitter us (think of the author of this Psalm, who resented the success of others); or we will sense our superiority in several of these areas, which will turn us into self-righteous, arrogant snobs (like the Pharisee in Jesus' parable). Either way, we will develop a distorted view of ourselves that damages our relationships with others and inhibits our effectiveness in God's kingdom.

We need to get over this obsession with comparing ourselves to others. But is that even possible? We interact with people every day of our lives, and those interactions provide constant reminders of the disparities between us and them.

We cannot escape the reality of different talents, achievements, and fortunes among us. But there is one thing we can change: *who* we choose to compare ourselves to.

Instead of comparing myself to other people, what if I focused on the life of Jesus—His holiness, His perfection, His power, His knowledge of every detail of my life? Such a comparison would deflate my pretensions of greatness. By reflecting on His majesty, I would come to realize that it really doesn't matter what advantages I may have over others. In His presence, I have no room to gloat about my achievements. He owns me, and that should humble me into the dust.

At the same time, if I study the horrible death of Jesus, not as a stale historical event, but as a personal gift I could not earn for myself, the knowledge of such a vicarious sacrifice would lift me from the gutter in which I find myself. "The Son of God loved ME and gave Himself for ME" (Gal. 2:20). In light of that cosmic truth, who cares how I measure up to the achievements of others? I am a child of the King! I have a mansion waiting for me in heaven! What more do I need?

Ultimately, there is only one comparison that really matters: my relationship with Jesus Christ. If I make that my primary concern in life, it will force my heart to embrace two essential truths: I am not worthy of God's blessings, so I can't get proud and haughty toward others. But at the same time, He has given me an enormous gift motivated by a love I cannot comprehend. I am valuable to God, regardless of what others think of me, so I have no reason to despair.

If I keep my eyes set on those two truths, there will be no need to compare myself to others. I won't have the time or the desire to play all the petty games that come with that futile exercise. I will be free in the truest sense of the word, liberated from the constant pressure to compete in a contest that means nothing in the end.

This World Is Not My Home

How we cope with the injustices of this life depends largely on our vision of the life to come. Which reality dominates our thinking?

You will guide me with Your counsel, and afterward receive me to glory. Whom have I in heaven but You? And there is none upon earth that I desire besides You (Psa. 73:24-25).

Albert Brumley is best remembered as the composer of the gospel hymn, "I'll Fly Away," first published in 1931. But for my money his arrangement of an earlier tune (usually attributed to A. P. Carter), "This World Is Not My Home," is more memorable. The first stanza is a beautiful echo of the 73rd Psalm:

*This world is not my home, I'm just a passing through.
My treasures are laid up somewhere beyond the blue;
The angels beckon me from heaven's open door,
And I can't feel at home in this world anymore.*

Read the entire Psalm, and the sentiment expressed in this hymn comes into sharper focus. Asaph was troubled by the unfairness of life that he saw all around him. While he struggled to live a good life and paid a dear price for his trouble (v. 13-14), the wicked prospered in their iniquities (v. 3-12). It's hard to trust God when it seems that He winks at the sin and injustice that infects this world.

But Asaph's downcast outlook took a positive turn when he opened his eyes to a more expansive view of what's going on. He realized that God has a far greater plan in motion, a plan that included providing a home in glory for him when this life is over. All the pain, the frustration, and the trauma that Asaph had to endure in the present would be swept away, and he would find rest at last in a beautiful abode far away from the ruthlessness of this world.

Like Asaph, we're stuck here in a broken world, having to grind out our existence day by dreary day, wondering why God doesn't do something about the wretchedness that surrounds us. Like Asaph, we have to learn how to think of this world as an aberration. Life on this old earth is merely a bumpy detour to our final destination, and when God receives us to glory in heaven, then we will realize . . . it was all worth it.

"This world is not my home, I'm just a passing through." If that line does not capture your current frame of mind, there is a high likelihood that you are struggling with your own doubts about God and the unfairness of life. Lift up your eyes from this barren wasteland and see with the eye of faith the joy that lies beyond. What else do you need?

When People Hurt Us

The closer the relationship, the greater the risk of devastating loss if it is destroyed. Only one relationship is worth building our life upon.

Whom have I in heaven but You? And there is none upon earth that I desire besides You. My flesh and my heart fail; but God is the strength of my heart and my portion forever (Psa. 73:25-26).

Human beings are social creatures. From the day we are born until the day we die, our lives are unavoidably intertwined with the lives of others. Ideally, those interactions are healthy, providing us with positive reinforcement and encouragement, helping us to cope with challenges we face along the way.

But life is not ideal, and most of us have to experience the bitter disappointment of people who hurt us. Often these episodes involve acquaintances only peripherally involved in our lives. In those breakdowns, we simply put the bad experience behind us and chose another path. But sometimes the experience involves relationships from which we cannot easily walk away: parents who berate and belittle us; life-long friends who betray us; a "dream" boyfriend or girlfriend who dumps us; a brother or sister in the Lord who fails to live up to their faith. When we encounter these problems, it is more than merely disappointing; our world is shattered, and our faith in humanity is crushed. As a result, families are broken, friends are alienated, jilted lovers jump off bridges, and churches are split. All because someone said or did something that hurt us.

God understands the pain of these experiences. Much of the Bible was written precisely to help us cope with this kind of hurt. These passages address the subject from a variety of directions, but they all arrive at a single message: *Our faith should be in God, not people.*

The 73rd Psalm addresses directly the debilitating emotional effects of pain inflicted by others. The author was depressed by the fickle performance of the people around him. But he found strength in the conviction that "there is none upon earth that I desire besides You." Once he elevated God to the place of ultimate devotion in his heart, the disappointments in his other relationships became more bearable.

Does that statement accurately describe your view of life? Is God *really* the one Person, above all others, who dominates your existence? If you have to struggle with that question, then your faith is almost certainly misplaced. As long as the important people in your life treat you decently, you'll be fine. But if any of them, for whatever reason, should abuse you or end their relationship with you, the impact will be ruinous.

If, on the other hand, you put God first in your life, and keep Him there, it really doesn't matter what others do. God is the one Person who will never forsake you, never let you down, never betray you. And He is the only One who will be with you even through death.

This does not mean, of course, that if God is first in your lives then you can ignore your friends and family. Your primary relationship with God provides the foundation upon which all your other relationships should be built. Those other connections are enriched and enhanced because you are not leaning on them to provide more than they can bear. Your self-respect is tied to God, not to other people.

When people hurt us, we will still cry. But we can get on with our lives, knowing that our strength is in God.

Seeking God in Darkness

Whatever the root causes of depression, one Psalm gives the depressed person assurance that God understands and is available to help.

You have laid me in the lowest pit, in darkness, in the depths. . . . Loved one and friend You have put far from me, and my acquaintances into darkness (Psa. 88:6, 18).

The heading to this Psalm identifies the author as "Heman the Ezrahite," considered by some commentators to be the grandson of Samuel the prophet (compare 1 Chron. 6:33 and 15:16-17). His father, Joel, was a priest whose immoral conduct scandalized the priesthood (1 Sam. 2:12-17). Somehow Heman survived what must have been a tumultuous childhood to become a godly man and author of this Psalm.

We do not know the details of the trials Heman was struggling with, but we do know that it had pushed him beyond the point of hope. Again and again, he cries out to God for relief (v. 2, 9, 13)—but God is silent. He even blames God for his predicament: "You have afflicted me" (v. 7); "Lord, why do you cast off my soul?" (v. 14); "Your terrors have cut me off" (v. 16). The key word used repeatedly in this Psalm is "darkness" (v. 6, 12, 18)—the classic symptom of *depression.*

Victims of depression can instantly recognize other signs documented in this Psalm. Notice the language:

"I am like a man who has no strength, adrift among the dead" (v. 4-5). Depression *robs its victims of the motivation to function* in the simplest routines of life.

"You have put away my acquaintances far from me" (v. 8). "Loved one and friend You have put far from me" (v. 18). The anxieties of the depressed person often *drive away those closest to him.*

"My soul is full of troubles, and my life draws near to the grave" (v. 3). "I have been afflicted and ready to die from my youth" (v. 15). Depression also fosters a sense of hopelessness and abandonment so overwhelming that it *erodes a person's will even to live.* Tragically, many depressed people are driven to act on that impulse to end it all.

Whatever the underlying causes of depression, this Psalm informs us that depression is a very real illness. Telling someone who suffers from depression to just "snap out of it" or "cheer up" doesn't work; in fact, it usually makes the problem worse.

Many other Psalms contain similar cries of despair, but those cries are usually accompanied by words of hope or reassurance. This is the only Psalm that does not offer a single word of comfort. The only consolation that we can glean from its melancholy mood lies in the subject to whom it is addressed; the Psalm is *a plea to God for help.* "O Lord, God of my salvation, I have cried out day and night before You" (v. 1, 13). Like Job, Heman did not understand what was happening to him, or how to process the pain. But also like Job, he refused to abandon God for nihilism, or seek refuge in a bottle or a needle. Instead, He flung himself across the chasm of gloom, reaching out for the God he still believed was there.

Therapy and medication can play a legitimate role in the treatment of depression, but a stubborn diet of faith and prayer will also go a long way toward relieving the pain. On those days when your sanity is hanging by a thread and it appears that all is lost, spend time reading and pondering this Psalm. It will articulate the pain in your heart, and give you the strength to grasp the invisible Hand of the God who is never far from your side.

The Clock Is Ticking . . .

The passing of time in our lives is so slow that we fail to recognize how quickly it goes by. The wise person uses his days for tasks that really matter.

For all our days have passed away in Your wrath; we finish our years like a sigh. The days of our lives are seventy years; and if by reason of strength they are eighty years, yet their boast is only labor and sorrow; for it is soon cut off, and we fly away. . . . So teach us to number our days, that we may gain a heart of wisdom (Psa. 90:9, 10, 12).

"I must work the works of Him who sent Me while it is day; the night is coming when no one can work" (Jn. 9:4).

Moses likely wrote Psalm 90 during Israel's forty years of wandering in the wilderness. Day after day, he witnessed the slow extermination of an entire generation. The daily mortality reports were a grim reminder of the fragility of life. His reflections on life and death can help us appreciate the fleeting nature of our own lives, and how best to use them.

Moses knew that no matter how long we may live, in the end our lives will have gone by far too quickly. He compares our life to a "sigh," a brief, imperceptible exhalation of air that nobody notices. To a young person, life seems to be almost endless; there are so many years yet to come that it is difficult to see the urgency of using them carefully. But as the young person grows older, the passing of time seems to accelerate until finally he moans, "Where did the time go?" It's a simple mathematical certainty: Even if you lived eighty years, and had a penny for every day you lived, you would end up with less than $300. Indeed, our life "is soon cut off," and all those years spent cannot be retrieved or relived. Whatever regrets we have at the end cannot be undone.

Jesus also knew the limitations of time. His ministry covered less than four years, and He died before His thirty-fourth birthday—what many of us would consider "young." He knew from the beginning that He had only a short time to finish His mission, so He threw Himself into His work with an urgency befitting its value. He compared His ministry to a single work day, limited by the approaching nightfall. He had to achieve His life's work *now*, not "someday," and His work habits reflected that compulsion.

Moses saw the same lesson in the parade of futility that passed before him. Life may be short, but it is still a life, an opportunity to do something with the precious gifts God has given us. If we can learn to appreciate the brevity of our time on this earth, we will exercise greater wisdom in the decisions we make. Instead of squandering our days in trivial pursuits that produce nothing of value, we will focus on activities that have eternal consequences. We will see our relationships for what they are, as bridges that we are building for future generations. We will, through a lifetime of good deeds and unselfish service, lay up treasures in heaven rather than on earth. It's true that our names may not be preserved in the history books, but they will be preserved in the only book that matters, God's Book of Life.

Sadly, there are many people whose lives are much like those of the Israelites in the wilderness. They live for nothing and die without purpose. But it doesn't have to be that way. If you embrace the fact that your time on earth is short, and that your life does have meaning, if only briefly, then you will be empowered to do something meaningful with it. Strengthen your relationship with God; dedicate your resources to helping others; get involved in activities that make a difference. Life will still be short, yes, but it will be rich with meaning. You will be remembered by all those whose lives you touched—and rewarded by God in the life to come.

The Multitude of My Anxieties

Being a child of God does not insulate us from
the hardships of life. But it does provide us with
an antidote to the worry that accompanies them.

Unless the Lord had been my help, my soul would soon have settled in silence. If I say, "My foot slips," Your mercy, O Lord, will hold me up. In the multitude of my anxieties within me, Your comforts delight my soul (Psa. 94:17-19).

This psalm was written by a righteous man, but his confession of struggling with "the multitude of my anxieties" provides a good lesson for dealing with our own struggles with worry.

In this context, the author was particularly anxious about the attacks of personal enemies (v. 16). But there are many other sources of worry in life: illness, accident, the loss of a job, the welfare of our children, economic decline, and so on. Then there are the pains that we inflict upon ourselves by the foolish mistakes we make. We like to think of the godly life as a long stretch of serenity, but in fact, it can be a wild ride of emotional peaks and valleys. In rare cases, the afflictions can be so intense that our soul can "settle in silence"—the silence of death. We can despair of life itself.

We have to acknowledge up front that God does not wave a magic wand and make all our problems and anxieties go away. We may be children of God, but we are still creatures of flesh who live in an imperfect world, so we can never entirely escape the crises of this life. We do not know if David was the author of this psalm, but his life is certainly reflected in it. His persecution at the hands of Saul, the treachery of his friends, his vexing family problems, and the burden of his own sins in the incident with Bathsheba—all were sources of great anxiety in his life.

David was not unique in this regard. All Bible heroes dealt with similar struggles. In writing to one church, Paul confessed to an episode when he was "troubled on every side. Outside were conflicts, inside were fears" (2 Cor. 7:5). His whole career as an apostle was marked by "weariness and toil . . . sleeplessness often" (2 Cor. 11:27). Even the Son of God, when facing the greatest challenge of His life, experienced extreme mental anguish. His agony was so intense that "His sweat became like great drops of blood falling down to the ground" (Lk. 22:44). I've had some anxious moments in my life, but nothing like that.

The fact that we encounter these periods of distress in our life is not a sign of weakness or failure. The issue here is *how we deal with it*. This Psalm not only acknowledges the fact of anxiety in our life, but also tells us how to respond to it: "*Your mercy*, O Lord, will hold me up. . . . *Your comforts* delight my soul." The author managed the stress in his life by concentrating his mind on the good things God had done for him. God is a benevolent and kind Creator who wishes the best for us, and has gone to extraordinary lengths to provide for our eternal welfare. In view of that special relationship, the struggles of this life fade in significance and become more manageable.

This relationship with God is not merely a masking of our pain. His comforts "delight my soul"; that is, they impart a genuine joy to our inner spirit, whatever the external problems we are dealing with in our life. "If God is for us, who can be against us?" (Rom. 8:31). Indeed, we never had it so good. Our state of mind should reflect that reality.

Two Kinds of Heart

> Like steaks, human hearts are either tender or tough. The condition of our heart makes all the difference in our quality of life.

Do not harden your hearts, as in the rebellion, and as in the day of trial in the wilderness, when your fathers tested Me; they proved Me though they saw My work (Psa. 95:8-9).

"Because your heart was tender, and you humbled yourself before God when you heard His words against this place and against its inhabitants, and you humbled yourself before Me, and you tore your clothes and wept before Me, I also have heard you" (2 Chron. 34:27).

൞

In Hebrew nomenclature, the "heart" is the source of the will, the fountain from which all our decisions spring. In these two accounts, we are given a sharp contrast between two kinds of hearts and the outcomes they produce.

The Psalmist attributes the catastrophic failure of the Israelites during their wilderness crossing to their "hard" heart, a poor attitude that led them repeatedly to challenge God's rule. Even as God was providing for them, they complained about the poor accommodations and resisted His guidance. Nothing was good enough for them, so they finally lost their opportunity to enter the Promised Land.

Centuries later, when King Josiah heard the words of the newly-found Book of the Law, his response was quite different. He was overcome with remorse, realizing how far his people had wandered away from God's law. The prophetess reassured him that his "tender" heart was acknowledged by

God, and he would be spared the judgment that was coming upon the evil nation. His eyes would "not see all the calamity which I will bring on this place and its inhabitants" for their sins (v. 28).

Like steaks, human hearts can be tender, pliable, easily cut; or they can be hard, tough, resistant to penetration. Knowing the difference can spare us a great deal of trouble.

A *tender* heart is sensitive to the will of God, eager to order his life under God's direction. On those occasions when he realizes that he has erred in this commitment, the tenderhearted person is pained at the thought of damaging his relationship with God and seeks reconciliation. Repentance and growth are constant companions in the life of the one whose heart is receptive to truth.

A *hard* heart, on the other hand, is stubborn and defiant, challenging God on whatever details do not conform to its own preferences. The hard-hearted person is not necessarily an atheist; he just prefers God not to interfere with his selfish intentions. God's word has little effect on this person's heart. Like the Israelites, the hard heart is blinded to even the most obvious evidence of God's authority.

Whether hard or tender, the condition of our heart not only influences our decisions, it shapes the trajectory of our lives. Our worldview, our relationships with others, our moral character, our lifestyle choices—*everything we do* is governed by how sensitive or insensitive our heart is to the guidance of God.

That's why, above all else, our primary challenge in life is to keep our hearts open to God's influence. "Keep your heart with all diligence, for out of it spring the issues of life" (Prov. 4:23). Having made that decision, we must take care not to be distracted going forward: "Beware, brethren, lest there be in any of you an evil heart of unbelief in departing from the living God" (Heb. 3:12).

How is *your* heart health?

Cheerful People Are Beautiful People

True beauty is not achieved by gilding the outside, but by building character. One character trait is especially useful at making us attractive.

Honor and majesty are before Him; strength and beauty are in His sanctuary (Psa. 96:6).

Honor and majesty are before Him; strength and gladness are in His place (1 Chron. 16:27).

These verses are from two versions of the same psalm, recorded in different parts of the Old Testament. The longer version in Chronicles (perhaps the original?) was composed by David on the occasion of the tabernacle's move to Jerusalem. The version we know as Psalm 96 is an abridged variant. Our purpose here is not to parse out all the differences or their origins, but to highlight one distinction that carries a practical message regarding personal attractiveness.

Notice that where Chronicles uses the word *gladness* (or *joy*, NASB), the Psalm uses *beauty*. We do not know why an anonymous editor made the change, but the word choice suggests a deliberate connection between the two concepts. People whose personalities radiate *gladness* are truly *beautiful* to behold.

This connection is not hard to understand. As humans, we crave acceptance. We desperately want others to like us, and will do all sorts of things to make ourselves more appealing. For most people, that means addressing their physical appearance. They will spend gobs of money on clothing, hair styles, make-up, cosmetic surgery, weight loss programs, and so on, all in an effort to make themselves appear beautiful to others. Some people (at least those who can afford it) will adopt an opulent lifestyle, convinced that living in a gorgeous house, driving a luxury car, and throwing lavish parties will earn them a place among the glitterati.

Good looks and platinum credit cards may turn a few heads, but they don't make us beautiful. A cursory glance at the chaotic lifestyles of Hollywood celebrities should disabuse us of that notion. True beauty comes from within. It is a product of the personality we exude. And these verses suggest that a major factor in developing a beautiful personality is a glad or cheerful spirit.

The person whose personality is characterized by gladness tends to be more upbeat, optimistic, pleasant, and happy. This spirit is not just a plastic smile that is artificially turned on or off, but a deep-seated part of her character. She is genuinely glad to be alive and greets every new day and new experience as gift from heaven. Her words are consistently positive and encouraging. Her cheerful demeanor lights up a room when she walks in.

Moreover, this joyful countenance is not doused by the negativism of others. She is not easily discouraged by the difficult circumstances that come her way. She is convinced that all of life, including other people around her, are basically good—and she will treat them accordingly.

One whose personality exudes gladness may not have movie star looks or a fat bank account, but most people will never notice that. She will have more admirers than she can know. Her pleasant personality is a magnet that draws others to her, and she will never lack for friends. This is the person who has learned the secret of true beauty.

Which form of beauty are *you* pursuing in your life?

God and Me

Whatever else we may know, our knowledge of God (or lack thereof) will have a dramatic impact in every other area of our life.

Know that the LORD, He is God; it is He who has made us, and not we ourselves; we are His people and the sheep of His pasture (Psa. 100:3).

Everything we do in life is calibrated by an underlying worldview that we embrace. Our worldview may encompass a number of metaphysical assumptions, but the first assumption is our view of God. This verse declares three simple truths that should inform our perception of God.

First, *the Lord is God.* Yahweh, Jehovah, the God of the Hebrews—this is the Supreme Being who rules over all. He has no competitors, no challengers, no substitutes. Do we really believe that? Or do we seek to replace Him with other objects of affection, such as physical riches, pleasures, or people? Or maybe we exalt ourselves as the god of our own life? Everybody takes a position on these questions. Do you recognize the Lord as the God of your life, or have you ditched Him for something else?

Second, *the Lord made us, not we ourselves.* Many in our modern age simply shrug their shoulders at the question of ultimate origins, claiming not to know or care where they came from. But that's an intellectual cop-out. *Something* or *someone* made us, and it is worth our trouble to find out who or what that Creator is. Moreover, who we are as His creatures is embedded in our nature, and we cannot alter that nature without damaging the purpose for which we were made. Just as an exquisitely crafted automobile must be used as it was designed to be used, so we must live our lives within the parameters our Creator has set for us. When we deviate from those norms, we do great harm to ourselves and others. It's a simple question that each one of us must face: *Who* made me, and for *what purpose* was I made?

Finally, *we are His people and the sheep of His pasture.* He is the Great Shepherd, and we belong to Him. It is in our best interest to follow His lead, to let Him decide where we should go for pasture and protection. Once we declare our independence from Him, we expose ourselves to all the dangers of life in a hostile wilderness, where our chances of survival are nil. The Lord holds Himself out as our shepherd. Do we accept His guidance, or do we reject it and choose to navigate life on our own?

The truth claims about God made in this little verse are simple, but their implications in our lives are far-reaching. We are free to accept or reject these claims—and must take the consequences that come with our decision. But decide we must.

What role does God play in *your* life?

It Starts at the Top

Human communities need leadership, but the effectiveness of that leadership depends entirely on the caliber of their character.

He who works deceit shall not dwell within my house; he who tells lies shall not continue in my presence (Psa. 101:7).

For the LORD brought Judah low because of Ahaz king of Israel, for he had encouraged moral decline in Judah and had been continually unfaithful to the LORD (2 Chron. 28:19).

❧

When a nation's leader insists on a high standard of moral conduct among his lieutenants, and sets an example of it in his own personal life, that influence percolates down to the population at large. People are inspired to greatness by the integrity of a ruler who has the courage to stand firm for truth and justice, even when it costs him personally to do so.

Conversely, when a ruler openly embraces corruption and moral sleaze, the people on the streets have an incentive to behave just as selfishly. After all, if it's good enough for the guy at the top, why can't I grab some of the fun, too?

Psalm 101, written by King David perhaps early in his reign, describes the kind of principled leadership that will serve a nation well. Read the entire Psalm, and ask yourself: What would our country look like if all our politicians behaved this way?

- "I will behave wisely" (v. 2), rather than selfishly.
- "Whoever secretly slanders his neighbor, him I will destroy" (v. 5), instead of rewarding his libels.

- "He who walks in a perfect way, he shall serve me" (v. 6), even though it may be hard to find someone of such noble character.
- "He who tells lies shall not continue in my presence" (v. 7), because *truth* is the foundation of good government.

The lofty principles David lays out here evoke chuckles, because we know that this standard of integrity in government is rare. By definition, institutions of power attract the crooked, the corrupt, the treacherous. It's always been this way.

Even so, David's fidelity to these principles, while not perfect, set a high bar for those who followed him. Sadly, long after he penned this Psalm, Judah descended into a maelstrom of decadence and depravity under the leadership of a king, Ahaz, who actively "encouraged moral decline" in his people. His evil influence hastened the destruction of the nation a few years later.

What is true in the realm of politics is also true in families, businesses, and churches. The whole enterprise takes on the character of the person(s) at the top. Husbands, fathers, CEOs, owners, elders, preachers—anyone in a position of authority over others sets the tone for those who labor under their leadership. Leaders who conduct themselves with integrity and honor tend to inspire the same among their followers. Leaders whose primary interest is looking out for Number One should not be surprised to see their followers descend into cynicism, immorality, and infighting.

Social communities need leadership, but it must be the right kind of leadership, or the whole enterprise will collapse. Those who lead—and those who are in a position to choose leaders—should act accordingly.

In the Day of Trouble

When we face troubles in life, we want God to step in and fix them. But often the best solution is simply a changed attitude on our part.

Do not hide Your face from me in the day of my trouble; incline Your ear to me; in the day that I call, answer me speedily (Psa. 102:2).

The opening lines of this Psalm should sound familiar. How often have we encountered a "day of trouble" and gone to God begging for answers? In this Psalm, God provides a speedy answer—but with an unexpected twist.

The opening section (v. 1-11) is dominated by an inward focus: how the Psalmist feels in his life right now. The circumstances are not revealed, but they must have been quite severe. He lost his appetite (v. 4), endured sleepless nights (v. 7), and wept inconsolably (v. 9). Worse, his enemies took advantage of his vulnerability and persecuted him without mercy (v. 8). He felt as though God Himself had cast him away (v. 10). The prospect of death overwhelmed him with a deep sense of gloom: "My days are like a shadow that lengthens, and I wither away like grass" (v. 11). All he could see was a life of suffering ending in an ignoble death.

But that inward focus was itself a major contributor to his problems. By fixing his attention exclusively on I/me/my, he could see nothing beyond the span of his own wretched years.

So beginning in verse 12, the author broadened his perspective to include another character in his story: "But You,

O Lord, shall endure forever, and the remembrance of Your name to all generations." He realized that "from heaven the Lord viewed the earth" (v. 19). By moving his locus of attention from his own problems to God's vantage point, he began to see life in an entirely new way. No longer was he consumed with frustration over his own problems, but with the welfare of the larger community of believers (v. 13-14, 16, 21). He gained a renewed hope for "the generation to come, a people yet to be created" (v. 18). He looked forward to a time when the nations would fear the Lord (v. 15), and the kingdoms of the earth would serve Him (v. 22). More importantly, his own children would be established before the Lord (v. 28).

By lifting his eyes to see God's role in the wider scope of history, even extending beyond his own life, the author came to understand that his problems were not the all-consuming catastrophes that he once thought them to be. Sure, his life may have been difficult and brief; but it was part of a larger plan that God was working out, a plan that would ultimately end in glory.

This Psalm offers a remarkable lesson in how to deal with life's hardships. Happiness and misery are determined not by what we experience in life, but by *how we choose to look at life*. If we view our time on earth entirely in terms of our own little dramas, we will magnify our struggles far out of proportion to their real significance—and make ourselves miserable in the process. If, on the other hand, we open our eyes to a broader view of time and see the hand of God guiding everything to a majestic conclusion, life becomes easier to bear.

So when the day of trouble comes, don't freak out. Look at your problems against the larger backdrop of God's work in ageless time, and take comfort in the knowledge that someday He will make everything right.

Benefits

Just as our relationship with an employer includes special privileges, so our relationship with God comes with incredible perks. Do we value them?

Bless the LORD, O my soul, and forget not all His benefits: Who forgives all your iniquities, who heals all your diseases, who redeems your life from destruction, who crowns you with lovingkindness and tender mercies, who satisfies your mouth with good things, so that your youth is renewed like the eagle's (Psa. 103:2-5).

When someone applies for a job in a corporate setting, one of the considerations in taking the job is the benefits package. Standard benefits often include things like health insurance, an employee stock purchase plan, 401(k) investment plans, and paid vacations. Some companies offer more exotic perks like gym memberships or on-site game rooms for breaks. Companies know that incentives like these can make the difference in keeping employees happy and productive.

But when we sign on with God, we get a benefits plan like no other. In this psalm David itemized many of the privileges he enjoyed as a child of God: forgiveness, healing, mercy, renewed strength, compassion, and hope. Companies can provide services that address our physical comfort, but only God can grant gifts that nourish our souls. It is this constant spiritual and psychological refreshment that keeps us young at heart.

This benefits package is still available today to anyone who wants it, but with one catch: They are available only to "those who fear Him . . . such as keep His covenant, and to those who remember His commandments to do them" (v. 17-18). Like corporate benefits, we have to join the team before we can participate. We have to show up for work, and do the job we were "hired" to do. In a world that mocks God and everything He represents, that commitment requires courage. Even after we come on board, sometimes we can get so bogged down in the daily grind that we lose sight of who we're working for and the value of the privileges available to us. And if we drop out of the team? Well, we forfeit the benefits that came with it.

Forget not all His benefits. Remember how fortunate you are to have God as your boss, and serve Him with all the enthusiasm such a generous employer deserves.

Oh, and one more thing: About that retirement plan . . . .

God and Harvey

It's easy to take cheap shots at God following a deadly hurricane. But the wise will view such calamities in the larger context of God's creation.

You who laid the foundations of the earth, so that it should not be moved forever. You covered it with the deep as with a garment; the waters stood above the mountains. At Your rebuke they fled; at the voice of Your thunder they hastened away. They went up over the mountains; they went down into the valleys, to the place which You founded for them. You have set a boundary that they may not pass over, that they may not return to cover the earth (Psa. 104:5-9).

Skeptics use natural disasters like Hurricane Harvey to mock belief in God. Surely a good and all-powerful God, if He really existed, would not allow such tragedies to occur. Watching the news reports of the thousands of people whose lives have been upended by this catastrophe, it's easy to understand the appeal of this argument.

But Psalm 104 invites us to take a more comprehensive look at the natural order. It is a poetic retelling of the six days of creation in Genesis 1. These five verses describe the events of the third day—the separation of the oceans from the dry land (see Gen. 1:2, 9). God has "set a boundary" that the waters cannot pass over. He has overruled that boundary just once in history (Noah's flood), but promised that it would never happen again—and despite some awful floods here and there, it hasn't. Nature is subject to limits, and humanity does not fear total annihilation from its awesome power.

As terrible as the destruction wrought by hurricanes, earthquakes, tsunamis, and similar events might be, they do not define the character of God's creation. They are rare exceptions in a world governed by natural forces that display remarkable regularity. Natural disasters are newsworthy precisely because they are so infrequent. The fact that we can sit back and philosophize on the reasons for such anomalous events is itself a compelling argument for a master intelligence that keeps everything running smoothly.

Think about it. Humanity thrives precisely because nature is so predictable and resilient. The rest of the Psalm describes the hydrological cycle (v. 10-13), botanical laws (v. 14-18), and the cyclical nature of days and seasons (v. 19-23), all of which makes life on this earth not just possible, but pleasant. The earth and everything in it are expressions, not of God's capriciousness, but of His care for His creation (v. 24-28). Even the cycle of life itself, with generations coming and going, is a demonstration of God's commitment to "renew the face of the earth" (v. 29-30).

Hurricane Harvey was a major disaster, and the lives of those who were impacted by it will never be the same. Yet at this writing the skies have cleared, and the clean-up and rebuilding has already begun. Millions of people will get on with their lives, relying on the resources of an abundant and self-healing earth. It's almost like Somebody designed it for that very purpose.

Yes, hurricanes are a part of God's creation, and they remind us of how puny we are in this enormous universe. But the rest of His creation, with all the beauty and bounty it provides, is an even greater reminder of how much God loves and cares for us. Embrace it!

Leanness of Soul

When we become emotionally wilted, even as we partake of God's blessings, something is amiss in our attitude. We'd better fix it, fast.

They soon forgot His works; they did not wait for His counsel, but lusted exceedingly in the wilderness, and tested God in the desert. And He gave them their request, but sent leanness into their soul (Psa. 106:13-15).

This psalm is a poetic retelling of the story of Israel's early history, especially their journey from Egypt, emphasizing the longsuffering of God in dealing with His people's mistakes. The passage quoted here likely refers to an incident recorded in Numbers 11, when the people "yielded to intense craving" and demanded meat to eat (11:4), instead of their daily ration of manna. God gave them vast quantities of quail, and the people gorged themselves on the meat. But the delicacy was tainted, and many people died of a terrible plague (11:31-33).

Of special interest in this story is the people's original complaint to Moses: "Now our whole being is dried up; there is nothing at all except this manna before our eyes!" (11:6). The King James Version renders that first phrase more literally, "now our soul is dried away." The wording in our text, that God "sent leanness into their soul," reflects that parched spirit.

This "leanness of soul" was not a lack of food, but a lack of *contentment*. They already had everything they needed to sustain themselves, but their souls were poisoned with discontent and ingratitude. It really made no difference what they had to eat; with the attitude they had adopted, they would have complained about *anything* God gave them.

There is an important lesson here for us who live in an affluent society. The self-centered person will always crave more, yet always be starved for satisfaction. Once we convince ourselves that the game is rigged and we are mistreated victims, we will be satisfied with nothing—even when we have everything we need. We will complain bitterly about our outward circumstances, when the real problem lies within our own hearts.

The solution to the problem, of course, also lies within our hearts. The secret to happiness in life does not lie in achieving some arbitrary level of prosperity, but in learning how to be content with whatever we have. It's a personal choice, a decision of the mind that is independent of our financial statement.

This is not an argument against working hard or enjoying the fruits of our labors. Prosperity is often a consequence of a godly life, and there is nothing inherently wrong with doing well (Prov. 3:9-10). But when times are good, we must constantly remind ourselves that our happiness is a function of where we are *going*, not where we are *at*.

Arming ourselves with that attitude will prepare us for those days when, for whatever reason, life does not go as well as we would like, and we find ourselves struggling at the bottom of the ladder. When those days come we should be able to say with Paul, "I rejoiced in the Lord greatly . . . I have learned in whatever state I am, to be content" (Phil. 4:10-11).

When life gets you down and you detect "leanness in your soul," take a hard look at your attitude. Remind yourself that your place in God's plan is good; learn to be happy with that.

Why We Forget God

Failure to honor God is often not a deliberate decision, but a benign neglect. Remembering God's role in our lives requires conscious effort.

They soon forgot His works; they did not wait for His counsel, but lusted exceedingly in the wilderness, and tested God in the desert. . . . They forgot God their Savior, who had done great things in Egypt (Psa. 106:13,14, 21).

So the children of Israel did evil in the sight of the Lord. They forgot the Lord their God, and served the Baals and Asherahs (Judg. 3:7).

A voice was heard on the desolate heights, weeping and supplications of the children of Israel. For they have perverted their way; they have forgotten the Lord their God (Jer. 3:21).

These are only a few of the many passages in the Old Testament describing a problem that repeatedly got Israel in trouble: forgetting God. In most cases their rebellion against God was not a conscious decision based upon a reasoned examination of the evidence. Rather, it was a careless drifting away from God, a long term failure to keep Him foremost in their minds and lives. That forgetfulness, of course, led to disobedience, and eventually to destruction.

Human nature hasn't changed since then, and the same problem that led to Israel's downfall still plagues us today. Like Israel of old, we tend to forget God, both in our individual lives and as a culture. And like Israel, that forgetfulness leads us to marginalize God and His word. Sooner or later, we pay a heavy price for our neglect.

Why do we forget God? How can people who once had such deep reverence for God develop such a cavalier attitude toward Him? The Bible pinpoints two root causes for this phenomenon.

The first cause is *complacency*, or a failure to grow. Peter encourages us to "be diligent" to grow in qualities such as faith, virtue, knowledge, self-control, perseverance, godliness, brotherly kindness and love. Then he warns, "he who lacks these things is shortsighted, even to blindness, and has forgotten that he was cleansed from his old sins" (2 Pet. 1:5-9). In other words, either we pursue improvement, or we forget why we're in the game. Christianity is not a label we wear; it is an active commitment to a program of personal growth and development. It requires hard work, sacrifice, and study. The result of that diligence is a steady improvement in our quality of life, and a deeper appreciation for the God who made it possible.

But conquering the first source of forgetfulness only sets us up for the second, namely, *prosperity*. "When they had pasture, they were filled; they were filled and their heart was exalted; therefore they forgot Me" (Hos. 13:6). One of the great ironies of life is that by honoring God's will, we usually end up being blessed for it; then we become so comfortable with the blessings that we lose sight of how and why it happened. That sequence of events is not inevitable. If we are careful to thank God, often and fervently, for all that He has done for us, we are less likely to forget Him.

How can we not forget God? It's really quite simple—by *choosing* to remember Him.

A Complaining Spirit

Life is tough, we all know that. But chronic complaining about our hardships reveals a deeper problem that threatens our relationship with God.

Then they despised the pleasant land; they did not believe His word, but complained in their tents, and did not heed the voice of the Lord (Psa. 106:24-25).

. . . Nor complain, as some of them also complained, and were destroyed by the destroyer (1 Cor. 10:10).

Do all things without complaining and disputing (Phil. 2:14).

◈

After witnessing God's power in delivering them from Egypt, the Israelites immediately started grumbling about the travel accommodations. There was no potable water: *Complain!* (Ex. 15:24; 17:3). They got hungry: *Complain!* (Ex. 16:2). Even when God gave them food from heaven, it was too bland. *Complain!* (Num. 11:1; 21:5). The land of Canaan was everything God had promised, but it was occupied by powerful enemies: *Complain!* (Num. 14:2). Rebels challenged Moses' leadership and were punished in dramatic fashion: *Complain!* (Num. 16:41). Are we starting to see a pattern here?

The story of the Israelites' journey to the Promised Land is a lesson in how *not* to handle hardship. But we need to look beyond the surface behavior and understand why this kind of grumbling became their default response to every difficulty they encountered. Doing so can help us avoid their mistake.

The author of Psalm 106 reveals a couple of important details about the Israelites' behavior that we should consider.

First, he says that "they did not believe His word." Which is to say, their complaining was merely a symptom of an underlying heart of disbelief in God and His promises. Oh, they believed that God *existed*; but they did not *trust* Him. They had no confidence that He was willing, or even able, to help them. They saw God the same way we view a disinterested DMV clerk or a customer service robo-answering machine: there to help, but of no practical value in actually solving our problem. Their complaining spirit was an outgrowth of their low view of God and His power.

The second detail is a natural outgrowth of the first: They "did not heed the voice of the Lord." Why should they obey God's instructions, if they had no confidence that God knew what He was doing? In their minds, this whole wilderness crossing thing was a fool's errand, and they were paying the price for God's incompetence. Expressed another way, complaining is the recourse of people who have no confidence in God to deliver on His promises. Why should I trust my life to a God who is out to lunch?

The implications of these two principles should be sobering to those of us who are given to complaining whenever things in our life don't go like we think they should. Do we believe in God? If so, great . . . but do we *trust* God? Are we fully confident in His ability and willingness to take care of us—as HE defines it? If we do, then there should be no place in our hearts for complaining. We should be willing to let God run the show as He determines and adapt our lives to whatever He sends our way, whether good or bad.

Life can be hard, and there's nothing wrong with crying out to God when it hurts (see: Job). But whenever we catch ourselves dwelling on the negatives, or obsessing over the obstacles, or lashing out at the unfairness of it all, we need to step back and reassess where we're at spiritually. A person who has truly put his faith in God has no room for that kind of negativity in his life.

The Blood of Innocents

> When a society reaches the point where it has no reservations about destroying the lives of its most innocent citizens, it has forfeited the right to exist.

They even sacrificed their sons and their daughters to demons, and shed innocent blood, the blood of their sons and daughters, whom they sacrificed to the idols of Canaan; . . . Therefore the wrath of the Lord was kindled against His people . . . (Psa. 106:37-38, 40).

When the Israelites came into Canaan, they were surrounded by a population whose moral standards were in the gutter. The Canaanites "burn[ed] even their sons and daughters in the fire to their gods" (Deut. 12:31). This culture of death represented a pathological disdain for everything right and good. Consequently, the land "vomited out its inhabitants" (Lev. 18:25). God could not allow this to continue.

Inexplicably, the Israelites became infatuated with the customs of the natives and adopted the practice of child sacrifice (2 Chron. 28:3; Jer. 32:35; Eze. 16:20-21). This "shedding of innocent blood" (v. 37) was one of the more outrageous sins in a range of social evils that angered God. When a nation has no problem slaughtering its own children —the most innocent of all humans—there is something seriously twisted in their thinking. In time, Israel paid a price for their sick ideology.

But sick ideologies never die; they just come back in different forms. Since the Supreme Court's Roe v. Wade decision in 1973, over sixty million babies have been killed in our nation by legalized abortion. These are humans who have been sacrificed to the false god of selfishness.

The controversy over abortion once centered on whether a fetus is a human being. Advances in genetics and obstetrical medicine have laid that controversy to rest. From a scientific standpoint, there can be no doubt that the child in the womb is a separate human being, with its own unique DNA and personality. It is a living soul, with all the rights and dignity of any other person. Abortion is the taking of human life.

Likewise, defining abortion as a "women's rights" issue ignores the history of feminism. Early advocates of women's rights condemned abortion as "child murder" (Susan B. Anthony). Many feminists today continue to reject abortion as an attack on women's well-being (see feministsforlife.org).

The push for abortion-on-demand in our society is driven by something more sinister than the right of a woman to choose. It is no coincidence that the demand for abortion rights grew in tandem with the sexual revolution of the 1960s. Both movements have been accompanied by a rise in mental illness, violence, family dysfunction, suicide, and declining faith in God. *This is a spiritual disease*, a disease with a host of social symptoms. We are witnessing the collapse of faith and reason on a civilizational scale.

In the early Roman Empire, parents who did not want to keep their newborn babies would simply toss them in the garbage dump, and nobody cared. But Christianity changed that. The early Christians rescued these little ones and adopted them as their own. They did this because they believed in the dignity of every human being. They promoted a culture of life, love, and compassion that extended to "the least of these." Over time, that culture slowly changed the thinking of the broader population, and abandoning newborns—even abortion itself—became socially unacceptable.

That culture of life is now being dismantled. In ages to come, when historians tell the story of our nation's fall, our eagerness to spill the blood of innocents will be part of that story. God help us.

Why Give Thanks?

In a world scarred by sin and suffering, it's hard to see the hand of God in any of it. But His hand is at work, if we will open our eyes to see it.

Oh, give thanks to the Lord, for He is good! For His mercy endures forever. . . . Oh, that men would give thanks to the Lord for His goodness, and for His wonderful works to the children of men! (Psa. 107:1, 8).

Skeptics mock the very idea of God because of the evil that saturates our world. Surely, they argue, if there was a God, He would not allow all the suffering we see around us.

For the moment we will set aside the question of why the atheist thinks that evil and suffering are "bad," rather than morally neutral outcomes in a universe governed by "pitiless indifference" (Richard Dawkins). Instead, let's examine what this Psalm says about God's active role in minimizing the effects of suffering.

The Psalmist argues that God is far from indifferent about our problems, and actively intervenes in our behalf. He gives four examples of divine deliverance: travelers lost in a wilderness (v. 4-9); prisoners doomed to hard labor (v. 10-16); the sick and diseased (v. 17-22); and mariners encountering dangerous storms on the high seas (v. 23-32). With two of these groups (the prisoners and the sick), the suffering might be the result of their own foolish choices (v. 11, 17). But regardless of the factors leading to their pain, all four groups are desperate for help and "cry out to the Lord in their trouble." God hears their cries, and "delivers them out of their distresses" (v. 6, 13, 19, 28).

But this outcome seems too simplistic. We can cite many examples of people in such circumstances for whom deliverance never comes, who perish in their sorrow. Why would God act to save some and not others? (Side note: Job struggled with this question, too.)

The short answer is, it's not our place to know why God acts as He does. God has a plan in motion that is more complex than we could comprehend, and we have to trust Him to know what He's doing.

But this Psalm does not leave the matter there. The closing verses describe a broad pattern of judgment and restoration that recurs throughout history. God "turns a fruitful land into barrenness, for the wickedness of those who dwell in it" (v. 33-34), and "pours contempt on princes" (v. 40). Then He restores the land that it might yield its bounty (v. 35-38), and "sets the poor on high, far from affliction" (v. 41). Judgment followed by restoration.

Look at the vast panorama of history and you'll see this pattern play out again and again. The wicked eventually are purged from the land, followed by a relative degree of peace and harmony. This pattern offers no guarantees for specific individuals, of course; but it does give assurance that good will always win out in the end.

The certainty of that divine template should cause us to "give thanks to the Lord for His goodness, and for His wonderful works to the children of men" (v. 8, 15, 21, 31). We must look beyond the irritations of our own selfish affairs to the grand sweep of human history, and realize that God truly is good. This world is not perfect, but neither is it hell, and we have God to thank for that.

"Whoever is wise will observe these things, and they will understand the lovingkindness of the Lord" (v. 43).

Why We Are Afflicted

We are obsessed with understanding the origins of the suffering that afflicts us. But perhaps we are asking the wrong question.

Fools, because of their transgression, and because of their iniquities, were afflicted (Psa. 107:17).

It is good for me that I have been afflicted, that I may learn Your statutes (Psa. 119:71).

☙❧

Suffering is a universal experience of humanity. Whether young or old, rich or poor, good or bad, all of us encounter pain at one time or another in our lives. Philosophers and theologians have struggled to explain the origin and purpose of suffering, but definitive answers are difficult to pin down.

There are two explanations that can be dismissed as too simplistic. First, some argue that all affliction is the result of *bad behavior*. This was the counsel that Job's friends offered to explain his pain. In their shallow worldview, good people are rewarded with good things, and bad people receive bad things. Job suffered horribly; therefore, he must have done something really bad to deserve it. The problem with their theory, of course, was that Job was "blameless and upright" (Job 1:1), a man who served God with all his heart and soul. Moreover, how does this theory explain the suffering of Jesus? At least some suffering seems to be arbitrary.

At the opposite extreme is a faulty hypothesis that attributes all suffering to *blind luck*. In this view, whatever happens to us in life is entirely the product of chance. Like the card player who sometimes draws a bad hand, we are victims of tough breaks that fall randomly across the population. This explanation plays well among those who seek to avoid responsibility for their actions, but it denies the unmistakable cause-and-effect relationship that exists between choices and their consequences: "Fools, *because of their transgression*, were afflicted." As much as we would like to dodge it, we cannot deny that at least some of our misfortune we bring upon ourselves by our poor decisions.

We are left, therefore, with a conundrum: Some—but not all—affliction is the result of our own poor choices, while other suffering—but not all—is entirely arbitrary in its origin, striking good and bad alike. There is no simple all-inclusive explanation that covers everything.

So where does that leave us? Instead of addressing directly the Gordian knot of *why* we are afflicted, perhaps we would be better served to spend our time learning *how to deal with it*. There are three simple principles that should guide our response to suffering.

First, we should learn the humility necessary to *see the flaws in our own character that may be contributing to our struggles*. If our foolish choices keep blowing up in our face, we should have the good sense to adjust our decision-making paradigm. Repentance is something we *can* control.

Second, *we mustn't become bitter and lash out at God or others for the hardships that intrude into our life*. Whatever the source of our afflictions, giving in to rage and anger will only exacerbate the problems. We must learn the value of patience and endurance.

Finally, at a deep intellectual level, *we must change how we view the afflictions in our life*. We must see them, not as setbacks or defeats, but as opportunities for learning. Like the soldier in boot camp or the athlete in a tough training regimen, we should see our problems as a discipline that God is using to make us stronger, wiser, and more effective in His service. When we can truly say "it is good for me that I have been afflicted," then we will finally have a satisfactory answer to why God has allowed suffering to come into our life.

The Lord's Volunteer Army

God does not force people to follow Him. Neither can we. That fact must always guide our efforts in advancing the Lord's cause.

The LORD said to my Lord, "Sit at My right hand, till I make Your enemies Your footstool." The LORD shall send the rod of Your strength out of Zion. Rule in the midst of Your enemies! Your people shall be volunteers in the day of Your power; in the beauties of holiness, from the womb of the morning, You have the dew of Your youth (Psa. 110:1-3).

This Psalm is clearly identified in the New Testament as a prophecy of the Messiah and His reign (Ac. 2:34-36; Heb. 1:13). Of special interest here is David's description of the manner in which the Messiah's subjects would come to serve Him: "Your people shall be *volunteers*" (or, "will offer themselves freely," ESV).

There is no conscription in the Lord's army. People enter this special relationship entirely through their own personal choice. Even if some form of pressure were applied to "persuade" them to sign up, their service would be meaningless to God, because service that does not come from a willing heart is not true service.

Compare, for example, how people converted to Christ in the first century, with how people converted to Islam in the seventh century. The apostles never forced anyone to convert at the point of a sword. No taxes on non-believers, no political coups, no military conquests. People were converted because they genuinely believed, nothing more.

When Paul encouraged the Corinthians to participate in the Jerusalem relief mission, he carefully avoided any coercive tactics. He knew there first must be "a willing heart" (2 Cor. 8:12). The gift would have to be prepared "as a matter of generosity and not as a grudging obligation" (9:5). "God loves a *cheerful* giver" (9:7), not one whose arm has been twisted to give.

Paul's plea to Philemon to release Onesimus was also based on this principle of free will. "Without your consent I wanted to do nothing, that your good deed might not be by compulsion, as it were, but voluntary" (Phe. 14). Notice that Paul delivered this message through the hands of Onesimus himself. He risked everything—including the slave's freedom—on the voluntary willingness of one man to do the right thing.

This principle has important implications in our work today. Preachers and elders who browbeat a congregation into submission are not advancing the Lord's work, no matter how "sound" the congregation may be. People must be truly convinced by the power of Biblical reasoning, or their "faithfulness" is a sham. And if people chose to walk away from their commitment to Christ, they are perfectly free to do so. They came of their own free will; they can leave of their own free will.

In our efforts to win converts and encourage faithfulness, we must be careful to respect this principle of voluntary service. It's the only service that pleases God.

A Broad Place

As we make our way through the madness of life, it is important that we pause to recognize those rare moments of beauty that God sends our way.

I called on the LORD in distress; the LORD answered me and set me in a broad place (Psa. 118:5).

Viktor Frankl was an Austrian psychiatrist who spent several years in Nazi concentration camps during World War II. He survived the ordeal, and later wrote a book about his life in the camps (*Man's Search for Meaning*, 1946). In the book, he recounts one experience that happened a few days after his liberation:

I walked through the country past flowering meadows, for miles and miles, toward the market town near the camp. Larks rose to the sky and I could hear the joyous song. There was no one to be seen for miles around; there was nothing but the wide earth and sky and the larks' jubilation and the freedom of space. I stopped, looked around, and up to the sky—and then I went down on my knees. At that moment there was very little I knew of myself or of the world—I had but one sentence in mind—always the same: "I called to the Lord from my narrow prison and He answered me in the freedom of space" (p. 111).

As a Jew, Frankl was familiar with this verse from Psalm 118. But after what he had been through, the words took on a new—and literal—meaning. His journey from a wretched concentration camp to a beautiful spring meadow taught him that whatever the circumstances we might encounter in this life, God is always in control.

Our distresses in life may not be as awful as a Nazi death camp, and our broad places may not be as beautiful as an alpine meadow in springtime, but the Lord has a way of directing our steps from one to the other, and like Frankl, those occasions should cause us to drop to our knees in gratitude.

When life turns hard and cold, and the temptation to scream out in anger ravages your heart, remember the lesson of this verse. Your job is not to critique how God runs His universe. Call on Him in your distress. Some day, at a time and place of His choosing, He will answer and set you in a broad place.

Then you will know: It's not about you or all the craziness that happens in this world. It's about God and His glory. And that's enough.

What Can Man Do to Me?

The fear of mistreatment at the hands of others can terrify us. But that fear melts away once we grasp God's role in our life and in the life to come.

The Lord is on my side; I will not fear. What can man do to me? (Psa. 118:6).

Actually, if history is any guide, others can do quite a lot to me. They can laugh at me, shun me, or slander me. They can rob me, beat me, or torture me to within an inch of my life. If they hate me enough, they can even kill me in any number of creative ways. I can be crucified, stoned, poisoned, gassed, shot, hung, beheaded, pulled apart on a rack, burned alive, or simply left to slowly starve. Oh, yes, man can do quite a lot to me.

Knowing that the world can be such a cruel place, we look for safe havens to protect us from the threats of man.

Some of us are fortunate to have strong, stable *families* to shield us from the chaos of this world. But many others do not have that advantage. And among those who do, even those families cannot shield us from every injustice. Sometimes entire families may share the same cruel fate (think of the Holocaust).

Some people put their confidence in the *government* to guarantee their security. But governments can become corrupt or be overthrown. What then? In all too many cases, the government itself is the instrument of oppression that seeks to ruin us.

Others seek to secure their own well-being through amassing *wealth*. Surely, they think, money will buy safe passage through any threat. But as so many have learned the hard way, money can be a treacherous friend, one that often brings its own set of problems.

The Psalmist offers another source of security, one that he claims will never fail: "The *Lord* is on my side."

Think about the implications of those words. God, the One who created and sustains all things, is my champion, my defender, my friend. His position is so far beyond that of the most powerful of men that He is not even in the same league. They can only hurt me in this life; He controls what happens in the next. If God is indeed on my side, then it really doesn't matter what man may do to me. Try as they might, they cannot touch the eternal reward that my Father has promised me.

The poet is not flippantly dismissing the awfulness of the pain that others can inflict upon me. It hurts. But compared to what God has prepared for me later, this pain is but a temporary discomfort. I can stand up against the tyrants who threaten me, and challenge them do their worst. Whatever they might do, they can never overcome the One who stands beside me and will deliver me in the end.

The challenge here, of course, is to inculcate in my mind a spiritual relationship with a Being whom I cannot see, hear, or touch. That requires a disciplined approach to thinking about life and its responsibilities. If I want God on my side, then I must make the effort to be on His side in the great cosmic struggle between Good and Evil. I must respect God's word, honor Him in all I do, and seek His guidance in fervent prayer.

Finally, I must learn what it means to love as God loves, even to those who seek to harm me. Nothing else so clearly defines my connection with Him.

Do Not Trust in Princes

Every election cycle, Americans agonize over who will lead our nation. The agony is misplaced, if we understood who is really in charge.

It is better to trust in the LORD than to put confidence in princes (Psa. 118:9).

Do not put your trust in princes, nor in a son of man, in whom there is no help (Psa. 146:3).

Our nation is currently being torn apart by partisan bickering, much of it centered on who will be our next President. Half the population believes that we are recovering from a corrupt administration riddled with illegalities and incompetence. The other half is convinced that we are descending into a nightmare that threatens the very existence of the republic. In the midst of this deep divide, nobody seems to be asking the most significant question of all: *Why is it that 300 million people are looking to one man to solve all our problems and make us all happy?*

No president, no king, no prime minister—however decent and well-respected—can fulfill the aspirations of an entire nation. Leaders can set a personal example for good or ill, and influence policy decisions that move the national needle one direction or another. But looking to elected officials to wave a magic wand that makes all our problems go away puts them on an impossibly tall pedestal. The cause of our societal ailments does not rest exclusively with our leaders, and neither does the cure. Our nation's character is an aggregate of the character of the millions of citizens who comprise it. And the character of the citizens is tied directly to how they relate to God. In other words, we all have a role to play in how this drama turns out.

As Americans, we are fortunate that we have a voice in electing our leaders. But these two psalms remind us that putting our trust in human rulers to resolve all the pressing issues of our lives is a dangerous delusion. Only God can fill that role. "The Lord is my strength and song, and He has become my salvation" (Psa. 118:14). "Happy is he who has the God of Jacob for his help, whose hope is in the Lord his God" (Psa. 146:5). The authors of these psalms knew that earthly rulers come and go, but God is the only constant—and a reliable one at that. He alone deserves our total confidence.

Until we can look past the pettiness of our current political turmoil to the King who rules over all the universe, we will never find the peace of mind that we need to guide us through the chaos of regime change. Regardless of who our next President is, put your trust in God and take personal responsibility for following His guidance. Only then can you sleep comfortably at night.

Happiness Is a Choice

Too many people link their happiness to the circumstances they experience in the moment. Believers find happiness in a different manner.

This is the day the Lord has made; we will rejoice and be glad in it (Psa. 118:24).

God had gone to extraordinary lengths to rescue the Israelites from Egyptian bondage. They had witnessed the devastating plagues upon the Egyptians, and walked through the midst of the Red Sea to freedom. God gave them manna from heaven and water from rocks. God personally guided them day and night. They had a leader, Moses, who had dedicated his life to helping them. God gave them a detailed Law to provide order and direction to their daily lives. No enemy could harm them, and no obstacle could stand in their way of reaching the Promised Land. All they had to do was endure a brief march through a rugged wilderness. It would be a hard journey, but they could do it.

But that was too much to ask of these people. Instead of marching with firm resolve toward their destination, they grumbled about every hardship they encountered. Even when they reached the border of Canaan, the report of their spies triggered an open rebellion. Their rejection of God's gift cost them entrance into the land, and they spent the next forty years dying off in the wilderness. That generation never did reach their goal.

Many years later, inspired writers summarized the Israelites' failure as a *faith* issue. "They despised the pleasant land; they *did not believe His word*" (Psa. 106:24). "Beware, brethren, lest there be in any of you *an evil heart of unbelief* in departing from the living God" (Heb. 3:12).

The Israelites had their own version of our opening psalm: "This is the day the Lord has made; we will complain and be miserable in it." No matter what God did for them, they were determined to be unhappy—and they succeeded in that goal. They were not miserable because of the hardships they encountered; they were miserable because of *how they chose to deal with* those hardships.

The story of the Israelites' march to the Promised Land serves as a metaphor for our own lives. Like the Israelites, we have our own rescue from bondage, our own Promised Land, and our own journey of faith. We also have our own hardships and struggles to deal with along the way.

And now, also like the Israelites, we have a simple choice to make: Do we accept with courage the challenge before us and rejoice in each new day that God gives us? Or do we obsess over our problems and live in a perpetual state of discontent?

The secret to a happy life is not hard to figure out, once we grasp this simple truth: Happiness is not a product of what we encounter in life; it is a product of *what we choose to think about life*. If we greet each new day with a determination to "rejoice and be glad in it," that is exactly what we will find. If instead we choose to feel sorry for ourselves and give in to discouragement and gloom, we will find that, too. It's our choice.

Does this deny the reality of our present troubles? Not at all. Rather, it embraces a greater reality: We have a future home in heaven that far surpasses anything we may experience in this life, and *nothing* will stand between us and reaching that home.

The Lord has given you this day. What you do with it is up to you.

Why Do Young People Give Up Their Faith?

Our young people are easy targets for a godless world, but we can save them from Satan's clutches if we prepare them for the battle.

How can a young man cleanse his way? By taking heed according to Your word (Psa. 119:9).

❧

Recent studies indicate that about 70% of young people raised in Christian homes abandon their faith after leaving home for college. A sizable number return to their faith after graduating from college, but that is still a troubling attrition rate. Why are we losing so many of our young people? There are four major factors at work here.

Obviously, *the influence of a hostile culture* plays a major role. Despite our best efforts to shield them, our children are growing up in a deeply secular society that ridicules God, the Bible, Christianity, and traditional morality. Public education, music, movies, social media, and current events are all overwhelmingly dominated by a godless worldview, and we're kidding ourselves if we think this environment has no impact on their thinking. When they go off to a secular university, the aggressive secular indoctrination they encounter there finishes the job.

Inconsistent parenting is a contributing factor. When parents demonstrate in their personal lives that their own faith is shallow, they should not be surprised to see that it means nothing to their children. When sports and school activities trump worship services, or when parents' personal vices are not tempered by gospel teaching, kids quickly figure out that religion is just for show. Parents may not intend to send that message, but the kids are definitely learning it.

Clueless church leadership must share some blame. Preachers, elders, and Bible class teachers may have the best of intentions, but if their teaching does not directly address the hard questions that young people are thinking, the world will answer those questions for them. We may not like the world's answers, but from the kids' point of view, at least somebody is taking their questions seriously. The church loses the battle, because it was never in the war.

Finally, *personal choice* is the ultimate determining factor. By the time our children head off to college, they are old enough to think for themselves. There are plenty of resources available online and in bookstores to research the ultimate questions about reality. Young people are capable of digging for those answers themselves . . . if they really want to know the truth. Ultimately, they will be held responsible for the life decisions they make.

My advice to young people: Read the Bible regularly, with an open mind, and give it a chance to answer the questions you're struggling with. You might be surprised how relevant it is to your life.

The Value of Affliction

We tend to view suffering as a trauma to be avoided at all costs. But the wise recognize a deeper principle in play—and appreciate it.

It is good for me that I have been afflicted, that I may learn Your statutes (Psalm 119:71).

David knew a thing or two about affliction. There were days in his life when he dared not ask, "What else could go wrong?" for fear that he would find out. Betrayal, sickness, personal failure, rejection, the death of loved ones—David experienced it all, and more. The pain was sometimes more than he could bear: "I drench my couch with my tears" (Psa. 6:6).

And where was God in all of David's troubles? He was right where He always had been, patiently guiding David's steps through the tortuous maze of life, toward a final home that would make it all worthwhile. Somehow, David had that awareness of a larger purpose: "And now, Lord, what do I wait for? My hope is in You" (Psa. 39:7).

That hope made all the difference in how David dealt with the hardships in his life. He learned that the afflictions God sent his way were not retribution or random bad luck, but chastening designed to cleanse away the dross and refine his character. The hard times drove David deeper into God's arms, forging a stronger faith in God's power to make it all work out in the end. Rather than blame God for giving him a crummy life, he thanked God for giving him the wake-up calls he needed to keep his priorities straight.

We see this principle of fatherly discipline play out in the lives of many Bible characters. Joseph's rise to prominence in Egypt was facilitated by a long series of injustices and setbacks. Only at the end could he look back at all those sorrows and realize that "God meant it for good" (Gen. 50:20).

Job suffered horribly, without a word of explanation from the God who allowed it to happen. Yet he remained convinced that the experience would make him a better man: "When He has tested me, I shall come forth as gold" (Job 23:10).

Paul saw his sufferings, which were considerable, to be nothing more than a "filling up what is lacking in the afflictions of Christ" (Col. 1:24). It was a privilege to partake of the life of Christ in the interest of a greater cause.

In a society that is so pampered by pleasure and ease, God's people have likewise become desensitized to the value of affliction. We expect our life of obedience to bring us only good things, all the time. So when calamity shatters our comfortable little world, our faith crumbles. Our myopic understanding of suffering leaves us ill-prepared to deal with it.

Affliction hurts, and it's okay to grieve when it strikes. Even Jesus, when faced with His final ordeal, called out to God "with vehement cries and tears" (Heb. 5:7). But underneath the anguish we need a foundation of faith that will enable us to know that, in the end, God will make it all right.

Until that day, we must learn to say—with conviction—"it is good that I have been afflicted." I will learn from this experience, no matter how painful it may be—and God will be glorified in my life.

Beware of Counterfeits

Satan's favorite tactic in confusing God's people is to flood the zone with phony imitations of God's gifts. We must learn to spot these counterfeits.

"Therefore I love Your commandments more than gold, yes, than fine gold! Therefore all Your precepts concerning all things I consider to be right; I hate every false way" (Psa. 119:127-128).

God has revealed in His word all that is good and right and true. When we follow that truth, our lives will be blessed and we will be prepared for life hereafter. Satan, however, will do all he can to obscure that truth with cheap imitations. These fakes will lead us away from God and cost us a home in heaven. The Bible identifies several of these counterfeits that we should beware of.

False christs are those who offer a different path to God. Their special insights are usually presented as extra-Biblical revelations, such as the Koran, the Book of Mormon, or some new age "inner light." Jesus warned that false christs arise in times of great uncertainty and confusion, feeding on people's fears (Matt. 24:24). Whatever shortcuts they may offer, Jesus Christ remains "the way, the truth, and the life"; no one comes to God except through Him (Jn. 14:6).

False teachers—also called false prophets or false apostles—may not appeal to other sources of revelation, but they distort the one source of revelation we do have. Like wolves in sheep's clothing, they come across as pious messengers of God (Matt. 7:15; 2 Cor. 11:13). Much of what they teach may even be true. But their creative interpretations, colored by selective exegesis, traditions, or human philosophy, twist the scriptures into saying things that God never intended. These misguided leaders, by their sheer numbers, pose the greatest danger to God's people (2 Pet. 2:1; 1 Jn. 4:1).

False brethren are oh-so-close to the truth, but their faith is corrupted with hidden agendas and personal grudges. They have a zeal for the truth, and may even teach it correctly; but they view the truth primarily as a tool for personal advancement, not personal enlightenment. Paul warned that these people will come in "by stealth," subjugating others to their self-centered schemes (Gal. 2:4).

False churches are dominated by all of the above. They claim to follow Christ, but that loyalty is in name only. They are based on error, not truth. Like the church at Laodicea, Christ has spewed them out of His mouth (Rev. 3:16)—if they ever belonged to Him in the first place. No church is perfect, but false churches have set a deliberate course of rebellion against God and His word.

How can we protect ourselves from all these counterfeits? Remember the words of David: "All Your precepts concerning all things I consider to be right." The only way we can protect ourselves is to arm ourselves with a balanced knowledge of God's word. Only by knowing the truth can we avoid the false.

Early Risers

The wise use of our time starts with how we begin each day. Those who get up early have a more serious perspective on life, and accomplish more.

I rise before the dawning of the morning, and cry for help; I hope in Your word (Psa. 119:147).

Albert Barnes was a Presbyterian minister who, between 1832 and 1851, wrote an eleven-volume commentary on the New Testament (*Barnes Notes*) that remains a best seller down to the present day. In his Preface to the final volume in the series (Revelation), he explained how he found the time to do his prodigious writing alongside a busy ministerial career. All his books were written "before nine o'clock in the morning, and are the fruit of the habit of rising between four and five o'clock." He counseled younger preachers that "much may be accomplished by the habit of early rising, and by a diligent use of the early morning hours."

Many of the heroes of the Bible were also early risers. Moses rose early in the morning to confront Pharaoh (Ex. 8:20). The habit of rising early was a trademark of Joshua's leadership (Josh. 3:1; 6:12, 15; 7:16; 8:10). Job would often "rise early in the morning" to offer sacrifices for his children (Job 1:5). Jesus would arise "a long while before daylight" to pray (Mk. 1:35). Even His resurrection occurred "very early in the morning, on the first day of the week" (Mk. 16:2,9). There is a pattern here that we would do well to study.

Early risers have a different perspective on time than the rest of us. For these people, "rise and shine" is not an empty catchphrase; it epitomizes a sense of urgency that affects everything they do in life. By getting an early start on their day, they are able to tackle critical tasks while their minds are fresh, rested, and sharp. That time is generally free of interruptions, so they can concentrate more fully. Unsurprisingly, these people tend to accomplish more with their lives.

Perhaps you have no ambition to publish a multi-volume Bible commentary. That's okay. But how often have you read the Bible, cover to cover? If your usual excuse is, "I don't have time," then try this challenge: Get up a half-hour earlier than usual every day, and use that sliver of time to read a chapter or two and have a quiet conversation with God. If you establish that habit, you will accomplish something you never thought you could accomplish. And you will be a better person for it.

Rise before the dawning of the morning, and see if it doesn't transform your life.

Perspectives on Truth

Truth exists. But its effect on people's lives, for good or bad, depends on the perspective from which they approach it.

The entirety of Your word is truth, and every one of Your righteous judgments endures forever (Psa. 119:160).

The dictionary defines "truth" as "that which conforms to fact or actuality." It presupposes some external, objective standard that is independent of whatever we might believe about it. In the physical realm, there are laws of nature that are true, regardless of whether or not we understand or believe them. The law of gravity, to offer an obvious example, is a "truth" that we early learn to respect. We ignore it to our peril.

In the spiritual realm, God's word is the source of truth. If we honor it, that truth will enlighten our eyes and guide our steps. But the benefits of truth are realized only by those who respect it and choose to live by it.

To many people, however, this view of truth is too burdensome, too simplistic. So they adopt strategies for avoiding the demands that truth lays upon them. They view truth in ways that circumvent the role that God intends truth should have in their lives. Let's consider some of these alternative perspectives.

The *sophist* views truth as a plaything for intellectual manipulation. In his mind, "truth" is whatever his convoluted logic can make it out to be. Principles that are so obvious to ordinary people somehow get turned upside down by the time the sophist gets through with them. Isaiah bemoaned those in his day "who call evil good, and good evil; who put darkness for light, and light for darkness; who put bitter for sweet, and sweet for bitter" (Isa. 5:20). Truth was turned into a tortured pretzel, worthless as a guide for living.

The *cynic* views truth as an elusive phantom, a noble ideal that can never be realized. This was the position of the Roman governor Pontius Pilate when he heard Jesus' claim that He came to bear witness to the truth. Pilate responded with a dismissive shrug, "What is truth?" (Jn. 18:37-38). To the cynic, the complexities of life render truth an unrealistic luxury; so why even bother pretending to honor it?

The *hedonist* views truth as an annoying obstacle to personal satisfaction. The only thing that really matters is feeling good, so if truth stands in the way of instant gratification, then truth is simply tossed aside, or redefined to fit one's personal preferences ("*my* truth"). When such a view becomes widespread in a society, the result is a law of the jungle where there are no rules, and human relations are dominated by injustice, oppression, and falsehood. In such a society, "truth is fallen in the street" (Isa. 59:9-15).

The *hypocrite* views truth as a vehicle for selfish advantage. He acknowledges that there is "truth" out there, and will even honor it—so long as it is convenient for him to do so. But the hypocrite reserves the right to pick and choose which elements of truth apply to him. Some truth he obeys, and even chastises those who do not share his commitment to it. But other elements of truth he conveniently bypasses. Like the scribes and Pharisees, the hypocrite goes to great lengths to "appear beautiful outwardly," but inwardly is full of uncleanness (Matt. 23:27).

To the sincere *believer*, however, truth is a beacon of light from heaven, a guide to help him navigate the difficult pathways of life. It may take time and effort to learn, but his quest to build the truth into his life will reward him richly.

Treasures on Earth

What we value most in this life will determine what we inherit in the next. God has placed a hoard of riches at our disposal—if we want it.

I rejoice at Your word as one who finds great treasure (Psa. 119:162).

"Do not lay up for yourselves treasures on earth, where moth and rust destroy and where thieves break in and steal; but lay up for yourselves treasures in heaven, where neither moth nor rust destroys and where thieves do not break in and steal" (Matt. 6:19-20).

ଛଚ

In 1982, archaeologists working at the site of an eighth century home in Capernaum made a remarkable discovery. As they dug down through centuries of accumulated debris, they determined that the occupants had been people of modest means; their belongings were few and simple. But as they began removing paving stones from the floor to access a lower level, they were astonished to find a cache of 282 gold dinars. Scholars surmise that the home originally had been occupied by a wealthy owner who had hidden the coins, then disappeared. The later occupants of the site had no idea of the fabulous wealth that lay just inches below their feet (*Biblical Archaeology Review,* July/August 1983).

Before you start ripping out the floorboards in your home, take a moment to reflect on two major lessons from this bit of history.

First, it reminds us once again that we can't take our wealth with us. The archaeologists were able to determine that the home where this treasure was hidden likely had been leveled in the great earthquake of AD 746. Was the wealthy owner killed in that earthquake? Or was he the victim of a marauding gang of bandits? Or did he die a natural death without revealing the whereabouts of his life savings? We have no idea of the details of his disappearance, but we do know this much: He didn't take the money with him. He left this world the same way he came in: empty-handed. No matter how hard we work and how much we save, whether we bury it under our house or entrust it to an investment firm, our portfolio will stay here after we leave. That fact should temper our passion for accumulating earthly possessions.

The second lesson is equally compelling. This story of a poor family living so close to life-changing riches without ever enjoying them illustrates the role that the Bible plays in the lives of many people today. Here is a book that contains a wealth of wisdom that could transform their lives for the better—but they don't bother to read it. Like that poor family in Capernaum who never knew the value of what lay right under their feet, people are so busy scratching out a living that they are clueless to what the Bible could do for them.

Wherever the original owner of that cache of gold coins is now, it no longer means anything to him. Someday everything you own will mean nothing to you either. Think about it.

"God Wants Me to Be Happy"

Trying to enlist God's blessing for a selfish pursuit never ends well. True happiness comes from honoring God's will, not abusing it.

Blessed is every one who fears the Lord, who walks in His ways. When you eat the labor of your hands, you shall be happy, and it shall be well with you (Psa. 128:1-2).

༺༻

I have often heard people defend their action in leaving an unhappy marriage or entering into an illicit relationship by declaring, "God wants me to be happy." That statement has been used so much that it has passed into popular culture as a universal "given." Nobody questions it.

If you have used this defense yourself—or are thinking about using it—please take a few moments to ponder a couple of questions.

First, *how do you know* that God wants you to be happy? Where and how did He reveal this to you? Do you have some kind of message from God to this effect, or are you just *assuming* that God wants you to be happy?

Second, let's assume for sake of this discussion that God does want you to be happy. Have you considered *how* He wants you to find that happiness? In other words, the course of action by which you hope to find happiness may not be God's preferred choice. Perhaps He wants you to find happiness by another route. Again, how can you be sure that this path you are on is God's will for your life? Where and how has God communicated this to you?

If you cannot give concrete answers to these two questions, there is a good chance that your reasoning is just wishful thinking based on a passing emotion. If you have no solid evidence for that conviction, then you are trusting your soul to a hunch—and that's dangerous. Remember, "the way of man is not in himself; it is not in man who walks to direct his own steps" (Jer. 10:23).

With these two questions before us, let's return to our opening text. It directly addresses both questions.

First, note that happiness is indeed a gift from God. "You shall be happy" is clearly identified as a blessing from the Lord. So it's fair to seek happiness as a goal in life.

But notice also that this happiness is promised only to the one "who fears the Lord, who walks in His ways." In other words, the happiness that God gives us is the outcome of pursuing a higher objective: obeying His word. "Happy is he *who keeps the law*" (Prov. 29:18).

The lesson here is not hard to figure out, but it is difficult to accept: *Happiness is not our ultimate objective in life.* True happiness is merely a by-product of a life dedicated to honoring God. When we live the way God wants us to live, we will find a joy that the storms of life cannot touch. Happiness achieved by any other means is only a cheap imitation.

Because this happiness is predicated on submission to God's will, it will likely involve some sacrifice. Sometimes doing God's will can be counterintuitive, even painful. But we must trust God to know what is best for us.

Now go apply this new knowledge to your current situation. God wants you to be happy, yes; but first He wants you to be *good*. He has not left it up to you to define happiness. Instead of chasing an ephemeral emotion, focus your attention on just one thing: *What is the right thing that God wants me to do?* Do that, and you will find a joy beyond compare.

On Raising Kids

Raising children successfully is a challenge, but not impossible, if parents arm themselves with a few key strategies.

Behold, children are a heritage from the LORD, the fruit of the womb is a reward (Psa. 127:3).

Every parent has had occasion to question this description of parenthood. If raising children is a reward from God, what must a punishment look like?

Raising kids is hard, thankless work. Especially in their younger years, children are messy, lack common sense, have no self-control, and are utterly selfish. They are a threat both to themselves and to everyone around them. Not to mention, they are *terribly* expensive. For these and other reasons, some adults choose to live their lives without them. It's just not worth the trouble. Of course, if someone truly feels that way about kids, it's probably best that they avoid that career track.

But for those who choose to take on the challenge, how can it be done well? How can parents raise the next generation without losing their sanity? There are several essential ingredients that parents must bring to the game:

Sacrifice. Children require an enormous investment in time, money, and energy, and those resources must come from somewhere else in their parents' lives. Parents must be willing to pay the price to secure their kids' well-being.

Affection. When parents frequently cuddle, hug, and play with their children, the kids are more likely to grow up well-adjusted and happy. They will learn from an early age that they are valued. Not to mention, a close bond with their parents will be forged, a bond that will serve them well throughout the rest of their lives.

Patience. Children require a lot of discipline, but it must be measured and composed. Parents must choose their battles wisely, distinguishing between childish mistakes and deliberate defiance. An authoritarian one-size-fits-all response to all misbehavior will crush a child's spirit.

Love. When parents pour themselves into the lives of their children, they are teaching their kids one of the most important life lessons they will ever learn: I am loved and appreciated. Even when the kids respond with ingratitude and insubordination, the pain parents experience gives them a deeper appreciation of the Biblical story of God's love for His disobedient children.

Spirituality. Parents must create a home environment in which the Bible informs every decision, guides every behavior, and confronts every crisis. Parents who do not put God first in their lives cannot train their kids to put God first in theirs.

Someday we will see the little urchins who gave us so many sleepless nights develop into responsible young adults. When that day comes, we will know that it was all worth it. That will be our reward.

Family Traditions

Happy homes are not a myth from 1950s television shows. They are the product of following God's best practices for the family.

Blessed is everyone who fears the Lord, who walks in His ways. When you eat the labor of your hands, you shall be happy, and it shall be well with you. Your wife shall be like a fruitful vine in the very heart of your house, your children like olive plants all around your table. Behold, thus shall the man be blessed who fears the Lord (Psa. 128:1-4).

This passage portrays the image of a large family gathered around the dinner table, talking, laughing, and enjoying one another's company. And it's not a special occasion, but a scene that is repeated night after night. The joy of living in such a warm family environment is indeed one of the great benefits of the godly life.

But I would suggest that the very practice of having the family gather daily around the dinner table is itself not just a *benefit* of godliness, but a *contributor* to it. In our busy lifestyles today, it takes some discipline to get everybody together at the same time every day to eat a meal. But once established, this habit provides a forum in which family members can interact with each other and reinforce the love that binds them together. It is the one time during the day when they can tune out the rest of the world, and give each other their full attention.

The daily family meal is not the only opportunity that families have to interact and reconnect. There are other important activities that, experienced frequently, will help maintain a strong and healthy family relationship.

With younger children, for example, *nightly prayers* are a great way to teach them the basic mechanics of prayer. Instead of just sending them off to bed, if Mom or Dad will take a few minutes to tuck them in, and listen to their simple little prayers, the children will not only become comfortable with the practice of praying, but respect the value that their parents place upon that spiritual activity. As a side benefit, those nightly sessions will sometimes turn into discussions of questions that the kids are pondering. A lot of informal but powerful teaching can be realized in those last waking moments of a child's day.

Families are also strengthened by *sharing pastimes* as a family, rather than as individuals. The opportunities are limitless: camping, shopping, visiting museums, theme parks, trade shows, movies, dinner theaters, gardening, home remodeling projects, hobbies, and so on. The specific activities that a family shares are not as important as the fact they are doing it as a family. This does not prevent individuals from having their own unique interests, especially as the kids get older. But regardless of the individual preferences, at least some time should be spent on a regular basis doing things as a group, just for the sake of doing it as a family unit.

These and other family traditions have short-term practical benefits, to be sure. But the greater benefit is cumulative, built up over years of repetition. Children who grow up in a family that is rich with such traditions will be happy and well-adjusted, armed with a conviction that life is basically good. They will go into adulthood with a strong desire to repeat that experience in their own families. They learned this conviction, not because their parents lectured them, but because they lived it every day in the simple traditions that defined their family's identity.

God and Family

> The role of the family as the foundation of an orderly society is not the result of mindless evolution, but of a divine mandate.

Your wife shall be like a fruitful vine in the very heart of your house, your children like olive plants all around your table. Behold, thus shall the man be blessed who fears the Lord. . . . May you see the good of Jerusalem all the days of your life (Psa. 128:3-5).

༄༅༅

The Biblical model of the family consists of a husband and wife and their children, connected to a wider network of relatives—grandparents, aunts, uncles, and cousins. The Bible's treatment of this social unit is extensive and consistent.

In the Old Testament, humanity's very first appearance on the planet took the form of a marriage between a man and a woman (Gen. 2). God's plan for redeeming the human race grew out of a chosen family (Gen. 18:17-19). Three of the Ten Commandments given to Israel directly address family relationships—and several others have at least an indirect bearing on how families function (Ex. 20:1-17). Moses pointed to the family as the primary agent in transmitting values from one generation to the next (Deut. 4:9; 6:6-9). The Wisdom literature is saturated with praise of faithful husbands and wives, parents and children (Job 31:9-12; Prov. 1:8; 5:18-20; 6:20; 18:22; 31:10-31).

In the New Testament, Jesus was a vocal advocate for family cohesion, attacking divorce and adultery (including the mental variety), while honoring the value of little children (Matt. 5:27-32; 19:1-15). The writings of the apostles frequently promote strong marriages and family units (Eph. 5:22-6:4; Col. 3:18-21; 1 Tim. 5:8, 16; 1 Pet. 3:1-6).

Recognizing the fallenness of this world, the Bible also enjoins special consideration for widows and orphans, in an effort to preserve the benefits of the family unit as much as possible (Deut. 24:19-21; Jas. 1:27).

The last line of our opening text—"may you see the good of Jerusalem all the days of your life"—hints at the much broader social influence of healthy families. Strong families make strong nations. That's why the Bible condemns departures from this standard model, such as polygamy, adultery, rape, homosexuality, rampant divorce, and so on. These aberrations are consistently portrayed as having a negative impact on social order. Always, the traditional model is held up as the ideal.

The fact that the Bible devotes so much attention to this subject suggests a strong correlation between a society's respect for family life and its respect for God. Historically those societies that have held to a deep faith in Biblical truth also have encouraged stable nuclear families. Conversely, those societies that have lost respect for Biblical truth usually suffer from widespread family breakdown and dysfunction—and pay a steep price for the chaos.

The conclusion is simple: If we want to have happy, harmonious, and successful lives, both individually and as a society, we should do all we can to promote respect for God and His vision for the family.

And it starts with me and my own family.

Keep It Simple

The universe is filled with mysteries that challenge our thinking. It's okay to pursue these questions, but not to the detriment of what is knowable.

My heart is not haughty, nor my eyes lofty. Neither do I concern myself with great matters, nor with things too profound for me" (Psa. 131:1).

Humans have a fascination with the mysterious. Given that we live in a universe of mysteries, we will never run out of questions to occupy our attention. Consequently, we are always pushing the boundaries of our knowledge, seeking to understand everything about everything.

This pursuit of the unknown is generally healthy; our learning contributes to our growth. But there is a danger that this fascination with the hidden can become an obsession that blinds us to the most obvious realities of our existence. The problem is not the pursuit of these questions, but pursuing them to the neglect of more fundamental truths that we can and should understand. That imbalance can be deadly.

That's why David placed limits on his consideration of such matters. He recognized there were some things in life that were simply "too profound" for him, no matter how much energy he expended trying to unravel them. Humility dictated that he simply accept the limits of his knowledge, and concentrate on what he did understand.

When Paul addressed the Greek philosophers in Athens, he was speaking to people who "spent their time in nothing else but either to tell or to hear some new thing" (Ac. 17:21).

This thirst for new knowledge generally served the Greeks well. Indeed, even today we benefit from the ventures of the Greeks into philosophy, politics, mathematics, science, architecture, and other disciplines. But in their pursuit of all these areas of knowledge, the Greeks lost sight of the most basic truth of all: the nature of God. That's why Paul's lecture to them was devoted to that foundational proposition (v. 22-31). Until they got that first principle sorted out, their great learning was merely groping in the dark (v. 27). (Which explains, by the way, why the glory of Greece was only a fading memory by Paul's day. Their failure to grasp the nature of God and His standard of moral righteousness resulted in a level of corruption that debased their culture.)

The same threat faces us today. There are many questions that God has not directly answered in His word, and the evidence of nature is inconclusive: Is there alien life elsewhere in the universe? How old is the earth? How can we explain the deity of Christ?

Some people have the answers to all these questions, and are not hesitant to share them with the rest of us. But this kind of certitude reveals a pride that runs counter to the humility of David.

Others go in the opposite direction: They not only admit they do not have the answers, but are so enthralled by the unknowable nature of these questions that they see *everything* in life as unknowable, complicated by hidden meanings and alternative explanations. These folks can't see the obvious right in front of their noses.

In our exploration of life, it is good that we ask questions, seek understanding, and grow in our knowledge. But we must be careful that we not let the things that are "too profound" become a stumbling block to knowing and doing the things that are simple.

Wonderfully Made

For all the diversity that exists among humankind, there is one trait we all share in common that should influence how we treat each another.

You formed my inward parts; You covered me in my mother's womb. I will praise You, for I am fearfully and wonderfully made; marvelous are Your works, and that my soul knows very well (Psa. 139:13-14).

This passage is often used in the abortion debate to highlight the humanity of life within the womb. Among those who respect the Bible as God's word, it's a powerful argument against the slaughter of millions of unborn babies.

But there is another truth hidden in this passage that deserves our attention, especially in a society that is now tearing itself apart over a variety of innate differences. Notice what is *not* included in this description of the unborn child: its skin color, its gender, its ethnic background, its nationality, its heritage, or any number of other genetic or ancestral identifiers.

Let the significance of this omission sink in. Every one of us, regardless of the attributes we possess, is a creation of God, "fearfully and wonderfully made." By virtue of that divine origin, every one of us have equal value in His sight. We ought, therefore, to value each other as equals.

Racism in all its forms is a denial of this basic truth. This applies not just to the antebellum slavery of the Old South, but the reverse racism that is being peddled by modern Critical Race Theory. Any time we argue that one race is superior or inferior to another based solely on the color of their skin, we are denying the value of human beings made in the image of God. Nothing good will ever come of such a scheme.

Ethnic differences may be deep-seated, but they are not grounds *per se* for demeaning whole populations. A melting pot cannot function if the ingredients refuse to mix.

Gender differences are real and unalterable. But they do not grant license to one-half of the human race to belittle and denigrate the other half. Whatever their differences, each sex provides unique skills and strengths that benefit the other. We should appreciate the beauty of that symbiotic relationship.

By elevating all these superficial characteristics as the ultimate measure of human worth, our society is descending into a hell of our own making. It's simply a modern version of the same old tribalism that has plagued humanity throughout our history.

But it doesn't have to be that way. In the gospel of Christ, these characteristics are minimized, and individuals are esteemed as creatures made in the image of God, simply for who they are.

I am fearfully and wonderfully made. So is every other person I encounter. Whatever differences I may have with others in the realm of politics, religion, or philosophy, God expects me to treat them with dignity and respect.

After all, that's what He did for me on the cross.

No One Cares

Loneliness and depression are not the curse of losers. In fact, even the best of people struggle with this darkness. That should encourage us.

Look on my right hand and see, for there is no one who acknowledges me; refuge has failed me; no one cares for my soul (Psa. 142:4).

They have heard that I sigh, but no one comforts me (Lam. 1:21).

৩৩৩

Have you ever felt unappreciated, ignored, or unwelcome? Have you had days where it seemed that nobody cared whether you lived or died—and as a result, you struggled with the same apathy about your own life?

If so, you're in good company. David and Jeremiah had days like that, too, and wrote about their depression in these verses. In fact, this kind of loneliness is a common theme throughout the Bible.

For forty years Moses got nothing but grief for all his trouble in leading the Israelites toward their Promised Land. When the people were not cavorting with idols and pagan women, they were complaining about Moses' incompetence. More than once God got fed up and wanted to destroy them, but Moses interceded and saved their bacon. In return, he got not even a "thank you" from the people; just more exasperation. Why didn't he quit?

After facing down the prophets of Baal at Mt. Carmel, Elijah reached the end of his rope, convinced that all his labor had been in vain. Whatever victories he won, his enemies came back stronger than ever. The people for whom he was waging this lonesome war were fickle and unreliable. Unlike Moses, he did quit, and the Lord had to gently nudge him back into the game.

Even Jesus at the end of His short life had little to show for all His sacrifices. The crowds who once thronged around Him had evaporated. His enemies remained firmly in control. Even His own apostles got cold feet and ran away. The only thing His years of good works and wise teaching got Him was death on a Roman cross—the fate of a criminal. At the end all He could do was cry out, "My God, My God, why have You forsaken Me?" (Matt. 27:46).

There is a message in all these stories that we need to process. God has not promised us a life of ease in this broken world. In fact, He warns us that it will not be easy. Like David, Jeremiah, Moses, Elijah, Jesus, and countless others, we will face our own dark days when it seems that nothing goes right, and worse, nobody cares about our struggles. It's perfectly natural that we feel discouraged and alone, just as they did.

But when you find yourself in that melancholy spirit, think of those who have gone before you. David eventually became the king of Israel. Jeremiah laid the foundation for a restored nation, and went on to his reward. Moses achieved his mission, and was rewarded with a personal burial by the hand of God Himself. Elijah set in motion a series of events that finally exterminated the threat of Baal, and ascended into heaven in a chariot of fire. Jesus rose from the dead in a dramatic reversal of everything that had gone wrong up to that point.

Even if nobody else cares for you, *God cares*, and someday He will reward you, too. Don't let the indifference of others drag you down. Look to God for your reason for living, and you will have ample reason to smile.

God Cares

It's easy to convince ourselves that nobody cares about us. But that gloomy outlook betrays a lack of faith in a God who cares more than we know.

Look on my right hand and see, for there is no one who acknowledges me; no one cares for my soul (Psa. 142:4).

Therefore humble yourselves under the mighty hand of God, that He may exalt you in due time, casting all your care upon Him, for He cares for you (1 Pet. 5:6-7).

David wrote Psalm 142 "when he was in the cave," probably the cave of Adullam (1 Sam. 22), during the years that he was running from King Saul. After his brilliant but brief career as a military hero, his new life as a fugitive was a hard blow for David to take. His lament that "there is no one who acknowledges me" was a sad departure from the glory days when he listened to the women of Israel chant, "Saul has slain his thousands, and David his ten thousands." David was no longer a hero, but a cast-off, a nobody. "No one cares for my soul" captured the dark sense of abandonment that David felt.

There are countless people today who can relate to David's depression. Convinced that no one cares about them, these people trudge through life burdened with an overwhelming feeling of worthlessness. The emptiness in their hearts drags down whatever ambitions or dreams they once had—after all, what's the point of trying, if no one cares one way or the other? The loneliness affects their relationships, too, as they (often unconsciously) push away the few people who might legitimately care about them. Once we become convinced that we are truly alone in this world, life loses a lot of its meaning, and motivation becomes harder to muster.

But that miserable self-assessment is not based on reality. David's declaration that "no one cares for my soul" is refuted by Peter's assurance that "God cares for you." In David's case, we know from our vantage point that, even as he was writing these words, God was carefully working out a long-term plan to bring David to the throne of Israel. It took David several years to see it, but God very much cared for him, and eventually exalted him above his peers. David's lonely cry of despair turned out to be a groundless exercise in self-pity.

David's story should serve as an encouragement to anyone who feels shut out, left out, rejected, or scorned. What other people do to us (or fail to do for us) does not influence in the slightest what God thinks of us. If a sparrow does not fall to the ground without His awareness (Matt. 10:29), surely He is familiar with our deepest anxieties and is willing to act in our behalf.

Our biggest problem in such moments is a lack of faith. Notice that Peter's promise of God's care is preceded by the caveat, "in due time." God operates on a different timetable than we do, according to a much bigger plan than we can see, so it is unreasonable to expect Him to jump at our every whimper. God's care may not come to us in a manner that we recognize or at a time that we want, but it's there all the same. We must arm ourselves with the conviction that no matter what happens to us in this life, God really does care, and some day will make everything right.

After all, He cared enough to send His Son to die for us. Believe that, and you'll never feel lonely again.

When God Doesn't Answer Prayer

We believe in the power of prayer, but sometimes that power comes up short. God has reasons why He will not always give us what we ask for.

Hear my prayer, O Lord, give ear to my supplications! In Your faithfulness answer me . . . (Psa. 143:1).
"I cry out to You, but You do not answer me" (Job 30:20).

※

One of the great privileges of the believer is the right to approach God in prayer, with an expectation of having one's petitions granted. God has promised that He is interested in our needs, and will respond to our call (Matt. 7:7-11; Mk. 11:24; Jas. 1:5-6).

But despite that promise, every believer has experienced the frustration of unanswered prayer. Every one of us has had occasions in which we could complain with Job, "You do not answer me."

Why does God sometimes not answer our prayers? Does He not care? Is His promise fickle? Fortunately, we do not have to speculate about the reasons for unanswered prayer. The Bible gives us several examples of prayers that went unanswered. A study of these cases provides valuable insight into why God does not answer every prayer.

Some prayers are not answered because *sin is involved*. Following David's adultery with Bathsheba, the baby that was born to them was stricken with a fatal illness. David grieved for the infant and begged for the child's life. But God had already decreed that the child would not live because of

David's sin (2 Sam. 12:14). David's prayers could not reverse the punishment that God had decided. When we act foolishly and get in trouble, it is not reasonable to expect God to bail us out. In such cases, we just have to take our lumps and learn our lesson. In some cases, letting us bear the consequences of our misdeeds might even be God's best possible response to our prayer. Nothing teaches us humility better than tasting the bitter fruit of our own mistakes.

Some prayers are not answered because *it is in our best interest that we not get what we want*. Paul had a "thorn in the flesh" that gave him trouble—apparently some kind of health problem. Paul prayed to God at least three times that this impediment be removed (2 Cor. 12:7-8). But God refused to remove it, explaining to Paul that "My strength is made perfect in weakness" (v. 9); that is, Paul's infirmity made him a stronger, better man. Paul learned to live with his infirmity, and even glorify God with it. Sometimes that's what we have to do, too, and trust that God knows what is best for us.

Some prayers are not answered because *God has a higher purpose in view*. Before He died, Jesus prayed to His Father to "take this cup away from Me" (Mk. 14:35-36). He didn't want to die. But even though Jesus "was heard because of His godly fear" (Heb. 5:7), His request was not granted. Jesus' death was necessary to fulfill the broader plan that God was seeking to accomplish. Today, of course, we can be thankful that God did not answer that prayer. We do not know all the details in God's master plan or our place in it, but we can trust that our unanswered prayers are contributing to some higher objective that God has in play.

God has legitimate reasons for not answering every prayer. But whether or not He answers, we can be assured of one thing: *He hears us*, and like a loving Father, is keenly interested in our long-term welfare.

When Faith Grows Weak

A flagging faith is nothing to be ashamed of, but it does need to be addressed. There is a simple strategy for managing it.

My spirit is overwhelmed within me; my heart within me is distressed. . . . Answer me speedily, O LORD; my spirit fails! (Psa. 143:4, 7).

༄

Even the strongest believers have episodes in their lives when their faith begins to crumble. Study the lives of Elijah, Moses, Peter, Paul, and many other Bible characters, and it is obvious that our heroes of faith were not immune to difficult episodes that tested their souls. Discouragement, failure, loss, betrayal, and doubts took them into dark places that caused them to question God's care.

So when we sense that something is going awry in our spiritual lives, we should not be surprised. Now it is our turn to fight our own battle with unbelief. Fortunately, David—another Bible character who had his own faith struggles—wrote this Psalm especially for you.

The first step in reclaiming our faith is to *talk about the problem*: "Hear my prayer, O Lord!" (v. 1). This entire Psalm is a cry to God for help in driving out the demon of despair. Disbelief, like a fungus, thrives in darkness, and the longer we refuse to talk about the problem, the bigger it grows. So pour out your anxieties to God. Your prayer does not have to be eloquent or verbose, just honest. There is no shame in confessing a weak faith.

Second, *force yourself to reflect on God's role in the universe.* "I meditate on all Your works; I muse on the work of Your hands" (v. 5). If you can recognize God's hand in all the grandeur and orderliness of the creation around you, can you not also see His power to manage the little troubles that weigh down your life? A small faith is evidence of a small God; so think big.

Finally, *seek the Lord's counsel in His word.* "Cause me to know the way in which I should walk. . . . Teach me to do Your will" (v. 8, 10). The Bible is a magnificent volume of wisdom that can calm the troubled soul and soothe the anxious mind—but only if we read it. Dedicate time to read the Psalms, or the Sermon on the Mount, or Paul's ode to joy in Philippians. These compositions are chicken soup for the soul, nourishment that can heal a distressed heart.

A weak faith can be repaired, but it takes effort. God has given us resources to get us back on the right track. And our faith will be even stronger for having survived the experience.

Happy People

Happiness in life is achievable, but not in the manner in which most people seek it. The secret is quite simple, if we're willing to embrace it.

Happy are the people whose God is the LORD! (Psa. 144:15).

Like arrows in the hand of a warrior, so are the children of one's youth. Happy is the man who has his quiver full of them (Psa. 127:4-5).

◈

The Hebrew word translated "happy" in these two verses is not the same word that is translated "blessed" elsewhere in the Old Testament. This word—found mostly in Psalms and Proverbs—is used only of humans, never of God. It denotes "a state of bliss," an experience of being happy, joyful, euphoric. It's a state of being to which we all aspire. But how? These two passages reveal the secret.

Happiness is not a function of what we possess, but of *the quality of our relationships*; specifically, to God and to family. Like many Old Testament proverbs, this is not an absolute guarantee but a pointer to a path that offers the best hope for a positive life. Simply stated, if we want a happy life, we should strive to build good relationships with God and with our family.

Our relationship with God is the foundation of everything else. Money, possessions, career, pleasure, education, even family—all these things have their rightful place, but if any of them displace God as the foremost object of affection in our lives, we will be disappointed. Without God, we are cut off from the one thing that can give our life purpose. A passion for God is the only thing that can provide hope in the face of death itself. Get right with God, and you can handle anything life throws at you with confidence.

The biblical model of family—ideally consisting of husband, wife, children, siblings, uncles, aunts, grandparents, cousins—is our primary human support group. We invest far more of our lives in them than with any other, and they in us. It is in our family that we are most likely to find unconditional love and support. Families are not perfect; sometimes they are downright dysfunctional. But to the extent we can develop a close bond of familial love with these people, we will always have someone with whom we can share our lives. (Side note: This does not mean that single people cannot find happiness. Even without a spouse and/or children, our parents, siblings, nieces and nephews, and other extended family members can be a source of tremendous joy.)

Young people, take a clue from these Psalms. If you want to plan your life so as to increase your chance of finding happiness, here is the blueprint: Seek God, and build close ties to your family. Both will require a lot of hard work, patience, forgiveness, and even a few tears along the way. But the payoff will be so worth it.

You'll be happy you did.

Why Worldview Matters

> What we think about God and the world sets the tone for everything else in our lives—even if we deny that we think about these abstractions at all.

The fear of the Lord is the beginning of knowledge, but fools despise wisdom and instruction (Prov. 1:7).

The fear of the Lord is the beginning of wisdom, and the knowledge of the Holy One is understanding (Prov. 9:10).

The book of Proverbs—indeed, all the Bible—starts with the concept of "the fear of the Lord." This fear is not a terror at the prospect of getting blasted by God, but a positive reverence, respect, and admiration for God, an awe that lifts us up and enables us to appreciate the order in His creation. Until we grasp what it means to "fear the Lord," we will always fall short of the discernment we need to live well.

This principle hints at a deeper truth that explains so much of the human behavior we see around us: *Whatever* we think about God, whether good, bad, or indifferent, sets the parameters for how we live our lives. We act out of the deepest convictions of our heart.

Philosophers call this underlying mode of thought a *worldview*. A worldview is defined as "a collection of beliefs and ideas about the central issues of life. It is the lens through which we 'see' all of reality" (Chad Meister, *Building Belief,* 2006). For his purposes, Meister (following the lead of philosopher Ronald Nash), organizes all worldviews into three categories: theism, atheism, and pantheism. That's a useful scheme, but many people don't fit neatly into any of these categories of belief. Start talking about worldview with these folks, and they will simply shrug it off. They are too busy dealing with work, relationships, recreation, and household drama to bother with all this academic mumbo-jumbo. Try to talk to them about their worldview, and you'll get a blank stare in return. They have no worldview.

Except they *do* have a worldview—they just don't realize it. By focusing all their attention on the mundane details of this life, they display a worldview of self-centeredness. Everything in their lives is measured against the paramount question, "How does this benefit ME?" If it doesn't serve, soothe, or entertain ME, then it doesn't exist. All this extra philosophy talk is just wasted brain cells. But that way of looking at worldview *fits the definition of a worldview*.

The world in which we live operates according to a complex system of cause-and-effect relationships. The wise life is one in which we recognize these connections and align our decisions with their demands. That's why we do not stick our hand in a fire, or punch someone unprovoked, or steal our neighbor's horse, or a thousand other destructive actions. Some behaviors are just plain dumb—or as Solomon says, "foolish."

In some cases, however, the consequences are too subtle to recognize at first. That brings us back to "the fear of the Lord" as the foundation of knowledge and wisdom. We do not have to figure this out on our own. God has given us His Word as a source of guidance on how we should behave, speak, and even think. It's a complex book, yes; but we are complex creatures, and the path to wisdom is long and arduous, requiring a lifetime of study and practice. The payoff is worth the effort, if we're willing to accept the challenge and take God's lead in our decisions. But it all starts with "the fear of the Lord."

Until we recognize God as the central focus of our existence, our alternate worldview will lead us into dead ends again and again. What is your worldview? And how is it working out for you?

Solomon on Fools

> On April Fool's Day it is appropriate that we pay homage to the honoree by looking at what Solomon had to say about him in his Proverbs.

The fear of the LORD is the beginning of knowledge, but fools despise wisdom and instruction (Prov. 1:7).

The wise shall inherit glory, but shame shall be the legacy of fools (Prov. 3:35).

⚜

April Fool's Day is a good occasion to consider the observations of the wisest man who ever lived on what makes a man a fool. Such a study can help us avoid the fool's mistakes and his fate.

If foolishness is the antithesis of wisdom, then the dominant character trait of the fool is his dismissive attitude toward wisdom. He "despises wisdom and instruction" (1:7), whether that wisdom comes from his parents (15:5) or his friends (23:9). He is so convinced of his own intellect and insights, that he prefers to figure things out on his own. "A fool rages and is self-confident" (14:16). He "trusts in his own heart" (28:26), confident of his ability to chart his own way in life. His way is "right in his own eyes" (12:15); why does he need anyone else's opinion? Even when he is chastened for his folly by those who want to help him, he refuses to listen to their rebuke (17:10).

Naturally, his DIY approach to life is a disaster. Again and again, his go-it-alone decision-making results in beatings, whether metaphorical or literal (19:29; 26:3). He never learns from his mistakes. He may be stuck on a trajectory of futility, but he will never admit that his own stubbornness is the cause (27:22; 13:19). He will ride the train wreck all the way to the bottom before he'll acknowledge his error. It's a sorry sight to behold: "As a dog returns to his own vomit, so a fool repeats his folly" (26:11).

The fool has plenty of opinions, and is more than happy to share them. "A fool has no delight in understanding, but in expressing his own heart" (18:2). He "vents all his feelings" (29:11), to no good purpose. His mouth "pours forth foolishness" (15:2), and everyone but him can see it. His rash talk is good at starting quarrels (20:3), but not much else. He could do himself a favor by simply keeping his mouth shut (17:28), but is too enamored with his own genius to recognize the wisdom of that approach.

Why can't the fool see the damage he is doing to himself? Solomon attributes his blindness to self-deception: "The wisdom of the prudent is to understand his way, but the folly of fools is deceit" (14:8). There is a perverse kind of reasoning that allows the fool to rationalize his troubles. "The eyes of a fool are on the ends of the earth" (17:24); that is, his thinking is so abstract, so theoretical, so "out there," that he fails to see the obvious right in front of him.

What the fool refuses to see is usually glaringly obvious to others, who prefer to steer clear of him (14:7). They know that he cannot be trusted with important tasks (26:6), and that hanging around with him will bring nothing but trouble (13:20).

Whatever advantages the fool may possess through the course of his life will be squandered by his inability to see beyond himself (21:20). Sadly, his fate is predictable: shame (3:35), bondage to others (11:29), and ultimately destruction (1:32).

Before we get too smug in our criticism of the fool, let's remember that there is a little foolishness in all of us. The overarching message of Proverbs is simple: *Learn to listen to the counsel of others, especially God.* Don't be a fool.

To Be a Parent

Parenthood is an adventure like no other. Doing it well demands a commitment that will alter one's life forever. But the payoff is worth it.

My son, hear the instruction of your father, and do not forsake the law of your mother (Prov. 1:8).

There is no experience in the world like being a parent. It is an awesome responsibility with profound implications in the lives of others. The book of Proverbs provides a good commentary on what it means to be a parent.

To be a parent is to be a leader. "When I was my father's son, tender and the only one in the sight of my mother, he also taught me, and said to me: 'Let your heart retain my words; keep my commands, and live'" (4:3-4). A parent is charged with the most fearful task imaginable: Take a completely helpless and ignorant infant, and turn him or her into a model human being within twenty years. This task requires all the skills of a teacher, a coach, a psychiatrist, a Marine drill sergeant, a CEO, a librarian, an accountant, a nurse, and a few dozen other disciplines. Some basic rules may be fixed, but most of the time a parent must make decisions on-the-fly, based on imperfect information. It is the ultimate test of decision-making ability. The stakes in this game are huge: "Train up a child in the way he should go, and when he is old he will not depart from it" (22:6).

To be a parent is to experience pain. Sometimes, for a variety of reasons, the training fails and parents experience the nightmare of a child in rebellion. "He who mistreats his father and chases away his mother is a son who causes shame and brings reproach" (19:26). "A foolish son is a grief to his father, and bitterness to her who bore him" (17:25). There is no pain like that of parents whose love and sacrifice are rejected and thrown back in their faces. Even if this is "just a phase" and the child eventually straightens out, the frustration of dealing with this irrational willfulness will keep a parent awake at night. And this does not include dealing with all the usual traumas of childhood: broken toys, broken limbs, broken hearts. Multiply these tragedies by the number of kids in the family, and it's no wonder that a parent's hair turns gray. Someone once described the adventure this way: "Once you become a parent, you will never be happier than your unhappiest child."

To be a parent is to know joy. "The father of the righteous will greatly rejoice, and he who begets a wise child will delight in him. Let your father and your mother be glad, and let her who bore you rejoice" (23:24-25). For all the hassles of parenthood, the joy of seeing one's children grow up to become responsible citizens—and parents of their own children—is beyond worth. Whatever else a father and mother might accomplish in their lives, to have successfully raised a child will always rank as their greatest achievement. It is the one thing that validates their contribution to the human race. Their home, their money, and their careers may influence a few people for a short while, but their children will influence generations yet unborn.

No life is complete without having served as a parent. Take the role seriously, and accept it as the challenge it is—scary, but exhilarating.

Choices Have Consequences

Our world operates on a fairly simple cause-and-effect principle. The sooner we figure that out, the quicker we will learn how to live life well.

They would have none of my counsel and despised all my reproof, therefore they shall eat the fruit of their own way, and be filled to the full with their own fancies. For the turning away of the simple will slay them, and the complacency of fools will destroy them; but whoever listens to me will dwell safely, and will be secure, without fear of evil (Prov. 1:30-33).

The book of Proverbs is based on the premise that choices have consequences, and that the relationship between these choices and consequences is predictable and understandable. It doesn't take a bolt of lightning from Mt. Sinai to figure out these connections. Notice that it is not God who is speaking in the verses above, but rather "Wisdom" (v. 20-21), the feminine personification of what we would call "common sense." Anyone with normal intelligence should be able to recognize, both through thousands of years of human history and through his own experience, which choices are "good" and which are "bad."

But there are many people who are convinced that the usual rules don't apply to them. Influenced by our modern notions of freedom and toleration, they choose to engage in behaviors that their grandmothers could have told them were bad news. When their folly lands them in big trouble, they have no idea what went wrong.

A young woman begins hanging around with the wrong crowd because of the great parties they have. Drugs and alcohol are readily available, so before long she has a drug habit. She dresses in skimpy clothes to make herself attractive to the guys, and her strategy works—she sleeps around with several guys, none of whom have any respect for her. A string of abusive boyfriends leaves her with a couple of kids and a lot of bitterness. Between the drugs, late night parties and crazy living arrangements, she struggles to hold down a steady job. She moves from one dump to another, sometimes with the kids, sometimes without. One of the boyfriends abuses the kids, so the state finally takes custody of the kids, and she winds up in the hospital with a drug OD. And she has no idea why her life has ended up in such an awful mess.

Radical feminists blame her problems on the patriarchal society that encourages men to subjugate women. Psychologists see the cause of her problems in her troubled childhood relationship with her father. Bleeding heart politicians focus on the economic hardships she's had to endure; free rent and a bigger welfare check should save her.

"Wisdom" says, get a clue, girl. You make dumb choices, you pay the price. Of course, compassion and grace are available to those who are willing to learn from these life lessons. Even the vilest sinner can find redemption. Moreover, life is not always fair, and sometimes bad things happen to good people. But even when life pulls the rug out from under us, we can choose behaviors that enhance opportunities to overcome the hardships.

Whatever our current circumstances, the first step toward healing is to hearken to Wisdom's plea: "Listen to my voice."

A Father's Discipline

Adversity in life can make us bitter or it can make us stronger. The difference depends on how we choose to look at our distresses.

My son, do not despise the chastening of the LORD, nor detest His correction; for whom the LORD loves He corrects, just as a father the son in whom he delights (Prov. 3:11-12).

This admonition follows a lengthy list of character traits that, if followed faithfully, promise a long and good life: respect for authority (v. 1-2); mercy and honesty (v. 3-4); love of God (v. 5-6); humility (v. 7-8); and generosity (v. 9-10). The message of these preceding verses is simple: do well, and life will go well. Got it.

But in the next two verses, the author throws us a curve ball. Part of a life well-lived is the willingness to accept what he calls "the chastening of the Lord." In the New Testament (Heb. 12:3-11), this passage is used as the starting point for a larger excursus on dealing with trials—which is another way of saying, life doesn't always go the way we expect it to, even when we've done everything right. Life is not a cosmic vending machine that dispenses goodies in response to our payment. Sometimes bad things happen to good people.

That aspect of brokenness in our world troubles people. It's easy to become cynical, even bitter, when life is unfair. But the author likens these distressing experiences to a father's discipline: it's painful in the moment, but in the long run, it's for our good. Without these discomforts to test our fortitude, we become soft, spoiled, and self-centered. The rough edges of life are not easy to endure, but we are better people because of them.

That's a great concept in theory—but theory provides scant comfort in the face of heart-wrenching tragedy. How can two parents possibly see the hand of God in the kidnapping and murder of their little daughter? What good can thousands of people ever find in the fiery crash of an airliner that snuffs out the lives of hundreds of loved ones?

There are no easy answers to these mysteries. But if we reject God when these grievous blows rock our world, what do we have left to fall back on? Our souls will become shriveled with bitterness, consumed by a resentment that slams the door on any hope or joy. By treating the chastening of the Lord with contempt, we will descend deeper into a darkness that will devour us.

Whatever life throws at us, we must arm ourselves with the conviction that God is still in control, and that someday the twists and turns of this life will all make sense. In the meantime, our task is to take on the adventure with courage, and allow God's chastening to shape us into better people.

Walking in the Light

If life is a journey, it's important that we see the path we are walking. But the illumination on the path—or lack thereof—is of our own choosing.

The path of the just is like the shining sun, that shines ever brighter unto the perfect day. The way of the wicked is like darkness; they do not know what makes them stumble (Prov. 4:18-19).

If we walk in the light as He is in the light, we have fellowship with one another, and the blood of Jesus Christ His Son cleanses us from all sin (1 Jn. 1:7).

The Bible often compares life to a long journey. That journey may be pleasant or it may be hard, depending on how we choose to prepare for it. This proverb seeks to influence our decision by contrasting the two strategies that are available to us.

The first strategy is likened to a hiker who chooses to travel in the light of day. The sunshine enables him to see the obstacles and dangers in his path and make necessary adjustments in his course. Not only is this man's path easy to travel, it becomes easier as the day advances. In the gray light of early dawn, his way may be somewhat dim. But as he journeys on, the increasing light gradually brightens his way, and he moves with a quicker, surer step.

This is a fitting metaphor for the righteous man whose godly character allows him to discern foolish mistakes before he blunders into them. Like the daytime hiker, he moves through life with a minimum of trouble and worry. Moreover, his faith matures as he grows older. He becomes better equipped to handle the temptations and disappointments that ensnare lesser men. His spiritual discernment improves with time, and makes the going easier.

The second approach is compared to the poor fellow who waits until dark to start walking. Without any light to illuminate his way, he gropes along the trail, stumbling over the smallest obstructions in his path, not even knowing what the obstructions are. That is a fitting illustration of the man who ignores his spiritual destiny and lets fleshly impulses guide his affairs. His life will be marred by bitter experiences and broken dreams. Saddest of all, he is oblivious to his own role in creating the problems. Like the midnight hiker who becomes frustrated and thrashes about even more awkwardly, the wicked man will often vent his anger on other people, circumstances, or "fate." Life becomes increasingly bitter and hopeless for this fellow.

This proverb informs our understanding of John's injunction to "walk in the light." The apostle is not demanding sinless perfection, but a commitment to *growth* in knowledge and wisdom. Divine forgiveness is promised, contingent on maintaining a walk in the gradually expanding illumination of God's word.

Every word and deed in my life is another step down the path to my eternal destiny. Which path are my steps taking me on?

The Social Cost of Sin

Rejecting God's moral order is not a simple lifestyle choice. It's a deal with the devil that will inflict enormous costs on our social fabric.

The way of the wicked is like darkness; they do not know what makes them stumble (Prov. 4:19).

"The Lord will send on you cursing, confusion, and rebuke in all that you set your hand to do until you are destroyed and until you perish quickly, because of the wickedness of your doings in which you have forsaken Me. . . . The Lord will strike you with madness and blindness and confusion of heart. And you shall grope at noonday, as a blind man gropes in darkness, you shall not prosper in your ways, you shall be only oppressed and plundered continually, and no one shall save you" (Deut. 28:20, 28-29).

Justice is far from us, nor does righteousness overtake us; we look for light, but there is darkness! For brightness, but we walk in blackness! We grope for the wall like the blind, and we grope as if we had no eyes; we stumble at noonday as at twilight; we are as dead men in desolate places (Isa. 59:9-10).

In all three of these passages, God is describing the state of moral and social confusion that occurs when men choose not to follow Him. The "freedom" we think we have discovered actually turns out to be moral darkness. With no sure guidelines to follow, we are left to thrash about, trying to find the best way to live. Like a blind man groping for the wall, we end up stumbling around, tripping over the simplest obstacles. Our lack of moral clarity renders us incapable of making wise judgments on behaviors that will result in the greatest good for all.

Indeed, what is at stake here is "what is good" for all men. Sin comes at a steep price, and that is especially true in those matters that involve our relationships with others. God's laws concerning marriage, family, labor, money, envy, honesty, and a host of other social issues have all been handed down, not to shackle us in chains, but to make our lives easier. These instructions contribute to a stable social framework that benefits everyone involved. Paul summarized it well in a passage emphasizing moral purity: "These things are good and profitable to men" (Tit. 3:8). Abandon these principles, and everyone suffers for it.

This is especially true in regards to the greatest institution of all, marriage and family. Our current experimentation with easy divorce, cohabitation, and gay marriage, while promising freedom, will end up costing us dearly. "The consequences of our current retreat from marriage is not a flourishing libertarian social order, but a gigantic expansion of state power and a vast increase in social disorder and human suffering. . . . There is scarcely a dollar that state and federal government spends on social programs that is not driven in large part by family fragmentation" (Maggie Gallagher, "The Stakes," *National Review Online*, July 14, 2003).

The sages of old were right: Abandon God, and we become stragglers blindly groping in the dark. There is only one way out of this self-imposed nightmare: Humbly return to the God who made us and knows best how we should live.

Words Children Should Hear

Children thrive in a home environment where they are exposed to language that will shape their character in a godly direction.

My son, give attention to my words; incline your ear to my sayings (Prov. 4:20).

❧

Parenting is the most difficult job a person can take on in life. If the outcome is positive, it can also be the most rewarding. There are many skills and strategies that are required to be a good parent, but the one tool that will make the biggest difference in raising a child is the *words* a parent chooses to use in his or her interactions with the child.

This past week, the public was treated to a sorry example of words a parent should never use with a child. An audio clip of a phone message from actor Alec Baldwin to his young daughter was released. It was a profanity-laced diatribe, berating the poor girl, calling her names. Clearly, these were words that a parent should never use with a child. (This incident, by the way, says a lot about looking to Hollywood for role models.)

But there are other words that a parent *should* use when communicating with a child. If a child grows up hearing these words often, they will bolster his self-image and significantly influence the direction of his life.

In no particular order, here are several words that every child should hear.

"No!" A child is born without any sense of self-restraint, and as he grows older, that ability must be taught. But saying

"no" is meaningless unless it is (1) used consistently, and (2) enforced consistently—physically, if necessary. A child who is trained to respect boundaries at home will respect boundaries in society.

"You can do it!" and *"Well done!"* Along with the "no's" should be frequent encouragement to take on difficult tasks, and praise when those challenges are met. Adjustments have to be made for a child's limited knowledge and ability, of course. But frequent encouragement and praise strengthen a child's confidence to take on life's challenges.

"Life's not fair." A wise parent strives to create an environment of justice in a child's life, a respect for the principle that we get what we deserve. But in the real world, that rule doesn't always work. That's why children need to learn to expect some disappointment, and to deal with it without complaining or blaming. Patience is forged in the crucible of frustration.

"I love you." The world can be a hard, cold place, especially for a little one who is encountering it for the first time. Verbal reminders from parents of their unconditional love provide a haven of security for a child.

"I'm sorry." Like everyone else, parents are not perfect and will make mistakes. There is no shame in admitting our failures to our children. If those stumbles affect them directly, a sincere apology can even enhance their respect for us.

"Because God said so." A variation on the more popular, "because I said so," these words point the child to a more reliable source of authority in their life. Respect for God begins in a home where God is the undisputed arbiter of all decisions.

There are many other words that a child should hear throughout his early years, but these give a good indication of the kind of verbal environment that produces healthy, well-adjusted young people.

All of this assumes, of course, that any words are used at all. So Rule #1 should be: *Parents, talk to your children!*

Godliness and Good Health

The life of the righteous is concerned with more than just beliefs and emotions. Our bodies also benefit from our spiritual commitment.

My son, give attention to my words; incline your ear to my sayings. . . . For they are life to those who find them, and health to all their flesh (Prov. 4:20, 22).

Religion is popularly regarded as the province of emotions, beliefs, hopes, and other elements of an intangible nature. As a result, religion is usually the last place people will look for help with their medical problems. But body and spirit are not isolated components of life. They are so closely intertwined that what affects one is certain to affect the other. We should take seriously, therefore, the Bible's claim of providing "health to all their flesh" for those who obey it.

In 1967, Dr. S. I. McMillen published a little book entitled *None of These Diseases*. As a practicing physician, Dr. McMillen saw countless patients whose physical ailments were directly or indirectly caused by spiritual defects in their lives. Medicines and treatments might offer temporary relief from the physical symptoms, but the underlying spiritual diseases were beyond the doctor's ability to treat. Leaning heavily on the Scriptures, McMillen detailed numerous ways in which our physical health could be dramatically improved by simply applying age-old principles of godly living. A few examples:

- Avoiding alcohol and other mind-bending drugs eliminates drug-related diseases and injuries.

- Avoiding tobacco greatly reduces the risk of several cancers.
- Avoiding fornication prevents socially transmitted diseases (STDs).
- Proper diet and exercise strengthen the cardio-vascular system and minimize other weight-related problems.
- Replacing worry, anger, bitterness, fear, selfishness, and so forth with their mental opposites—contentment, love, cheerfulness, trust, generosity, and so on—will dramatically reduce the risk of heart disease, ulcers, nervous disorders, and other psychosomatic conditions.

These "cures" prescribed by the doctor were promoted by God ages ago, long before the modern medical profession discovered them. In the years since Dr. McMillen wrote his book, advances in medical science have strengthened his case: Those who adopt a Biblical lifestyle are generally healthier, happier people.

"Godliness . . . holds promise for the present life and also for the life to come" (1 Tim. 4:8). Religion may be the domain of the spiritual life, but all of life benefits from its influence.

Be Careful!

There are many behaviors the Bible warns us about, but the greatest caution is reserved for the one area of life that controls all the rest.

Keep your heart with all diligence, for out of it spring the issues of life (Prov. 4:23).

I have no idea who originally wrote it (and Google was no help), but the children's song "Be Careful Little Eyes" has a wonderful message that all children need to learn—and we older folks, too. Consider the first line of each verse:

Oh, be careful, little eyes, what you see , , ,
Oh, be careful, little ears, what you hear . . .
Oh, be careful, little tongue, what you say . . .
Oh, be careful, little hands, what you do . . .
Oh, be careful, little feet, where you go . . .

This song encourages us to be careful about everything we do in life. But the last line of each verse gives the reason for this caution: "There's a Father up above, and He's looking down in love . . ." Which is to say, God sees every detail of our lives and will judge accordingly.

It occurs to me, however, that the song is missing an important component. There should be another verse that goes, "Be careful little *minds* what you *think* . . ." Perhaps the original author thought that might be too abstract for kids. Or maybe it was in the original, and later editors dropped it for the same reason.* Whatever the history, it's a concept to which children should be introduced early in life.

Everything we do in life springs from the desires of the heart. The thief steals because he covets in his heart. The grumbler complains because of envy in his heart. The unfaithful spouse cheats because of lust in his heart. The liar deceives because of fear in his heart.

Conversely, the good Samaritan goes out of his way to help someone in need because of compassion in his heart. The frazzled mother keeps on sacrificing for her children because of the love in her heart. The martyr clings firmly to his convictions in the face of death because of the faith in his heart.

Good or bad, we are all what we are *because of what we choose to be in our minds.* We need to train our eyes, ears, tongues, feet, and so forth to do the right thing, of course; but that training regimen starts in the heart, where our ultimate destination is set.

"Be careful little minds what you think" . . . and the rest will be easy.

---

* For the record, I did locate one online version of the song that includes this additional verse. Look up the Cedarmont Kids version on songlyrics.com. Good for them.

The Wife of Your Youth

In their quest to remain loyal to their wives, husbands can do themselves a great favor by reflecting on the early days of marriage.

Let your fountain be blessed, and rejoice with the wife of your youth. As a loving deer and a graceful doe, let her breasts satisfy you at all times; and always be enraptured with her love (Prov. 5:18-19).

The Lord has been witness between you and the wife of your youth, with whom you have dealt treacherously; yet she is your companion and your wife by covenant. But did He not make them one, having a remnant of the Spirit? And why one? He seeks godly offspring. Therefore take heed to your spirit, and let none deal treacherously with the wife of his youth (Mal. 2:14-15).

൭൭

Both of these passages are found in contexts warning men not to mistreat their wives, either by committing adultery against them (Proverbs) or by divorcing them (Malachi). In both passages, the authors bestow an unusual title on the woman in the relationship: "the wife of your youth." This expression should cause men to pause and reflect on the value of their wives.

A young man is attracted to a young woman by her good looks, her character, her personality, her cooking, common interests—or if he's really lucky, all the above. When he proposes and she says "yes," he's the happiest man in the world. He has a companion who makes his life complete, who brings him more joy than he could have ever imagined.

Over time, the initial excitement wanes. Her beauty fades, and he learns all her idiosyncrasies and irritating habits. Their relationship settles into a routine. It is easy in this mundane environment for a man to "fall out of love" with his wife, and begin looking for excitement elsewhere.

When those days come, guys, remember that she is still "the wife of your youth." She is the same woman who turned you on so wildly in your younger days. There are several things you can do to honor her in that role.

First, fantasize about her, not other women. Recall the passion of the early days, and let those memories rekindle the desire that should be reserved for her alone.

Respect all she has done for you through the years—raising the kids, sacrificing her interests for your career ambitions, giving you unqualified encouragement and moral support. She helped you get where you are today. Is that not worth something?

Above all, cherish the memories of the early years, when you were young and in love and the whole world was an exciting adventure the two of you were eager to take on together. Remember the dates, the walks in the park, the little disasters that you survived together (and laugh about now). She may have put on a few pounds and wrinkles since then, but she represents a link to the happiest days of your life. Don't throw it away for a cheap trinket.

She is the wife of your youth; she has earned the right to be the wife of your old age.

Christians and Sex

The caricature of Christians as sexually repressive has no foundation in Scripture. The Bible, in fact, is quite positive about the joy of sexual pleasure.

Let your fountain be blessed, and rejoice with the wife of your youth. As a loving deer and a graceful doe, let her breasts satisfy you at all times; and always be enraptured with her love. For why should you, my son, be enraptured by an immoral woman, and be embraced in the arms of a seductress? (Prov. 5:18-20).

In a culture that is increasingly hostile to religion in general and Christianity in particular, the beliefs of Christians are often caricatured as irrational and intolerant. By portraying Christians as out of touch with reality, the anti-Christian culture seeks to turn people away from the faith.

This is especially true in regard to the culture's portrayal of the Biblical view of sexuality. Christians are depicted as having a severe hang up with sex. Christians, we are told, are not comfortable with sex because they view it as inherently evil. So rather than enjoy this natural gift themselves, Christians spend all their time denying it to others. That's why they're always railing against premarital sex, homosexuality, adultery, pornography, and so forth. There are a number of convenient labels to reinforce this image of sexual intolerance, such as "Victorian prudes" or "sexual Taliban." Who wants to be associated with a bunch of misfits like that?

Of course, this depiction of the Christian view of sexuality, like most caricatures, is a gross misrepresentation of the facts. While it is true that some Bible believers may have a distorted view of sex, the majority have a very healthy respect for the subject.

First, the Bible itself addresses sexuality openly and honestly as a natural part of the human experience. Our opening text is just one of several passages that address, in a positive tone, the joy of carnal pleasure. Look also at the Song of Solomon, an entire book that is devoted almost exclusively to the subject of romantic love (with appropriately erotic language, too). Christian couples are specifically commanded not to forego this pleasure (1 Cor. 7:1-5). If anyone, Christian or otherwise, believes that sex is dirty, they didn't get it from the Bible.

Furthermore, an honest examination of how modern evangelical Christianity deals with sexuality will reveal a refreshing openness on the subject. A perennial best-seller on Christian book lists is *The Act of Marriage* by Tim and Beverly LaHaye (Zondervan, 1976; revised in 1998), a book that tastefully but graphically informs couples how to get the greatest enjoyment from the most intimate part of their relationship. Surveys have repeatedly shown that Bible believers have more satisfying sex lives than those who are more "enlightened." The popular depiction of Christians as sexually-repressed prudes is simply a lie.

But if Christians enjoy sex so much, why are they so rigid about keeping it within a traditional marriage relationship? Because the emotional and psychological dimensions of such a relationship—a permanent commitment between one man and one woman—is what allows sexual activity to reach its fullest potential. Without that framework, physical intimacy is not love, but lust—manipulative, exploitative, and destructive.

It is precisely because we enjoy sex so much that we insist on preserving the sanctity of traditional marriage. We wish everyone could enjoy it the way God intended it to be enjoyed.

Have an Affair!

> The secret to keeping a marriage healthy and positive is no secret at all: Treat one another as the lovers God intends you to be.

Let your fountain be blessed, and rejoice with the wife of your youth. As a loving deer and a graceful doe, let her breasts satisfy you at all times; and always be enraptured with her love. For why should you, my son, be enraptured by an immoral woman, and be embraced in the arms of a seductress?" (Prov. 5:18-20).

According to a study performed several years ago at the University of Chicago, as many as 25 percent of men in America and 17 percent of women admit to having had an extramarital sexual experience ("Adultery in America," *U.S. News and World Report*, August 31, 1998). These affairs, once uncovered, wreak havoc on marriages and leave deep emotional scars on spouses, children, friends, as well as on the cheaters themselves. The devastation of adultery is underscored by the fact that it is the only cause for divorce sanctioned by Jesus. When someone cheats on his or her spouse, they destroy the very foundation of marriage.

But if extramarital affairs are so bad, why do so many people engage in them? It's simple: Because they are *exciting*. Most marriages eventually settle into a pattern of behavior that can best be described as dull. The passion of the honeymoon is replaced by the boredom of familiarity, as a couple's life together turns into a perpetual struggle with bills, kids, and leaky faucets. Each spouse now sees the warts of the other all too clearly. In this environment of ho-hum acceptance, it doesn't take much temptation to cause a spouse to seek excitement elsewhere. That's why most cheaters justify their behavior with complaints of "she doesn't understand me" or "there's no love in our marriage anymore." The affair may be dangerous, but blinded by the hot lust of an illicit entanglement, the thrill is worth the risk. Only after the damage is done do the cheaters recognize the foolishness of their decision.

How can a couple make their marriage affair-proof? Considering the fundamental cause of infidelity just described, the answer should be obvious: *Have an affair with your spouse.* Your marriage was once alive with passion; do whatever it takes to rekindle that fire. Husbands, "the wife of your youth" is still your wife—treat her the same way you did back when you were trying to impress her. And wives, the same thing that once attracted your future husband to you—your physical features—can still fascinate him, if you still want them to. A husband and wife who both work hard to put passion into their marriage will get excitement out of it.

Paul summarized it well: "Because of sexual immorality, let each man have his own wife, and let each woman have her own husband. Let the husband render to his wife the affection due her, and likewise also the wife to her husband" (1 Cor. 7:3-4). In other words, work to keep your love affair alive, and you won't need to look elsewhere for happiness.

The Cords of Sin

Every addiction is a form of involuntary servitude, and the cure is not easy. But escape is possible, if the right resources are brought to bear.

His own iniquities entrap the wicked man, and he is caught in the cords of his sin (Prov. 5:22).

༺꧂

"Entrap... caught in cords." This language describes an individual bound against his will to a fate he cannot escape. He is a victim, powerless to save himself—except that the language in the rest of the verse pins the cause for his predicament entirely on him: "*His own* iniquities ... *his* sin." He is caught in the chains of a bondage that he brought upon himself.

This is a description of *addiction*. In his seminal work, *Addictions: A Banquet in the Grave* (2001), counselor Edward Welch defines addiction as "bondage to the rule of a substance, activity, or state of mind, which then becomes the center of life, defending itself from the truth so that even bad consequences don't bring repentance, and leading to further estrangement from God." Addiction is not a disease; it is sin gone to seed, the end result of a bad habit so deeply ingrained in our character that we have lost the will to defeat it. The addict is, in every sense of the word, enslaved to a master he cannot defeat.

Whether the habit is drug or alcohol abuse, gambling, pornography, workaholism, laziness, arrogance, explosive anger, or any other activity that has seized control of one's life, the result is the same: The addict is stuck in a death spiral of behavior from which he cannot break free, even though he recognizes its destructive effects in his life and in the lives of others. There is no easy escape from this bondage. Every aspect of the addict's life is held hostage to the controlling demon.

If the addict is helpless to save himself, then the only hope of deliverance is intervention from an outside source. That's where God comes in. But let's be careful here; the sinner doesn't need more laws, more lectures, more threats of punishment. He has already become impervious to that. What he needs is a motivation that reaches beyond the cravings and self-loathing to touch the last remaining spark of goodness buried deep within.

Once the addict stops denying his predicament and acknowledges that he has a problem, he is open to a change in his thinking. With the aid of a network of reformed addicts getting involved in his life (that's you and me), he can be introduced to a power that is stronger than his chains. The image of the Son of God dying on the cross for his sins, and the resulting awareness of forgiveness of his failures—providing a clean break from the past—will open his heart to the work of rehabilitation. He will experience a psychological liberation.

Will this rescue be easy and quick? No, escape from slavery is never easy and quick. Repentance will be a long road back to freedom; but it is possible, and the new life on the other side is worth the struggle.

Do Not Commit Adultery

Adultery is one of the few sins that most everyone agrees is wrong; yet so many men are guilty of it. Avoiding it requires a deliberate strategy.

The one who commits adultery with a woman is lacking sense; he who would destroy himself does it (Prov. 6:32).

§

Question: What do Eliot Spitzer, Mark Sanford, Bill Clinton, John Edwards, and John Ensign all have in common?

If you answered, they're all politicians, you get extra points for being up to speed on current events. Yes, they are politicians, but more to the point of this article, they are politicians whose careers were either tarnished or destroyed by marital infidelity. Democrats or Republicans, conservatives or liberals, these men risked everything on wild flings with mistresses or prostitutes, got caught, and paid a heavy price for their passion.

Politicians, of course, are not the only ones who cheat on their wives. I long ago ceased being surprised at reports of preachers and elders—yes, men of God—who were caught up in sexual scandals.

And the rest of us wonder, why do they do it? How could they be so careless and stupid?

Sadly, these high-profile cases of unfaithfulness highlight the pervasiveness of this sin in all levels of our society. Depending on which source you consult, experts suspect that up to one-half of all husbands cheat on their wives at some point in their marriages. The consequences of most of these affairs may not make the nightly newscast, but they are just as devastating to the individuals involved.

Clearly, the temptation to find excitement outside of marriage is a strong one. How can a godly man avoid making this mistake? The book of Proverbs provides a wealth of helpful advice to men on how to avoid adultery and its awful aftermath.

First, *be alert to the seriousness of this sin.* It is the "simple" man, the one who "lacks understanding" who is most susceptible to sexual temptation (9:16). The man who assumes that "it could never happen to me" is more likely to stumble into compromising situations.

Second, *avoid potentially enticing encounters with women.* "Remove your way far from her, and do not go near the door of her house" (5:8). The line between an innocent encounter and a romantic entanglement is easily crossed. Stay clear of it!

Third, *control your thoughts ruthlessly.* "Do not lust after her beauty in your heart" (6:25; see also Matt. 5:28-30). This includes your use of the internet. The heart that feasts on forbidden fruit cannot effectively control the flesh that desires to do the same (see Mk. 7:21).

Fourth, *think about the consequences.* "By means of a harlot a man is reduced to a crust of bread; and an adulteress will prey upon his precious life" (6:26). A broken home, a lost career, the wrath of a jealous husband, shame, disease, eternal damnation—is a few moments of illicit pleasure worth all that?

Finally, *work hard to maintain a strong and happy marriage.* "Let your fountain be blessed, and rejoice with the wife of your youth" (5:18). A man who is madly in love with his wife will have little desire to go fishing elsewhere. Whatever issues may exist in your marriage, do whatever it takes to deal with them, and keep the flame of passion alive.

Women and Clothing

As the temperatures go up and the clothing comes off, it's appropriate to revisit what the Bible says about women's clothing—and why it matters.

And there a woman met him, with the attire of a harlot, and a crafty heart (Prov. 7:10).

In like manner also, that the women adorn themselves in modest apparel, with propriety and moderation (1 Tim. 2:9).

In our politically correct climate, few topics generate more heated rhetoric than the subject of women's clothing. Any suggestion that women should be more discreet in their wardrobe choices is met with howls of outrage against the idea that women are "asking for" being treated as sex objects through the clothes they wear. At the same time, it cannot be denied that some women deliberately draw attention to their sexuality by dressing provocatively. "The attire of a harlot" is a timeless advertising technique that never fails to attract its target customers.

The Bible addresses women's clothing, but in a general way that leaves some room for cultural variation. This broad approach makes it difficult for some women—especially younger women—to know what is acceptable and what isn't. How can a godly woman make wise decisions in her choice of clothing?

To answer that question, we first must address a fundamental difference in the natures of men and women. Unlike women, men are visually attracted to the beauty of the female form. The more of a woman's body that is exposed or accentuated, the more likely she is to attract the attention of men as a potential mating partner. This explains why *Sports Illustrated* has an annual swimsuit issue featuring scantily clad women; why men visit strip clubs that feature women performers; why sports teams use cheerleaders in skimpy uniforms (trust me, the guys looking on are not admiring the complex choreography); and why pornography is an overwhelmingly male pastime. Feminists can protest all they want, but men are hardwired to look at women as sex objects, and it takes a lot of internal discipline for a man to keep his gaze from becoming lustful. (And the Bible demands that discipline, Matt. 5:28-30; Prov. 6:25).

But women have a corresponding responsibility not to aggravate that temptation. The Bible calls it "placing a stumbling block" before another (Rom. 14:13, 21). Whether by design or by carelessness, anyone who causes another to stumble in his weakness is subject to punishment (Matt. 18:6-7). Women must take that principle into account when choosing their wardrobes. Any clothing that draws attention to her bodily features—thereby attracting the lustful gaze of men—should be avoided.

So what are the specific types of clothing that women should avoid? We could offer such a list, but it would likely not match the list that preachers used to give a hundred years ago, or in another culture today. A more useful test would be for a woman to pose this question to herself: *Would this kind of clothing on another woman stir my jealousy if she were hanging around my husband or boyfriend?* If you'd be uncomfortable with another woman wearing that clothing around your man, then you shouldn't wear it around other men.

A woman's clothing should send a clear signal to men: "I respect my sexuality; I expect you to respect it too."

To Each His Own

As a general rule, we get out of life what we put into it. The sooner we learn that lesson, the better equipped we will be to live our life well.

If you are wise, you are wise for yourself, and if you scoff, you alone will bear it (Prov. 9:12).

ೲ

In the book of Proverbs, "wisdom" is the ability to recognize cause-and-effect relationships in life, and to choose behaviors that will achieve the best possible outcomes. The "scoffer" is the one who, due to stubborn pride, refuses to recognize those connections and makes mistakes that could have been avoided.

God's word is an excellent guidebook to mastering these principles. But one need not be a Bible scholar to learn them. Anyone who keeps his eyes open and studies human behavior —especially the mistakes that others make—should be able to figure out "wisdom."

Of course, the decision to be wise or to scoff at these basic truths is entirely our own. God will never twist our arm to do good or bad. He will persuade, plead, warn, encourage, instruct—but the final choice is always left up to us. By His own design, God's ability to enforce His will in our lives is somewhat limited.

But that doesn't mean God is powerless. The cause-and-effect relationships that God has built into His moral order are remarkably strong, and carry their own rewards and punishments. Whether or not we see the connections between our choices and the outcomes of those choices, the results are almost always predictable. "He who sows to his flesh will of the flesh reap corruption, but he who sows to the Spirit will of the Spirit reap everlasting life" (Gal. 6:8). We are free to live as we choose; but we are chained to the outcome of our choice.

Consider the rewards of a life of wisdom: a generally longer, healthier life; the esteem of those around us; peace of mind; prosperity; and in the next life, a home in heaven. If it seems that the godly man gets a few more breaks in life than the rest of us, it is no accident. His self-discipline and hard work have contributed to making those breaks possible. He is indeed "wise for himself."

Of course, we don't have to follow the wise man's example. If we choose to ignore God's instructions and let pleasure, greed, emotion, or blind tradition guide our steps, we are free to do so. Certainly it is much easier, and probably more fun this way. But don't go looking for a scapegoat when things go wrong, as surely they will. Health problems, financial troubles, poor relationships with others, chronic anxiety, and eternal torment in hell—these are the inevitable fruits of a life of self-indulgence. When this bitter harvest comes in, we cannot blame friends, parents, the preacher, God, or society. "If you scoff, you alone will bear it." We get what we deserve!

The fruits of our behavior, good or bad, are not always apparent at the first. The sacrifices that a life of wisdom requires can seem unduly harsh. Occasionally righteous people will suffer unfairly, and wicked people will profit from their wickedness. But these aberrations are only a temporary skewing of the natural order. Eventually the scales will balance out, and the chickens will come home to roost. "Do not be deceived, God is not mocked; for whatever a man sows, that he will also reap" (Gal. 6:7).

Sow accordingly.

After We Are Gone

Our reputation will live on long after we are gone. But that reputation is set by the countless little decisions we make while we are here.

The memory of the righteous is blessed, but the name of the wicked will rot (Prov. 10:7).

Death has a strange way of clearing away the fog of a person's life and allowing others to see us as we really are. While we are alive, we can win the favor of those around us with a variety of earthly stratagems—how we dress, the kind of home we live, in the kind of car we drive, maintaining the proper connections in the community, involvement in all the latest "cool" activities, and so forth. But when we die, such window dressing suddenly loses its importance, and people will remember us for what we really were—how we talked, how we treated others, our generosity (or lack of it), our moral strengths and/or weaknesses, and so on. In the hour of death, these weightier matters are remembered as the true measure of the man. The other details are soon forgotten.

"The memory of the righteous is blessed." Consider the example of Dorcas of Joppa, a widowed Christian whose death sorrowed many. We know nothing of the social or financial status of Dorcas. Neither do we know what she looked like. But we do know that she was "abounding with deeds of kindness and charity" (Ac. 9:36). The many items of clothing she had made for others was a testimony to her good heart (v. 39). Her friends remembered her with respect—and so do we—because she earned it.

"The name of the wicked will rot." A good example of this is Absalom, David's son. Absalom was handsome, rich, charming, intelligent (2 Sam. 14:25-26)—all the qualities that we equate with success. But Absalom's heart was blackened by a lust for power, and his life was a tragic tale of deception and violence, ending in his own death (2 Sam. 15-18). Today, Absalom's name is a symbol for treachery and evil. His surface qualities are forgotten.

Absalom no doubt performed a few good deeds in his life, and I'm sure Dorcas made some mistakes. But these exceptions could not offset the prevailing direction in their lives. It was this *general pattern* of behavior that defined the kind of people they were, and for which they are remembered. When they died, their reputations were fixed forever.

What will people remember about you after you are gone? Long after they have forgotten your looks, your home, and your money, they will remember your character. Will they remember a person who was friendly, patient, helpful, godly? Or will they remember someone who was cold, short-tempered, greedy, worldly? Or will they remember you as someone who couldn't quite make up their mind whose side they were on, a confusing mush of good and bad?

What people will remember about you after you are gone depends on the kind of person you are today. Live each day of your life in view of eternity.

Shut Up and Listen

If our mouth often gets us into trouble, then perhaps we should learn a lesson: Speak as little as possible, and listen to what others have to say.

In the multitude of words sin is not lacking, but he who restrains his lips is wise (Prov. 10:19).

A fool has no delight in understanding, but in expressing his own heart (Prov. 18:2).

Do you see a man hasty in his words? There is more hope for a fool than for him (Prov. 29:20).

If we will give an account for every careless word we speak (and we will, Matt. 12:36-37), then it makes sense that the surest way to avoid condemnation is to say as little as possible. But our tongues have hair triggers, and they usually go off before we have a had a chance to size up our shot. It is only after we have hurt a friend or embarrassed ourselves that we realize, "I shouldn't have said that." Many of these verbal blunders could be eliminated if we would master the fine art of keeping our mouths shut.

For example, hasty words frequently serve to reveal our ignorance. It is humiliating to make a confident assertion about a topic, only to find out later that our "knowledge" was all wet. Improved knowledge (if we really want it) comes through listening, not talking. If we have an opinion to express, a few thoughtful words, spoken with humility, will suffice.

Neither is it in our best interest to broadcast our talents. If such boasts are true, we won't have to tell others; they will be able to see it for themselves. If we fail to measure up to our bragging, then our own words will become egg on our face. It's hard to respect a man whose mouth outruns his performance.

Likewise, the person who is quick to criticize often has to eat his own words. There is a legitimate place for reproof, but so much of our criticism is just careless popping off that does more harm than good. Our disparaging commentary may be based on faulty information; or it may be demoralizing to a brother who needs our help; or it may be recycled by others and used against us. Criticize only when absolutely necessary, and with words carefully chosen and aimed.

James summarized these proverbs with a proverb of his own: "Let everyone be quick to hear, slow to speak" (Jas. 1:19). The fact that God gave us two ears and only one mouth ought to provide a clue as to how they should be used. Will we learn?

Before We Criticize Others

Constructive criticism has a place, but too much of our reproof is just mean-spirited carping. Before we criticize, we must ask: Is this really necessary?

He who is devoid of wisdom despises his neighbor, but a man of understanding holds his peace (Prov. 11:12).

※

It is important that we draw a distinction between the subject of this proverb and the unneighborly talk condemned elsewhere. Gossip (or slander) consists of unkind remarks about someone made behind their backs in an effort to disparage their reputation. That kind of talk is universally despised.

This proverb instead deals with hateful words spoken *directly to a neighbor's face*, words that would be better left unsaid. Delitzsch defines them as "arrogant criticisms . . . reckless condemnation." Other versions further clarify the idea: "He who belittles his neighbor" (RSV); or "the senseless man pours contempt on his neighbor" (TCB). It is this *eagerness to criticize another* that Solomon is warning against. Constructive criticism has a useful role to play in relationships, but the topic here is criticism that crosses the line into destruction.

Occasions for such attacks are common. Perhaps our neighbor has tossed a thoughtless barb in our direction, one that calls for rebuttal. He may insult us through some careless oversight, or treat us with indifference when we deserve better. Of course, his error may not involve us at all. Perhaps he blundered into a really dumb mistake, something he feels just as bad about as anyone. Or maybe his "offense" consists of a stroke of good fortune and we, green with envy, unconsciously desire to remind him of his place. There are any number of reasons why we may feel justified in criticizing.

Whatever the occasion, a verbal attack rarely does any good, and often works harm. First, such vindictiveness tends to boomerang on us. "Condemn not, and you shall not be condemned. . . . For with the same measure that you use, it will be measured back to you" (Lk. 6:37-38). If we are quick to criticize the shortcomings of others, we should not be surprised to find ourselves held under that same microscope. (See the story of Shimei for a good example of this, 2 Sam. 16:5-13; 1 Kgs. 2:8-9, 36-46). If we want others to be patient with our imperfections, then we should hold our peace when dealing with theirs.

Second, and more importantly, one who flings insults at others endangers his own soul. "Whoever says, 'You fool!' shall be in danger of hell fire" (Matt. 5:22). "For judgment is without mercy to the one who has shown no mercy" (Jas. 2:13). Our neighbor may not be perfect, but God doesn't need our help to know that. In fact, He resents our intrusion into His role as Judge.

If we are so eager to find fault, the best place to start looking for it is within ourselves. Goodness knows, there is plenty to work on there, and—more importantly—those are the only flaws we can actually do something about.

Gossip

Circulating dirt about others may be fun, but the long-term effects are destructive for all involved. Gossip is a serious sin, not an innocent pastime.

A talebearer reveals secrets, but he who is of a faithful spirit conceals a matter (Prov. 11:13).

Things which are not fitting . . . whisperers, backbiters (Rom. 1:28-30).

Love . . . does not rejoice in iniquity (1 Cor. 13:6).

Our word "gossip" comes from an Old English word *godsibb*, meaning "God relative (or sibling)." The original word described a close friend, someone with whom we can share intimate secrets. Over time, the meaning of the word shifted from the *friend* (person) to the *talking* (action) that friends engage in; hence, our modern definition of gossip.

The Bible uses a number of expressions that equate to our concept of gossip. "Talebearer" describes the activity of spreading unflattering information about others, while "whisperer" and "backbiter" emphasize the secretive nature of this talk. Whichever word we prefer to use, we're describing a well-known behavior: The spreading of defamatory details about someone behind their back. Whether those details are true or false is irrelevant. It is the act of *repeating this information about someone without their knowledge* that makes gossip so despicable.

The universality of gossip speaks to the influence of *pride* in the human race. Gossip is an easy way of promoting ourselves as superior to others. The more dirt we can dig up on others, the better we look—or so we think.

The Bible condemns gossip in the strongest language. If you've ever been the victim of gossip, you know why; it's terribly injurious. The information being circulated is almost always distorted, exaggerated, or filtered, making the victim look worse than he really is. By definition gossip is a form of injustice; it condemns someone as guilty based on flimsy evidence, without the victim having an opportunity to rebut the charges against him. It is a cancer that ravages the well-being of any social circle in which it is found.

How should we deal with gossip? For starters, don't do it! If we are privy to scurrilous information about an associate, we have two options: We can confront that person directly, privately and with a view to resolving the problem with a minimum of fallout; or, if it's someone with whom we do not have a relationship, we can just ignore the matter. We know so little of the facts involved that we would only make matters worse by getting involved—and it's none of our business anyway. Either way, the matter stays with us alone, and we do not spread the incriminating story.

What if someone comes to us with a juicy tidbit on a third party? The best course of action is to decline to listen to it. The one who gossips to us about others, will gossip to others about us. He has demonstrated that he is not above spreading ugly details of others' lives, and someday it may be details of *our* life that he is spreading. That person is not our friend. If more of us would politely but firmly refuse to listen to the whisperings of the talebearer, gossip would lose its appeal.

"Love does not rejoice in evil"—which is another way of saying, if we love our fellow man, we will not traffic in gossip. Integrity demands that we rise above this shameful behavior.

Gender Pathologies

Men and women are different—surprise! But one difference sets up a serious pathology that intensifies the conflict between the sexes.

A gracious woman retains honor, but ruthless men retain riches (Prov. 11:16).

As a ring of gold in a swine's snout, so is a lovely woman who lacks discretion (Prov. 11:22).

These two observations, separated by only five verses, highlight a quirk of human nature that explains much of the friction that damages relationships between men and women.

Verse 16 says that men get rich by being "ruthless." Other translations read "aggressive" or "violent." That is, they usually get what they want by brute force. Contrast that with the woman in verse 22, who is described as "lovely," or "beautiful" (ESV, NIV). Which is an oblique way of saying that women tend to achieve their goals by enhancing their physical appearance.

Simply stated, these two verses point to the different means by which men and women seek success in their lives. Men seek it by *projecting strength*. Whether in the military, in business, or in personal relationships, men tend to be more assertive, forceful, and aggressive, and others—especially women—are attracted to that strength. Women, on the other hand, seek success by *projecting beauty*. They spend inordinate amounts of time and money on their hair, clothing, makeup, and jewelry, all for the purpose of attracting the attention of men—who respond predictably.

These interrelated truths explain so much that we see in the relations between men and women.

Men rely on strength, partly because of biology, but also because it works. Women are attracted to athletes, Hollywood hunks, and even "bad boys," most of whom end up as lousy mates. Feminists can object all they want, but there's something about strong men that women find irresistible.

Similarly, the weakness of men for beautiful women is legendary. Like moths drawn to the flame, men succumb to the alluring curves and moves of a woman who knows how to dangle the bait. Even the best of men can be lured into disastrous liaisons based entirely on physical beauty.

So men and women each have qualities that appeal to the base instincts of the other; and neither is very good at recognizing the down side of what attracts them. This interlocking pathology is a dance of death that drags both into heartache and destruction.

There is a lesson in these proverbs that men and women would do well to learn. First, a wise woman will not be drawn to the macho posturing of a man who tries to impress her with his physique, money, status, or any other display of power. She will "retain her honor" and save herself for a man who has nothing to prove but will provide for her sacrificially.

Likewise, a man who is attracted to a woman strictly by her looks is like someone who grasps at a valuable gold ring, unaware that it is attached to a pig. He may get his ring, but he'll get a lot of ugly trouble with it. The wise man will look past the exterior to the character inside. If he can't find beauty in her character, he'll look elsewhere for companionship.

These verses do not disparage masculine strength nor feminine beauty. A good man will use his strength as a tool to serve others and protect the weak. And female beauty is a wonderful gift that makes up for a lot of the ugliness in the world. A woman is blessed who has it.

Whether male or female, how we find affirmation in life is based chiefly on *character*, both in ourselves and in our mates. Choose wisely.

Spend It or Lose It

The blessings God sends our way are provided for a reason. We only hurt ourselves when we selfishly hoard them for our own interests.

There is one who scatters, yet increases more; and there is one who withholds more than is right, but it leads to poverty (Prov. 11:24).
"It is more blessed to give than to receive" (Ac. 20:35).

❦

If this proverb sounds a little confusing, it makes perfectly good sense to the farmer. He regularly "scatters" in hope of an increase, and nature rarely disappoints him. Jesus had His own version of the proverb: "Give, and it will be given to you; good measure, pressed down, shaken together, running over, they will pour into your lap. For by your standard of measure it will be measured to you in return" (Lk. 6:38). The greatest rewards usually require long-term investments, but blinded by the lure of a quick profit, people often refuse to make the investment and end up cheating themselves.

It is a basic law of nature with countless applications. Consider, for example, our use of the material possessions with which God has blessed us. We are instructed "to do good, to be rich in good works, to be generous and ready to share" (1 Tim. 6:18). The resources so spent will probably never be seen again, but the child of God has not lost anything. Aside from his treasures in heaven (v. 19), he will receive the gratitude of a lot of people in a hundred small ways. True, some recipients may take unfair advantage of his generosity and hurt him. But if he uses that as an excuse to close his heart and pocketbook to all, he will die a bitter and lonely man, like Nabal (1 Sam. 25).

Local churches can learn from this proverb, too. Fearful of wasting the Lord's money, some congregations prefer to sit on their funds and watch them grow. It is no surprise that such churches are often plagued with internal friction, indifference, and declining memberships. They may be proud of the money they are saving, but that's a poor substitute for the souls they are neglecting to save. To increase—both spiritually and numerically—a church must scatter. This does not imply a blank check for every hare-brained scheme that comes along, but a commitment to a steady program of reaching the wider community with the gospel. Examine new methods, improve old ones, take a calculated risk now and then—but stay busy teaching the Word. The few mistakes a church makes in such an approach can be forgiven once the harvest comes in.

How much of my income should I give to the Lord's work? How can I show my wife that I love her? Which evangelism programs should we adopt? Detailed rules and regulations can answer such questions, but they are no match for a heart that knows "it is more blessed to give than to receive."

Wise Counselors

Navigating the complexities of life is a lot easier if we actively seek the wisdom of others who have traveled the path before us.

The way of a fool is right in his own eyes, but he who heeds counsel is wise (Prov. 12:15).

Without counsel, plans go awry, but in the multitude of counselors they are established (Prov. 15:22).

For by wise counsel you will wage your own war, and in a multitude of counselors there is safety (Prov. 24:6).

Very early in my career, I resolved to be guided solely by God's word in all my life decisions, especially in my work as a preacher. It was a noble commitment made with the purest of motives. However, being an introvert by nature, that decision gave me an excuse not to reach out to older preachers in managing the predicaments that inevitably arise in a preacher's work. After all, I had God's word; wasn't that enough? As I soon learned, it was *not* enough. I made some dumb mistakes in those early years that hindered my growth. I survived those stumbles and eventually gained the deeper insights into dealing with people that helped me be a more effective worker. But I could have learned those insights sooner and avoided some of the mistakes if, from the start, I had sought the counsel of older, wiser men.

In a book dedicated to the search for wisdom in living life well, it should come as no surprise to see so many references in Proverbs to the importance of seeking counsel from others in our decision-making. We are not nearly as smart as we think we are, especially in our younger days, and the experiences of older people who have seen far more of life than we have can be an invaluable source of guidance—if we are open to receiving it.

Who are these wise counselors? In our younger days, *our parents* should play a prominent role in shaping our thinking. As we mature, we can take advantage of the wisdom of *older friends* whose journeys have exposed them to a wider range of life experiences. In our professional careers, *mentors* can provide training on the intricacies of our craft and managing the office politics that are an inevitable part of work life. *Elders and preachers* who have demonstrated a mastery of spiritual disciplines can be helpful in getting our own spiritual and moral house in order. The young person who takes advantage of all these resources will be ahead of the game in preparing for life.

Wise counsel is not always easy to take. Sometimes the counsel may come in the form of a correction or a rebuke. Those episodes sting, because our pride takes a hit; we learn that our brilliance is a only figment of our misguided imagination. If the disciplinary advice is to be received, we will have to eat a generous portion of humble pie. Of course, we're free to reject the reproof and continue to go our own way. But we're likely to pay for our stubbornness farther down the road. Better to listen, learn, and improve.

Our personal study of God's word, of course, should play the primary role in shaping our life's trajectory. But we should never underestimate the value of wise counselors in helping us translate that divine guidance into daily living.

Depression: Cause and Cure

Not all depression is a medical condition. In many cases it is a spiritual problem, with a spiritual solution that is available to all of us.

Anxiety in the heart of man causes depression; but a good word makes it glad (Prov. 12:25).

According to one recent source, about one in five Americans adults—that's over 46 million people—suffer some form of chronic depression, ranging from prolonged sadness to psychosis. In some cases these unhappy people are victims of chemical imbalances that can be addressed by medication. They can and should take advantage of all the help medical science can provide them.

This proverb, however, suggests that the root problem often is not medical but spiritual. The mental gloominess is caused by *anxiety*, a state of mind that people bring upon themselves by how they choose to think about their life. The Hebrew word used here means "fear, dread, anxious care." When a person allows his mind to be consumed with worry over his problems—or potential problems—he is sure to become depressed.

Jesus viewed this kind of mental sickness as a behavioral issue that we can control. He cautions, "*Do not worry* about your life, what you will eat or what you will drink; nor about your body, what you will put on. . . . *Do not worry* about tomorrow, for tomorrow will worry about its own things" (Matt. 6:25, 34). Jesus knew that if people would simply change how they think about their possessions and their future, they would be happier.

Of course, that's easier said than done. How do you obey the command, "do not worry" when it seems that everything in your life is going wrong?

Solomon addresses this challenge in the second half of the proverb: "A good word makes it glad." We drive anxiety out of our hearts by forcing good words in.

Regular *Bible study*, for example, provides the best source of good words. Time spent reading and meditating on God's word can be a tremendous antidote to depressive thinking. Study the wonderful promises God has made to His people. Read the stories of godly men and women who struggled with problems worse than our own, and overcame them through their faith in God. A primary purpose of the Bible is to help people cope successfully with life, but that benefit is wasted if we do not read it.

Cheerful companions provide good words. Cultivate a close friendship with mature Christians who have learned how to be happy regardless of their circumstances. Take advantage of opportunities to share their company and conversation. Their words of encouragement will inspire you. More importantly, their optimistic spirit will rub off on you, and you will learn the secret of controlling your thinking to maintain a positive outlook on life. This social support is one of the key benefits of active membership in a local church. But that resource is wasted if you do not get involved!

Prayer generates good words. Verbalize your feelings to God. Let Him know about your needs and fears. The simple trust expressed in such an exercise will warm your soul and lighten your load.

God did not create us to be miserable. If we are, we must take the initiative to deal with the problem: "Be anxious for nothing, . . . and the peace of God, which surpasses all understanding, will guard your hearts and minds through Christ Jesus" (Phil. 4:6-7).

Pride and Counsel

Conflict is usually the result of wounded pride. The ability to set aside our pride and seek to understand others is essential to making peace.

By pride comes nothing but strife, but with the well-advised is wisdom (Prov. 13:10).

୧୨୦୧

Like most Hebrew poetry, the parallelism in this little proverb offers contrasting thoughts that clarify and explain each other. But the message in this couplet takes some effort to unpack.

The first line sets forth an obvious cause-and-effect relationship: Pride produces strife. That truism requires no explanation. In marriages, workplaces, and even churches we see what happens when warring parties are too proud to work out their differences. In the New Testament "selfish ambition" is often linked to contentions, outbursts of wrath, and so forth (see 2 Cor. 12:20; Gal. 5:20). So pride is destructive. That makes sense.

At this point our minds are conditioned to expect an obvious countervailing relationship, something along the lines of "humility brings peace." But that's not what we read. Instead of "humility" we find "well-advised," and in place of "peace" we find "wisdom." To see the contrast here requires some thought.

Let's look at the "cause" words first. "Pride" in the first line is set against "well-advised" (or, "those who take advice," ESV) in the second. A major character flaw of the proud person is his self-assurance. He knows everything already, and is not disposed to listen to contrary opinions. He is unwilling to consider the counsel of others. This sets up an obvious distinction: *Pride* and *the ability to take advice from others* cannot co-exist in the same heart.

Now consider the difference between the two fruits, "strife" and "wisdom." By definition, strife is the clash of two parties who cannot tolerate each other's viewpoint on some issue; all they can see is their own self-interest. But people who ask questions, seek advice from outsiders, and really try to understand all angles of the problem—who step outside their own self-interest—are far more likely to figure out a peaceful solution to the conflict. And as a bonus, they will also learn a lot. They will become wiser people.

This little proverb teaches us a major life lesson that can strengthen all our relationships: *The willingness to set aside our pride and listen to the viewpoints of others is essential to peace; and in the process of doing so, we will become a wiser person.* We will become the kind of counselor to whom others come for wise guidance.

How many of our relationship disasters could be avoided if we would all learn this simple lesson? When faced with a looming conflict, our first impulse should be to assume that we're missing something on our end, and start asking questions with a view to understanding the perspective of others. "Let every man be swift to hear, slow to speak, slow to wrath" (Jas. 1:19).

This simple strategy, so easy to articulate but hard to execute, would go far in defusing tensions and healing strained relationships. Maybe would should try it sometime.

Living Life the Hard Way

Much of the misery that plagues our race is the result of poor decisions that people make. The solution is simple, but not easy to implement.

Good understanding gains favor, but the way of the unfaithful is hard (Prov. 13:15).

The goal of every human life is happiness. But few people ever find that happiness. Many culprits get blamed for that failure, but in most cases the root problem is *sin*. We violate God's law, and pay the price for our decision. The irony here is that we ignore God's way because it's too much trouble, but the "easy" path we choose ends up costing us much more. Whether we realize it or not, we have chosen to live life the hard way.

Sin is the ultimate con artist. It offers glittering promises of pleasure, but only after we take the bait do we realize we've been deceived. There may be an initial spasm of excitement, but the fun is only temporary. The pleasure is soon replaced with pain, as the real harvest comes in: health problems, broken relationships, financial ruin, emotional trauma. In the end, we learn to our everlasting regret that we chose poorly. The way of the unfaithful is, in fact, quite hard.

Even after we realize we have made a mistake, we often compound the problem by trying to dodge the consequences of our error. Some folks, for example, will try to mask the first sin with other sins (consider King David's clumsy attempts to cover his sin with Bathsheba). Others look to science or legal maneuvering to lessen sin's impact (think of the gay lobby's efforts to legitimize their immoral lifestyle). Others simply redefine the sin as something other than sin, thereby perpetuating the notion that there is really no problem (alcoholism, gossip, pride). Ultimately, none of these denial strategies will accomplish what the sinner is looking for. In fact, in many cases, these strategies only make matters worse. Satan's noose will be drawn tighter.

The best way to avoid the consequences of sin should be obvious: Quit sinning! Notice in our text that "the way of the unfaithful" is contrasted with "good understanding." The first step in living right is to develop a healthy understanding of how God wants us to live. This is not a matter of merely memorizing Scripture. Rather, it is opening our eyes to the cause-and-effect principles that govern this world in which we live. Bible study is a good start; but also study the mistakes and successes of others. Seek to understand the unyielding connections between choices and outcomes, and live so as to achieve the best outcomes, rather than being guided by the whims of the moment. Of course, adopting this approach to life requires a fundamental shift in thinking, a mindset that is difficult to implement consistently.

Admittedly, in some cases the consequences of sin cannot be removed. Some sins in our past leave scars that will never go away, and we'll have to live with them the rest of our lives. But at least we can stop adding to the pain, and perhaps even lessen it.

Of course, the best course of action is to not sin in the first place. Resolve at an early age to serve God with all your heart, mind, and body, and learn the self-discipline necessary to make that commitment stick. It will require some sacrifices, and there will likely still be some rough patches along the way. But in the end you will find the happiness you seek.

The Bible and Economic Inequality

The Bible is not a textbook on economics, but it addresses the issues that play a role in economic inequality. The full picture may surprise us.

Evil pursues sinners, but to the righteous, good shall be repaid. . . . Much food is in the fallow ground of the poor, and for lack of justice there is waste (Prov. 13:21, 23).

These two verses in the book of Proverbs are separated by only one verse, yet their respective messages seem to contradict each other, offering competing explanations for economic inequality in society. One verse argues that prosperity is the reward of righteous living: Work hard, be thrifty, exercise self-discipline, treat others with integrity, and you will prosper. The second verse bemoans the fact that personal effort can be negated by injustice; that is, the strong enrich themselves at the expense of the weak ("swept away through injustice" ESV). It doesn't matter how hard you work, the deck is stacked and in the end it is the ruthless who will win.

So which of these two versions of economic reality is valid?

Our society is currently being torn apart by proponents of these two positions. Conservatives insist that socio-economic distress is the largely the result of a widespread failure of personal responsibility. People in increasing numbers are too lazy to get a job, so they mooch off the rest of society. In this view, the role of government should be to incentivize people to get to work. Liberals, on the other hand, argue that inequality is the result of built-in biases that rig the system against the disadvantaged, leaving them vulnerable to poverty and its evils. The role of government in this view is to eliminate the unjust social structures that serve as barriers to the little guy.

These two approaches to economic theory and policy are so incompatible, it seems there's no way they could ever be reconciled—except that they both find a home in the Bible, almost right next to each other. So not only is it possible to reconcile them, it is in society's best interest to figure out how to do it.

The Bible clearly advocates *personal responsibility*, diligence, hard work, and thrift. Generally speaking, those who adopt such a personal regimen will do better in life.

But the Bible just as clearly argues that this world is crooked, and sometimes good people get burned, despite their efforts to do right. *Justice for those who are oppressed*, therefore, is one of the identifying marks of a godly society.

The Biblical model, in other words, dismisses both of our modern perspectives as too simplistic and naive. The *conservative* approach that insists everyone make their own way in life fails the compassion test, abandoning some good people to an undeserved fate. But the *liberal* approach that tries to artificially eliminate all unequal outcomes squashes individual motivation for success, and rewards sloth.

A more nuanced approach can be found in the central theme of the gospel: salvation by grace through faith (Eph. 2:8). God has made accessible to us, at great cost to Himself, an undeserved gift (a very liberal idea). But that gift is based on the condition that we sacrifice everything for Him, starting with our heart (a very conservative idea).

This spiritual calculus not only defines our relationship with God, it also governs our relationship with others: Because of what God has done for us, we gratefully do the best we can with what we have—and that includes being generous with those who are suffering. The two concepts reinforce, rather than contradict, each other.

Lord, give us the wisdom to practice both.

Know Thyself

In our pursuit of knowledge in a world of exhausting complexity, the greatest challenge of all is to better understand ourselves.

The wisdom of the prudent is to understand his way, but the folly of fools is deceit (Prov. 14:8).

ಞ

At Delphi in ancient Greece, there stood a temple dedicated to Apollo. Carved over the entrance to this temple were two great principles of life: "Know thyself" and "Nothing in excess." We are concerned here with the first of these wise sayings. What the Greeks learned by experience, the Bible teaches by revelation: An individual cannot successfully deal with life and its problems if he does not first understand himself.

Our lives are spent in the pursuit of knowledge. Whether we are probing the deep mysteries of the universe or mastering the latest video game, we humans are hard-wired to learn. But of all the subjects we could try to comprehend, the most difficult is ourselves.

Let's start with the premise that our choices influence our interactions with the world around us, especially our interactions with other people. Stated another way, whether we succeed or fail in life is largely determined by how we think and how we behave. So success in life should be a simple matter of making the right choices and following through on those choices.

But reality is not that simple. Every human is a complex bundle of appetites, loyalties, beliefs, and desires. These motives often compete against each other for dominance in our lives. Knowing how all these factors interact with or against each other to produce a single pattern of behavior is the real challenge of life.

How many times have you done or said something foolish, and later chastised yourself with, "Why did I do that?" What you could see so plainly after the fact, was not so obvious in the passion of the moment. This complexity of human behavior led Jeremiah to observe, "The heart is deceitful above all things, and desperately wicked; who can know it?" (Jer. 17:9).

Understanding oneself may be difficult, but that does not release us from the obligation to try. Paul urges us to "examine yourselves as to whether you are in the faith. Test yourselves" (2 Cor. 13:5). God has given us an exhaustive diagnostic manual, the Bible, to help us perform this self-examination. The person who dedicates himself to studying this source of wisdom, and constantly monitors his own behavior and motives with a critical eye, will go a long way towards figuring himself out. He will become a better man, because he understands the passions that drive him, and makes progress in learning how to control them. When he makes a mistake, he deals with it and learns from the experience. His influence with others will expand, because having trained his heart to be honest with himself, he will also be honest with others.

The man is a fool who makes little effort to know himself. He may have fun for awhile, but life will become increasingly bitter for him. He stumbles blindly along, doing whatever feels good at the moment, trying to dodge responsibility for his errors, even as he repeats them. Such a man is only deceiving himself.

"Know thyself" is not an easy duty. But a lifetime of such self-examination will produce the mature, disciplined, unselfish character that is the goal of every Christian.

Sin Ain't Funny

Our society's dismissive mockery of the concept of sin has only intensified its destructive power. We must see it for the serious threat it is.

Fools mock at sin, but among the upright there is favor" (Prov. 14:9).

ఞ

The Bible portrays sin as the chief culprit in robbing humanity of happiness. Sin drove Adam and Eve out of the garden of Eden in the beginning, and it continues to reap misery among their descendants today. War, crime, divorce, drug abuse, drunkenness, poverty, disease, personal feuds—most of these ugly troubles can be traced back to human transgression. Clearly, sin is not a joking matter.

So why do some people treat it like a joke? Comedians get their biggest laughs mimicking drunks. Television shows and movies portray defiance of authority—parental, civil, or moral—as occasions of humor. The word "sin" is not even used by people today, except mockingly, because they are too sophisticated for such an old-fashioned idea.

Predictably, this light-hearted view of sin has resulted in a tacit acceptance of sin. One who laughs at sin will eventually reach the point where "to do evil is like sport" (Prov. 10:23).

Certainly there is a legitimate place for humor, even in dealing with sin. Humorous illustrations can sometimes teach sobering lessons on the ugliness of sin. But that's a far cry from the flippant attitude toward sin in general that weakens our opposition to it. One who sees sin as little more than a punch line is either woefully ignorant of sin's consequences, or callously indifferent.

In contrast to the moral insensitivity of the fool, Solomon describes the upright man as one having "favor," or goodness, holiness, purity. Derek Kidner summarizes the message thusly: "The whole proverb contrasts the unconcern of fools for the damage they do, Godward and manward, with the care of the upright to preserve good will" (*Proverbs: An Introduction and Commentary*, 1964). Unlike the fool, the upright man respects sin's destructive power. He not only doesn't laugh at sin, he despises it (Psa. 119:104; Jude 23). He seeks to offset sin's influence by promoting godliness in himself and others. His old-fashioned ways may attract a few chuckles, but he doesn't mind; he knows that his joy is deeper and more satisfying.

Sin is serious business. Why must we wait until we are victims of sin to realize that? It's for sure we won't laugh then.

A Nation in Decline

The rise and fall of nations is not the result of random luck, but of a predictable process of social development among its population.

Righteousness exalts a nation, but sin is a reproach to any people (Prov. 14:34).

The concept of "righteousness" and "sin" as representing opposite ends of a universal moral spectrum is now considered a relic from a more superstitious age. Truth is no longer an objective standard to be sought and followed, but a personal reality to be constructed as we see fit. Consequently, there is no righteousness to pursue nor sin to avoid. Everyone is free to follow the impulses of his own heart.

But while we may be free to choose our own path in life, we do not have the option of dictating the outcome of our choices. Whether we like it or not, behaviors have consequences. There are some behaviors that, by their very nature, tend to reward their owner with good health, prosperity, and the respect of peers. There are other behaviors that are more likely to result in misery and broken relationships. There is nothing arbitrary or oppressive in these cause-effect relationships. That's just the way human nature and the world operate, whether or not we choose to recognize it. People may scoff at Solomon's use of the terms "righteousness" and "sin" to describe this reality, but it's a truth that cannot be dismissed.

Applied on a larger scale, this principle also explains the rise and fall of nations. The strength of a nation is not to be found in its laws, its military, its economy, its natural resources, its system of government, judicial system, civic institutions, or any other attribute by which historians usually measure greatness. To be sure, all these elements have an impact on a nation's quality of life and its standing among its neighbors; but they are only symptoms of another, deeper measure of national strength: *the character of its people.*

A nation's strength, in other words, is the cumulative effect of millions of personal decisions made by its citizens every day of their individual lives. Are they honest and fair with each other? Do they respect each other's possessions and reputations? Are they motivated by selfish impulses or by more altruistic ideals? Do they honor or dishonor the institutions of marriage and family? A nation can tolerate a fringe element of non-conformists in these areas and remain strong. But if deviant behavior becomes the norm, a social rot sets in that gradually undermines the framework of a stable society. The result, as history shows with unmistakable regularity, is national decline and fall.

How can this process of national decline be reversed? Political elections have minimal effect on the cultural conditions among the population. Media campaigns to raise awareness of issues and educate the public can make a big splash, but rarely effect long-lasting change. These "solutions" are weak and temporary.

No, a nation's character is changed by changing the character of its people, one person at a time. That's the role of the gospel; that's the mission of God's people (Matt. 5:13-16). Our focus must be on reaching "every man" with the truth that can change his life (Col. 1:28), through a slow process of teaching and modeling that truth. It's not a glamorous process, and can be painful at times, but it's the only path to national righteousness.

And God expects His people to be busy in that mission.

A Soft Answer

Words carefully spoken can have a powerful influence on others. Learning how to speak with calm composure, therefore, is a critical life skill.

A soft answer turns away wrath, but a harsh word stirs up anger (Prov. 15:1).

He who has knowledge spares his words, and a man of understanding is of a calm spirit (Prov. 17:27).

By long forbearance a ruler is persuaded, and a gentle tongue breaks a bone (Prov. 25:15).

Let your speech always be with grace, seasoned with salt, that you may know how you ought to answer each one (Col. 4:6).

༺☙

James says that the fellow who can control his tongue is a perfect man, "able also to bridle the whole body" (Jas. 3:2). Perhaps that is why so many of the Proverbs deal with the wise use of the tongue. If we could learn how to say just the right words at just the right time in just the right way, everything else in life would be relatively easy.

Of course, controlling our tongues is *not* easy, especially when we are under pressure. Our first impulse is usually to blurt out whatever is on our mind, especially if we're dealing with frustration or anger. Too late do we realize that such passionate outbursts are like pouring gasoline on a fire. They serve only to make everyone else just as frustrated and angry as we are; the problem becomes worse, not better.

The wise man is one who restrains his passion and speaks with prudence. He understands the potential impact of his words on those who hear them, so his words are few and well-chosen. He speaks not merely to express himself, but to persuade others. His mind is always three steps ahead of his tongue, measuring the impact of every word on his audience. He wields language not as a weapon, but with the precision and finesse of a surgeon's scalpel.

This kind of self-disciplined speech is far more powerful than the verbal outbursts that so often characterize our exchanges with others. It has a calming effect on everyone, and melts the icy barriers that hinder communication. More importantly, it wins the respect of others. If a person displays such good judgment in his speech, he is likely to exercise good judgment in every other aspect of his life also. Indeed, even a ruler can be persuaded by a man who knows how to speak with discernment. That's why good communication skills are considered to be the most important trait of those who are in a position of influencing and leading others.

How do we train ourselves to speak with grace? There are several strategies for reaching this goal.

A steady diet of *Bible study* is a good place to start. A mind that is trained by divine wisdom possesses a humility that knows its limits. It will not be quick to express its opinion, nor easily swept away by emotion.

We can pick up some good pointers by *observing others* who remain calm under pressure, people who have a knack for choosing their words well in difficult circumstances. Listen closely to *what* they say and *how* they say it; analyze their words, and notice the impact on others. We can learn much from watching those who have mastered this skill.

But the biggest improvements will come only by *experience*, as we gradually develop the ability to "read" others and evaluate the impact of our words—and learn from our mistakes.

The product of utilizing these strategies will be a person who speaks judiciously—and is respected for it.

Violent Men, Nagging Women

How spouses deal with marital conflict is heavily influenced by gender differences. A wise couple realizes that fact, and responds accordingly.

A wrathful man stirs up strife, but he who is slow to anger allays contention (Prov. 15:18).

Better to dwell in a corner of a housetop, than in a house shared with a contentious woman (Prov. 21:9).

Among the many innate differences between men and women is their unique ways of dealing with anger. Men, with their higher testosterone levels, are more likely to resort to *physical* aggression. What women lack in strength they make up for in *verbal* skills; they are more prone to use words as weapons. While it is true that some men are very good at using cutting language, and some women can swing a rolling pen when pushed to the wall, the toxic combination of violent men and nagging women explains much of the marital strife that is destroying marriages and wrecking our culture.

In recent years, our society has turned the spotlight on the problem of violent men—and it should. There is *never* a justifiable reason for a man to physically abuse his wife, and it is appropriate that this kind of violence be criminalized.

However, the problem of nagging wives is not getting nearly enough attention. There are plenty of men who can testify to the emotional damage inflicted by wives who use their tongues as weapons. Some wives are experts at badgering, scolding, berating, belittling, and tormenting their husbands over every imperfection.

Sadly, these two behaviors usually reinforce each other. Men respond to nagging with physical threats, and women respond to mistreatment by lecturing. The result is a giant blowup that usually ends up in a divorce court—or jail.

The Bible has something to say to both parties about this phenomenon.

First, husbands and wives both must recognize that they are equally imperfect human beings who are prone to make mistakes. If I marry someone with the expectation that he or she will somehow "complete" me, I am setting up both of us for a major disappointment. My spouse will be no more perfect than I am, and I cannot expect forbearance for my shortcomings if I am not willing to extend forbearance first.

It follows, therefore, that *patience* is the name of the game if a couple is serious about making their marriage work—and patience starts with *me*, regardless of what my spouse does. When frictions arise in their relationship, husbands must get their physical aggression under tight control, and wives must put a leash on their tongues. Nothing will be gained by treating each other as enemies to be defeated.

In contrast to the destructive behaviors addressed in these two proverbs, the husband and wife of Proverbs 31 represent the ideal marriage climate. Here is a woman who honors her husband, rather than nagging him for his faults (v. 11-12). Her husband praises her hard work, rather than turning a spotlight on her imperfections (v. 28-29). With these matching behaviors supporting rather than tearing down each other, this is a couple who are an inspiration to their kids and a stabilizing influence in their community.

Best of all, they are companions who can spend the rest of their lives together as best friends.

The Simple Life

Cramming our lives with activities can be exciting, but it's also exhausting. There is a quieter, more satisfying joy available for those who want it.

Better to be of a humble spirit with the lowly, than to divide the spoil with the proud (Prov. 16:19).

The humble also shall increase their joy in the LORD, and the poor among men shall rejoice in the Holy One of Israel (Isa. 29:19).

Humility and pride manifest themselves not only in attitudes, but also in lifestyles. How we live our lives matters on multiple levels, but especially to our own peace of mind.

One reason life is so hard for many of us is all the obligations, activities, and pursuits that stretch our sanity to the breaking point. Everything we're involved in may be perfectly ethical and legal; but it's the *volume* and *scope* of our interests that undermine our mental health. We stretch ourselves so thin that we simply can't manage it all, yet we will kill ourselves trying.

In Biblical terms, the "humble" among humanity are those whose ambitions are modest, not because they are lazy or indifferent, but because they prefer the tranquility of the simple life. They are not necessarily poor, either. Whatever their chosen field of expertise, they are content to be good at that, and let the rest of the world pass them by. They limit their involvement in the myriad distractions this world offers in order to keep their lives uncomplicated and manageable.

It's a trade-off they're willing to accept, because of the serenity it purchases for them.

The simple life is not a dull life. The bounty of the humble is found in their "joy in the Lord." Because their treasures are of a more ethereal nature, their happiness cannot be snatched away by the uncertain tempests of life. A special kind of contentment grows from that mindset, an equanimity that the proud man cannot know in his mad pursuit of more and greater spoils.

As God's people, we must learn to focus our attention on what is truly important, and trim out the extraneous stuff that multiplies the worry and stress in our lives. Scale back on the hobbies and pastimes. Adopt more modest career ambitions. Volunteer only for those causes that provide lasting value. Say "no" to some of the kids' extracurricular involvements. The resulting lifestyle may be unadorned, even sparse; but it is more likely to be happy and satisfying.

If, of course, that's what we're looking for.

If It Seems Right . . . Look Closer

Humans have a bad habit of making important decisions based on flimsy evidence. We must learn to give God a greater voice in the process.

There is a way that seems right to a man, but its end is the way of death (Prov. 16:25).

୨୬

When Eve tasted the forbidden fruit, she was acting on an impulse that seemed to hit all the right buttons. Wasn't the fruit good for food? Pleasant to look upon? Desirable to make one wise? Why, the "facts" were so obvious! Surely there could be nothing wrong with it. Unfortunately, her sure hunch proved false, and the world has been suffering the consequences of that deception ever since.

It is easy for us to judge Eve harshly for her error, until we remember that we are her descendants, subject to the same impulse that undid her. If the history of the human race could be summarized in one word, it would be man's embarrassing vulnerability to *self-deception*. Ignoring every lesson of history and divine revelation, relying instead on emotions (usually fickle) or reasoning (often faulty), people create their own definition of "right" and make their decisions accordingly. Sexual immorality, lying, stealing, acts of vengeance, even murder—all these and other evils are routinely defended as legitimate according to a standard of ethics that seems right in the moment. Like Eve, people don't realize their mistake until the damage is done.

This quirk of human nature is not the sole possession of profligates and atheists. Even religious people can deceive themselves into accepting a false value system. King Saul "felt compelled" to bend the rules and offer a sacrifice before battle, because the circumstances seemed to warrant it (1 Sam. 13:8-14). His namesake, Saul of Tarsus, "thought within himself" that he had to persecute Christians as a matter of sacred duty (Ac. 26:5-11). Jesus warned that on the day of judgment He will reject many who sincerely believed they were right (Matt. 7:21-23). Confusing our feelings with God's will is a constant danger, and we must always be careful to distinguish between the two.

How do we accomplish this? David provides the answer: "I love Your commandments more than gold, yes, than fine gold! Therefore all Your precepts concerning all things I consider to be right" (Psa. 119:127-128). The heart that is trained to surrender completely to the higher authority of God's word is less likely to be swayed by the capricious appeal of what "seems" right. As we study, meditate, and learn God's word, our self-will becomes lost in the will of God, and what "seems right" will be that which *is* right.

Why Good Parenting Matters

God designed the family to function according to a well-defined pattern. The practical benefits of that pattern are significant, if we will honor it.

Grandchildren are the crown of old men, and the glory of sons is their fathers (Prov. 17:6).

This proverb looks at the rewards of a healthy family across three generations, but employs a curious strategy to make its point. By carefully unpacking it, we can learn an important lesson about the role of parents in a civilization.

This verse first addresses the joy of *grandparenthood*. Considering everything that a father and mother must go through in raising their kids, it's no wonder that both of them usually have gray hair by the time the kids leave home. (One battle-scarred mother hung this plaque on her kitchen wall: "Insanity is inherited; you get it from your kids.") But after the last chick spreads her young wings and leaves the nest, Mom and Dad have time to reflect back on the laughter, the tears, the conflicts, and the triumphs. Gradually, the realization grows that somehow, it was all worth it. When the little grands finally come along, Grandma and Grandpa are conditioned to see their newest offspring as a vindication of their life's work, the "crowning" achievement of all those years of toil and trouble. (And the pride shows. I recently saw a pair of coffee mugs in a store. One was inscribed, "If Mom says No, ask Grandma." The other read, "If Grandma says No, ask Grandpa." Who's going to tell a king how to wear his crown?)

The second half of the proverb starts from the opposite direction, bottom up, and looks at the family from the perspective of *the kids,* particularly how the kids relate to their parents, especially their father. There's much about life that children may not know, but there is one thing that they have absolutely no doubt about: "My Dad is the greatest!" Dad can fix a bicycle, play football, and answer almost any question. He can administer firm discipline when necessary, then buy an ice cream cone to show there are no hard feelings. This fondness for Dad may evolve and mature as a child grows older, but it will never go away. A father will always be the "glory" of his kids, someone to look up to and admire. A child who starts out life with a father to respect has a good chance of being a winner.

Having highlighted the oldest and youngest parties in this family dynamic, we must question why the verse does not provide the perspective of the middle party in the arrangement: *the father*, representing the husband/wife team who is responsible for raising the little ones. At first glance this scant treatment seems odd; aren't the parents the ones bearing the greatest responsibility in this arrangement? They are indeed—*and that's the key to understanding the verse.* This proverb fairly screams at parents (especially fathers) to take seriously their responsibility of raising their kids, for in doing so they will not only earn the respect of their kids ("glory"), but also set themselves up for pleasant twilight years with their grandchildren ("crown").

In a dystopian society plagued by dysfunctional families and feral kids, the intergenerational formula laid out in this little proverb lays out how the family is supposed to work. We would all do well to honor it.

The Basis of Friendship

A friendship can arise from the most unlikely connections. But there is one thing that is absolutely essential in making it possible.

A friend loves at all times, and a brother is born for adversity (Prov. 17:17).

There is a friend who sticks closer than a brother (Prov. 18:24).

What makes two people "friends"?

Some define a friend as someone with whom we share the same interests, values, or beliefs. Others say a friend is someone in whom we can confide intimate information about ourselves, without risking embarrassment.

These characteristics of friendship are generally valid, but they do not explain the real basis of friendship. The foundation of friendship is, quite simply, *shared experiences*. The more activities two people share together, the more they become friends.

Look at the friendships described in the Bible. David lamented the betrayal of a close friend, someone with whom he frequently talked and went to the temple (Psa. 55:13-14). Jesus called His apostles His friends, because of all time He had spent with them over their years together (Jn. 15:15). Paul and Timothy became closer than a father and son as a result of their years of work and travel together.

Soldiers become close friends because of the life-and-death experiences they have shared with each other on the battlefield—and this despite the very different backgrounds they come from.

Look at your own circle of friends. The one thing you have in common with them—and in many cases, the *only* thing—is that they all share some kind of life experiences with you. Whether work, church, or recreation, your friends are those people with whom you spend time talking, laughing, working, arguing, crying, building, playing, traveling, or just hanging out. Whatever else you may or may not have in common, life has somehow thrown you together, and the time you spend together doing things has allowed a relationship to develop that we call "friendship."

This principle also works in the opposite direction. Think of the people who were your friends in the past, but are such no longer. Whatever may have contributed to the parting, whether there was some disagreement or you just drifted apart, one thing is certain: You no longer share experiences with one another. Friendship cannot survive in the absence of shared experiences.

This principle has implications in maintaining our social well-being. If we want to have friends in this life, we must open ourselves up to sharing experiences with others. And to maintain those friendships, we must *continue* to share experiences. The experiences may evolve over time, but the nature of the experiences is less important than the fact that we *have* them. Otherwise, the friendships wither and die.

This is especially important for married couples. My spouse should be my best friend; but even that friendship cannot survive the lack of shared experiences. Husbands and wives who share few common interests, spend a lot of time apart, and do not actively feed their friendship through talking and doing things together, run a risk of losing their marriage.

Sharing experiences with others requires effort. We must sacrifice some of our own interests to align with the interests of others. But the result is a unique collection of people—our friends—who will truly enrich our lives.

To Be a Parent

> Parenthood is not for the faint of heart. The price we pay for being parents is high—but the rewards are even higher, if we commit to doing it well.

A foolish son is a grief to his father, and bitterness to her who bore him (Prov. 17:25).

Children's children are the crown of old men, and the glory of children is their father (Prov. 17:6).

◈

Several years ago, the CEO of the company I worked for took questions from employees in an all-hands meeting. Someone asked him a rather odd question: "What keeps you awake at night?" Without hesitation he responded, "My teenage son." The exchange drew nervous laughs from the audience, because everyone could instantly relate to his frustration as a parent.

Raising children is hard! When we choose to have children, we are giving up twenty years (or more) of our life to serve as a taxi driver, counselor, drill sergeant, cook, maid, cheerleader, tutor, coach, teacher, nurse, zookeeper, and psychiatrist. Whether we like it or not, we will often be forced to serve as a prosecuting attorney, judge, jury, and jailer (or executioner) all at once.

At the same time, we will have to be our child's number one advocate, an activist who fights to protect our kid from the evil influences of the world that would seek to destroy him or her. A thousand tough decisions will be thrust upon us, requiring the wisdom of Solomon to sort out. Sometimes we'll get it right, sometimes we won't.

That's not all. When we become a parent, we are taking on a life of sleepless nights, broken hearts, tears, disappointments, and exasperation. We are giving up date nights to become 24/7 babysitters. There's nothing glamorous about raising kids.

Oh, one more thing: For all our trouble, we will be judged by our offspring as incompetent boobs, and they will never pass up an opportunity to remind us of it.

Growing numbers of young adults in our society are looking at these challenges and deciding it's not worth it to have kids. Why bother with all that grief, when I can do whatever I want, without the hassles of having children around to get in my way of having a good time?

There are two reasons why having kids is worth all the headaches. First, having children in our lives fulfills our most basic purpose in life. Humans were put here by God to replenish the earth, and when we sacrifice a significant portion of our life to that task, we are doing what we were designed to do. There is something intensely satisfying about that.

Second, for all the hassles involved, there is also a deep sense of personal joy in raising children. We may not achieve greatness in business or politics, but if we do a decent job of guiding happy, well-adjusted kids into adulthood, we will have accomplished something truly great with our life. When our time comes to depart this earth, we can do so with the knowledge that a little piece of ourselves lives on in our kids.

These positives, of course, are predicated on the assumption that we take parenting seriously. We should seek the counsel of older parents, read books, and share our frustrations with other parents. We have one chance to do it right, so we should pour everything have into that endeavor.

One final thought. If we manage to survive parenthood and are blessed to see our children have children of their own, we will experience the joy of spending time with our grandchildren, an adventure that involves all the joys of parenting with few of the headaches. When that day arrives, we'll know it was worth it!

A Warning to Introverts

The desire to be alone is a perfectly normal personality trait. But introverts must be careful not to let this inclination dominate their existence.

A man who isolates himself seeks his own desire; he rages against all wise judgment (Prov. 18:1).

And the LORD God said, "It is not good that man should be alone" (Gen. 2:18).

I must begin this article with a disclaimer: I am an introvert myself. So this article is not a criticism from someone who just doesn't understand the world of the shy person. Believe me, I know all about it (and I'm a preacher, someone who makes his living dealing with people. How does that work? It's a long story . . .). Let's just say that this proverb has played an important role in my life, helping me to understand and deal with the challenge of the loner life.

Why are some people introverted? Genetics is the major factor, no doubt; some people are just naturally quiet and prefer to be by themselves. Extroverts don't understand that, but hey, this goes both directions; the introvert doesn't understand the extrovert's constant craving for socialization. These personality quirks are just part of the unique package with which God made each one of us. Neither one is right or wrong. Each type comes with its own strengths and risks.

This proverb is addressing specifically the danger to the introvert. To better understand what Solomon is saying, consider how other translations have rendered this verse: "Unfriendly people are selfish" (NCV). "Loners who care only for themselves spit on the common good." (Message). "Unfriendly people look out for themselves; they bicker with sensible people" (CEV). "The unsociable man is out to get what he wants for himself" (Beck).

This is brutal language expressing a message that is hard for introverts to swallow: Choosing to isolate ourselves from others is more than just a personality trait—it is a character flaw. And like most character flaws it is reinforced by poor decisions we make in trying to deal with it.

An introvert's reclusive lifestyle is a deliberate choice he makes, not a curse that fate somehow thrusts upon him. By allowing his natural disposition to dominate his behavior, he is robbing himself of the benefits of associating with others.

Those benefits are healthy and many. Being around others allows us to benefit from the wisdom they have learned in their own journeys. The different outlooks and ideas we are exposed to as we forge friendships with others helps us to grow. Facing difficult decisions is easier when we have close friends with whom we can discuss the options before us. God designed us to be communal creatures, and we only harm ourselves when we allow the frustrations of relationship-building to prevent us from getting close to others.

By nature, introverts need a lot of personal quiet time to decompress and recharge. There's nothing wrong with that. But at the same time, introverts must understand that, like it or not, God made us to interact with others; we really do need each other. Whatever the complexities involved in forming and maintaining relationships, those connections are essential to our mental and physical well-being. When an introvert allows his propensity for solitude to define every aspect of his life, he is yielding to his own version of humanity's oldest sin: *selfishness*.

So fellow introverts, listen up: It will not be easy, but force yourself to come out of your shell. You'll be a better and happier person for it in the end.

A Strong Tower

No matter how many layers of protection we try to build around ourselves, in the end we will lose everything. Where, then, can we find security?

The name of the LORD is a strong tower; the righteous run to it and are safe. The rich man's wealth is his strong city, and like a high wall in his own esteem (Prov. 18:10-11).

In ancient times, civilization was a thin veneer of peace pasted over an ugly and violent life. Marauding armies and bands of brigands roamed the countryside looking for plunder and rapine. Death lurked behind every corner.

In those days, security was everything. Every city had a strong wall to provide protection for its citizens and nearby residents. When threatened with attack, everyone fled inside the walls and shut the gates until the danger passed. In smaller villages that could not afford a massive wall, a fortified central tower served the same purpose. When a threat loomed, run to the tower! Get inside the walls!

These walls and towers became a metaphor for any place of refuge. In this proverb, the rich man's wealth is said to be like a city wall, a source of protection that insulates him from the chaos of life with which others must deal. Today we do not rely on walls and towers, but on strong locks, elaborate electronic security systems, or a well-trained police force. Surrounded by these bulwarks, we are protected from all harm—or so we think.

But this proverb adds a sinister footnote: the rich man's security exists "in his own imagination" (NASB, ESV). It's an illusion that sooner or later will fail him. Political or economic collapse can wipe out his investments. Or someday death will come, when no amount of money can buy another breath of life. To what sanctuary will the rich man flee then?

Today, as our large cities descend into chaos and anarchy, we are learning afresh that even our more sophisticated forms of protection have their limitations. Life in this world is fraught with risk, no matter how many layers of security we try to build around ourselves. Absolute safety is an illusion built upon faulty assumptions.

The only strong tower that can withstand every vicissitude of life is "the name of the Lord." The author is not describing a magical incantation that wards off bad luck. "The name of the Lord" refers to the strength of His promises, the guarantee of a final deliverance that transcends death itself. We have this hope "as an anchor of the soul, both sure and steadfast, and which enters the Presence behind the veil" (Heb. 6:19). Let the world do its worst; the believer looks to God for final liberation beyond the reach of whatever travails he may encounter in this life.

The walls and towers of this realm are doomed to crumble, leaving us exposed. To what strong tower will *you* flee when life closes in?

The Power of the Human Spirit

The spirit within can either make us stronger, or kill us with despair. The difference lies in how we see our future.

The spirit of a man will sustain him in sickness, but who can bear a broken spirit? (Prov. 18:14).
Hope deferred makes the heart sick (Prov. 13:12).

⚘

Happiness in life is only indirectly influenced by the physical circumstances around us. Some people are blessed with freedom, good health, and prosperity, yet are incurably miserable. Others are afflicted with bondage, sickness, or poverty, but somehow always manage to maintain a cheerful disposition. The author attributes these contrasting moods to the condition of the *spirit* within each of us—not the immortal substance that survives death, but the emotional "mainspring" that propels us through life, and over which we have a large measure of control.

The apostle Paul had a spirit that sustained him through his misfortunes. Despite the disappointments and dangers that plagued his work, he kept pushing on to his goal, "perplexed, but not in despair" (2 Cor. 4:8). He had a can-do attitude, one which kept him joyful and enthusiastic, even when times were bad (Phil. 1:18; 4:4, 13). It is that same spirit that has enabled businessmen to bounce back from failure and achieve success. Doctors credit such a spirit with helping some very sick people experience remarkable recoveries. Indeed, the spirit within us can be a powerful ally.

When that spirit is broken, however, the prospect of success plummets. The patient weakens and dies; the businessman seeks refuge in drinking and loses everything; the Christian is overwhelmed with discouragement and gives up trying. During his years as an inmate in Nazi concentration camps, Jewish psychiatrist Victor Frankl witnessed again and again relatively healthy people who simply gave up and died, long before malnourishment had a chance to finish them off (*Man's Search for Meaning*, 1946). Something inside them collapsed, and they lost the will to live any longer.

What causes the spirits of people to break? The problem here is *the abandonment of hope*. When people give up believing in the possibility of success, they are mentally already defeated. For the child of God, however, the setbacks of this life are outweighed by the hope of eternal life in the hereafter, a hope that serves as "an anchor of the soul" (Heb. 6:19). That confident spirit keeps them optimistic in the worst of circumstances.

As long as we live in this world, misfortune will be our bread. But if we arm ourselves with a spirit of confidence and courage, grounded in the sure promises of God, misfortune cannot beat us. "Therefore we do not lost heart. . . . for our tight affliction, which is but for a moment, is working for us a far more exceeding and eternal weight of glory, while we do not look at the things which are seen, but at the things which are not seen" (2 Cor. 4:16-18).

Believe that, and your spirit can remain strong, whatever life throws at you.

Truth and Testimony

Claimants in disputes are rarely impartial in their testimonies. Those who are in the position of resolving disputes must judge accordingly.

The first to plead his case seems just, until another comes and examines him (Prov. 18:17).

Every man's way is right in his own eyes . . . (Prov. 21:2).

Late in King David's reign, his son Absalom led a rebellion against his father. The rebellion was so strong that David and his loyal followers were forced to retreat from Jerusalem. In the midst of the confusion, David received word that a close friend, Mephibosheth, had deserted him and was seeking to seize the throne. Without seeking any corroborating evidence, David promised the messenger, Ziba—Mephibosheth's servant—all the possessions of the traitor once the revolt was put down (2 Sam. 16:4).

The rebellion was eventually crushed, and David returned to his throne. Only then did he discover that the crippled Mephibosheth had been framed by his greedy servant and left to his fate. But the damage had been done; David had given his word to the slanderous servant. Mephibosheth showed his true character by not challenging the judgment; having his friend safely back was sufficient for him (2 Sam. 19:24-30).

There is a lesson in this incident for those who will see it: An innocent man was unjustly punished, and a scoundrel unfairly rewarded, because a king in his haste forgot the age-old principle that *there are two sides to every story.*

Ziba's testimony was an outright lie motivated by covetousness. Certainly there is plenty of that kind of dishonesty around. But the greater danger arises from parties who unconsciously twist the truth. An accuser may honestly believe that his case is a just one. Even though there is no intention of deceiving others, he may be deceiving himself. His testimony may omit information that he considers trivial or inconsequential. Or he may tweak borderline evidence—in his favor, of course. Such subtle differences between the truth and what the accuser *thinks* is the truth can adversely affect the judge's decision.

Realizing this, every system of jurisprudence that strives to be fair recognizes the right of the accused to face his accuser before the bar of justice. If the truth can be determined at all, it will be determined when both sides in a dispute have an opportunity to present their cases and cross-examine each other. This principle is not limited to judges and juries. A preacher or elder seeking to help a couple work through marriage problems, or a manager who must restore harmony among feuding employees, or a parent trying to settle a squabble among the kids—all of these must take care to examine both sides before they render judgment. (This principle also explains why gossip is condemned as such a destructive evil. It is nothing more than telling only one side of a story, with the victim having no opportunity to defend himself.)

David's hasty judgment hurt a friend and rewarded a scoundrel. We can avoid similar mistakes in our decisions, if we refuse to take sides in a conflict until we have had opportunity to examine all the facts.

A Good Wife

A couple's golden anniversary is an opportunity to reflect on the journey they've taken together—and perhaps inspire younger couples to persevere.

He who finds a wife finds a good thing, and obtains favor from the Lord (Prov. 18:22).

౿⊶⊷ಌ

Fifty years ago today*, two starry-eyed teenagers said, "I do," having no clue what they were signing up for. After half a century of laughter and tears, struggles and triumphs, and a whole lot of "I'm sorrys," we're finally getting this marriage thing sorted out.

The Lord has blessed us with four beautiful children, along with two others who, sadly, we were never privileged to know. Together with their good spouses, these kids have blessed us with seventeen grandchildren. To young people today who think marriage and family is too much of a hassle, we can only say: Yes, it's a *huge* hassle—and so worth it! The best things in life are not free.

Our paths have crossed those of so many others over these years. With some we have lost contact. Others remain close friends to this day. Others have passed on to their reward. All have left their marks on our lives, and for that we are grateful. Hopefully we have reciprocated that influence.

And the adventures we have experienced together! Camping trips with the kids (and camping in our basement for a week when an ice storm knocked out the power), all-day ziplining excursions in Colorado, a trip to Nuremberg, Germany, remodeling several houses, soccer coach/mom, PTA president, graduate school, and countless other escapades that, had we been told on our wedding day that they were in our future, we would have responded with, "You're kidding?!"

It hasn't all been fun. Melissa has had to patiently endure several inexplicable (and costly) career changes in her husband's life. I, in turn, have had to fish a car out of the pond, because someone (ahem) did not know to leave the stick shift in gear. We early on learned that it does no good to complain or lecture one another about these mistakes. Some things we just have to laugh off and try to do better next time. But always, always, *always* as a team, never as competitors.

If there is one thing that has made the road easier to navigate, it's been our shared faith. From the beginning, our common commitment to the Lord and His guidance has been the bedrock that brought stability to everything else in our lives. We're not perfect, but we stay close to Someone who is. That makes all the difference.

Thank you, dear, for fifty years of unconditional love. May we have many more!

* Published on May 21, 2021

Choosing a Mate

After choosing to follow Jesus, choosing a mate is the most consequential decision a person can make. How can we choose the right person?

He who finds a wife finds a good thing, and obtains favor from the Lord (Prov. 18:22).

೪೦೪

Solomon observed (and with over 700 wives, he was a qualified observer) that a good wife is a gift from the Lord. From the woman's point of view, the same could be said of finding a good husband. The trick, of course, is finding the "right" mate, and not getting stuck in a relationship you will regret. For some folks, getting married is like going to a restaurant. They order what they think they want, but when they see what the other fellow has, they wish they had ordered that. Of course, by that time, it's too late.

Choosing a good mate is a challenge, but it need not be a blind roll of the dice. Follow a couple of key principles, and you can find a mate with whom you can be happy.

The first and most obvious rule is, *look for someone who shares your goals and values.* What do you want out of life? What is really important to you? Which behaviors are acceptable to you, and which are strictly off-limits? There is no person in the world who will have a greater influence on your ability to achieve your goals and live your values than the person with whom you choose to spend the rest of your life. If that person does not share your goals and values, your life will be wasted fighting a battle of competing convictions.

This assumes, of course, that you *have* a core set of values and convictions. Can you articulate your philosophy of life? If not, then your decision will more likely be governed by raging hormones than by reasoned judgment. Which is another way of saying, you're not ready for marriage. So before you start sizing up others, first figure out yourself.

A second rule is more practical, but just as vital: *Look for someone who complements your strengths and weaknesses.* Compatible convictions and values do not require a perfect match in abilities and interests. Each one of us has our own unique set of abilities. Some are genetic predispositions; some are related to our personality; others are artifacts of our raising or training. None of us is the best at everything. That's where marriage comes in. The ideal marriage is one in which the wife complements, or supplies what is lacking in, the husband, and vice versa.

For example, do you have trouble managing your money? Then look for someone who is very careful with theirs. A failure to consider such a mundane matter can result in two spendthrifts struggling to make ends meet—a recipe for disaster. Do you insist that your house be neat and tidy, always clean? Then find someone who respects that sense of order and will help you maintain it, even if they're not too good at it themselves.

Finding the right mate is not impossible, but like any other worthwhile challenge in life, it takes time and study. The payoff is a truly happy marriage—a "favor from the Lord."

Kindness in Marriage

> The secret to a happy marriage is quite simple, and really no secret at all. The trick is training ourselves to practice it consistently.

What is desired in a man is kindness . . . (Prov. 19:22).

She opens her mouth with wisdom, and on her tongue is the law of kindness (Prov. 31:26).

Be kind to one another, tenderhearted, forgiving one another, just as God in Christ forgave you (Eph. 4:32).

If we were to take all the books that have been written on the subject of "how to have a happy marriage" and boil their wisdom down into a single word, what would that word be? Emily Esfahani Smith, in a recent article ("Masters of Love," *The Atlantic,* June 12, 2014), argues that the word "kindness" would be the winner.

Smith based her conclusion on the work of researchers at The Gottman Institute, who have been studying happy and unhappy marriages for decades. John Gottman and his colleagues developed a number of innovative techniques to gauge the likelihood of a couple staying happily married or splitting up. They discovered that partners in a close relationship often send out what Gottman calls "bids"—ordinary little comments designed to elicit a reaction from the spouse. The response of the spouse is the key. If the spouse tends to ignore the bid, or shrug it off with a cursory response—or worst of all, rejects it angrily—the relationship is not healthy. If the spouse responds to the bidder with a genuine interest in the comment, the relationship is likely in good shape.

Gottman explained that in positive relationships, partners "are scanning the social environment for things they can appreciate and say thank you for. They are building this culture of respect and appreciation very purposefully." In the negative relationships, partners "are scanning the social environment for partners' mistakes." Gottman claims that he can predict with up to 94 percent accuracy whether a couple will remain together and happy years later, simply by observing this "bidding" behavior.

The researchers are approaching this subject from a secular perspective, but what they have discovered is a reflection of an age-old principle rooted in Biblical psychology: *Healthy human relationships are built upon a foundation of kindness.* How we treat others, including how we react to their behavior, has enormous influence on the quality of our relationships. The more kindness we display in our conduct —genuine and sincere, not shallow and phony—the more likely we are to build bridges with those around us, bridges that allow us to connect constructively and navigate whatever conflicts might arise in those relationships. The less kindness we display, the more likely our relationships are to crumble. It's that simple.

Happy marriages are not a product of luck or some kind of magical chemistry between two people. It's the result of two people committing themselves to a life of kindness. It's not surprising that, as a bonus, couples who practice kindness toward each other also tend to have a strong network of positive relationships with other family and friends.

Kindness is a lubricant that makes everything in life run more smoothly. Maybe we should try it more often.

Quarreling Fools

Before we allow ourselves to get dragged into a controversy, we need to gauge the benefits of the outcome. Sometimes it's best to just walk away.

It is honorable for a man to stop striving, since any fool can start a quarrel (Prov. 20:3).

Many years ago, an older preacher took a position that was unpopular with some of his brethren. His critics attacked him viciously, impugning his motives and misrepresenting his views. To the surprise of his son, the preacher made no attempt to respond to the smear campaign. "Why not?" the young man wondered. "It's so unfair!" "I know, son," replied his dad with a smile, "but you can't win a puking contest with a buzzard." The preacher knew what he was talking about. His critics soon discredited themselves by their malicious behavior, while his own reputation remained as strong as ever.

It's true that you can't win a puking contest with a buzzard—but that won't keep a lot of us from trying. It's a sad fact of life that so many of the quarrels we get embroiled in are a senseless waste of emotions and words. Pride will not let a silly insult go unanswered, and once the battle is joined, pride will not let us back down until we have whipped our foe. But in too many cases, our "victory" is as worthless as beating a skunk in a square fight; we smell just as bad as our defeated enemy. Indeed, wisdom sometimes demands that we walk away from a fight rather than lose our honor.

Personal squabbles are bad enough, but it is even worse when fools begin scratching and clawing in the name of "contending for the faith." To be sure, false doctrine must not go unchallenged. But before we attack the doctrine, we should carefully consider the character of the teacher. Jesus was quick to refute the popular errors of His day, but He didn't waste His breath when He knew that His opponents wanted not to discuss truth, but to merely argue. Paul "disputed daily" with anyone who cared to join him, but he shook the dust from his feet and went elsewhere when it became apparent he was wasting his time. When we press a fight with false teachers who have clearly shown their dishonesty, we are "casting our pearls before swine," and that useless exercise will do nothing toward advancing our cause.

Christians should not hesitate to defend their faith in honorable controversy. But neither should they hesitate to maintain an honorable silence when dealing with fools.

Humility in Godliness

No matter what progress we make in our pursuit of holiness, we must never consider ourselves to have arrived. Sin is an ever-present reality.

Who can say, "I have cleansed my heart, I am pure from my sin"? (Prov. 20:9).

૭✲૭

That's easy. The Pharisees said it all the time (Lk. 18:9-12). The Lord reached a different verdict, of course, and exposed such a boast for what it really was: self-deceptive pride. What the Pharisees gained in striving for righteousness, they lost by glorying in it.

One of the things that made the heroes of the Bible so great was their own sense of unworthiness in the presence of God. Some examples:

- David: "I know my transgressions, and my sin is ever before me" (Psa. 51:3).
- Solomon: "There is not a righteous man on earth who continually does good and who never sins" (Eccl. 7:20).
- Elijah: "Now, O Lord, take my life, for I am not better than my fathers" (1 Kgs. 19:4).
- Isaiah: "Woe is me, for I am ruined! Because I am a man of unclean lips" (Isa. 6:5).
- Peter: "Depart from me, for I am a sinful man O Lord!" (Lk. 5:8).

In their generations, these men stood apart as the people of God, the salt of the earth, a glory to their Creator. Yet everyone of them, when looking back on their performances, could say little more than Paul, "Wretched man that I am!

Who will set me free from the body of this death?" (Rom. 7:24). Their strength lay not in themselves, but in the God who promised to help them, a God to whom they clung in self-deprecating faith. They were great men, but they would have been the last ones on earth to acknowledge it.

In their zeal for God, the Pharisees lost sight of this humility, and that oversight corrupted their godliness. The same danger confronts us in our own quest for holiness. Great strides can be made in conforming to the divine standard, but absolute perfection will never be reached (Phil. 3:12). We will sometimes consciously stumble into sin; we will also sin unknowingly, due to natural restrictions in knowledge (Psa. 19:12-13). A person who realizes this will never for a single moment consider himself as standing by his own effort, apart from the grace of God. He will carry a petition for mercy in his heart at all times, painfully aware of his imperfections even as he is striving to overcome them.

The person who smugly assures himself that his performance is "good enough" for God is deceiving himself (1 Jn. 1:8, 10). It is the one who cries out, "God be merciful to me a sinner!" who will go down to his house justified (Lk. 18:13-14).

Idle Promises

Before we make a promise, we need to consider what we're committing ourselves to. Walking back that promise later will damage our character.

It is a snare for a man to devote rashly something as holy, and afterward to reconsider his vows (Prov. 20:25).

This proverb is drawn from the ancient practice of making vows to the Lord for granting some request. Jacob, for example, vowed to give God a tenth of all his possessions, if He protected him on his journey (Gen. 28:20-22). Jephthah vowed to sacrifice to God the first thing that walked out his door, if He would give him victory over the Ammonites (Judg. 11:30-31). Such vows were considered to be binding covenants with God, and one who made such a vow was under solemn obligation to fulfill it. The Law of Moses commanded, "If a man vows a vow to the Lord, or swears an oath to bind himself by some agreement, he shall not break his word; he shall do according to all that proceeds out of his mouth" (Num. 30:2). Again, "That which has gone from your lips you shall keep and perform" (Deut. 23:21-23). Breaking a promise to God (or to anyone) was considered another form of lying.

Since the breaking of a vow was such a serious offense, it made good sense for a person to carefully consider what he was vowing. A vow spoken in haste, with little thought given to the fulfilling of it, could prove embarrassing later—or worse. Jephthah's rash vow, mentioned above, became a terrifying sword when he saw his own daughter walk out the door (Judg. 11:32-40). Jephthah's horrible dilemma—keeping his vow and losing his daughter, or breaking his vow and offending God—was of his own making. Had he been more careful in making his promise, he could have saved himself a lot of grief.

The making of such formal vows to God, of course, is not consistent with the New Testament and its emphasis on simple honesty in everything we say (see Matt. 5:33-37). But Solomon's warning still has relevance today. Any ordinary promise that we make to others—whether to God or man—becomes a test of our inner character. Are we true to our word, or are we not? If we carelessly toss out idle promises, having little intention of carrying them out, we endanger our reputation and our soul. Wisdom demands that we carefully consider our promise before we make it, giving attention to our ability and/or willingness to carry through. Once we commit ourselves, it is too late to start looking for loopholes. "It is better not to vow, than to vow and not pay" (Eccl. 5:5).

Generational Sins

Every stage of life presents its own unique temptations. We will never outgrow the need for self-reflection and improvement.

The glory of young men is their strength, and the splendor of old men is their gray head (Prov. 20:29).

This proverb highlights obvious physical characteristics that accompany the different stages of life (strength versus gray hair). But behind these common *physical* distinctions lie some *character* differences that are just as obvious. Some sins, for example, can be more readily associated with various stages of life through which we pass.

Some sins are more common among *younger people*. David pleaded with God, "Do not remember the sins of my youth" (Psa. 25:7). Paul admonished his young friend Timothy to "Flee also youthful lusts" (2 Tim. 2:22). The combination of high energy, strong hormones, and inexperience in young people creates a zest for life that can sometimes lead to poor decisions, particularly in matters relating to their fleshy appetites. Most people, as they enter middle age, carry with them a number of regrets about mistakes made in their younger days.

Middle-aged people have generally learned to regulate their base human impulses, but have encountered a new set of temptations to deal with. By the time many people reach mid-life, they have accumulated a lot of possessions and have higher incomes with which they can purchase even more. So at this stage of life, materialism becomes a more serious problem. This preoccupation with material things interferes with the search for spiritual meaning in life. That's why many middle-aged people tend to lose interest in religion or spirituality; they're too busy accumulating and enjoying all their worldly goods.

Elderly people encounter a class of temptations that were not a problem in their younger days. As people enter their later years, the impulsiveness of their youth is a dim memory, and their material goods are no longer as important as they once were. But now they must navigate a new set of traps. The bad habits of their younger days have now become deeply embedded behaviors and attitudes, highly resistant to change. And a lifetime of dealing with the injustices of life sometimes leaves them jaded. That's why some older people have a reputation of being stubborn and cynical.

Of course, these observations are generalizations that do not always hold true. All the sins described above can be found among people in any age group. And every age group features a good many people who rise above their peers and buck the prevailing trends. Many young people, for example, are pillars of virtue and morality; many middle-aged people do an excellent job of balancing the spiritual and material interests in their lives; and nothing is more delightful than dealing with elderly people who have managed to keep a youthful outlook on life.

Nevertheless, these exceptions do not negate the fact that every stage of life comes with its own set of temptations. Our challenge, at whatever stage we find ourselves, is to maintain a strong commitment to personal growth based on the standard God has given us in His word.

The Joy of Doing Justice

> Going out of our way to help others can be a source of delight, but only if we have prepared our heart to see it as a virtue.

It is a joy for the just to do justice, but destruction will come to the workers of iniquity" (Prov. 21:15).

Some translations render this verse in a manner that suggests a passive experiencing of justice ("When justice is done, it brings joy to the righteous but terror to evildoers," NIV). But other scholars argue that this verse is not describing what individuals feel when justice is done *to* them, but when justice is done *by* them. Delitzsch summarizes the thought in this manner: "Right-doing is to the righteous a pleasure; and for those who have evil, and are devoid of moral worth, and thus simply immoral as to the aim and sphere of their conduct, right-doing is something which alarms them: When they act in conformity with what is right, they do so after an external impulse only against their will, as if it were death to them" (*Commentary on the Old Testament, Vol. VI*). In other words, the righteous get a genuine satisfaction out of doing the right thing. The wicked, when compelled by circumstances to do the right thing, are distressed; such behavior is alien to them, and they don't know how to deal with it.

This principle underscores a fundamental difference between how the righteous and the wicked view a life of righteousness. The godly man sees his life as a tool of service to others, an instrument by which good should be done. The wicked sees his life as the center of the universe, the object for which everything else exists. One behaves in such a way as to make the world a better place; the other behaves in such a way as to make the world serve his own selfish interests. Those contrasting perspectives yield contrasting outcomes. When the righteous man does what is right, his heart is uplifted by the service rendered to others. When the wicked man does what is right—by force of law or by social pressure—his heart chafes at the awkwardness of it all. He does not comprehend the larger meaning of what he is doing, and is uncomfortable with his role as a doer of good.

Consider two businessmen, one of whom has dedicated his life to serving society, the other to enriching himself. The former makes business decisions based criteria that extends beyond profit and loss: Is it ethical? Does it help or hurt my customers and my employees? Does it provide a benefit to the larger community? The latter makes business decisions based largely on one criterion: Will it make me money?

The first man's ideals may prompt him to pass up some lucrative deals. Some of his profit will go toward causes from which he will derive little or no reward beyond the satisfaction of knowing that he has helped others. But he will not regret his losses. The second man will shave corners, pad expenses accounts, and blur ethical lines in order to increase his profits—and even grumble when his accountant urges him to make a charitable contribution for a tax write-off.

One final thought: Despite his sacrifices, the first man will likely be more successful than the latter. Unselfish goodness has a way of returning to those who practice it, in a myriad of unexpected ways.

It is a joy to do the right thing, but only if one's mind is educated to appreciate the value of the right thing. Think about the purpose of your life. Why are you here? What do you live for? Find the right answer to those questions, and you'll discover a whole new source of happiness.

The Worship of Pleasure

Pleasure is not inherently evil, but it can easily become a substitute for God, short-circuiting the purpose for which God put us here.

He who loves pleasure will be a poor man; he who loves wine and oil will not be rich (Prov. 21:17).

I said in my heart, "Come now, I will test you with mirth; therefore enjoy pleasure"; but surely, this also was vanity (Eccl. 2:1).

Men will be . . . lovers of pleasure rather than lovers of God (2 Tim. 3:2, 4).

When God placed our original parents in a paradise filled with everything delightful and satisfying, He wanted them to enjoy their life. Even after sin corrupted that perfection, He still endorsed pleasure as the legitimate reward of hard work: "Every man should eat and drink and enjoy the good of all his labor—it is the gift of God" (Eccl. 3:13). So there is no Biblical basis for insisting that our lives must be spent in drab austerity.

Even so, there is a danger in handling this gift. This proverb warns against becoming so engrossed in chasing pleasure that we elevate it to the highest good. When we turn pleasure into our dominant ambition in life, our moral compass is no longer calibrated by "is it right?," but by "is it enjoyable?" We live for pleasure above all else—including God.

When pleasure becomes our god, we set ourselves up for three deadly outcomes.

First, a life dedicated to the pursuit of pleasure is *unproductive*. Poverty, warns the wise man, is the reward of the one who values pleasure above everything else. Lasting security is the product of diligent work, and bypassing that process in pursuit of sensuality is certain to end in financial ruin. In Jesus' parable of the prodigal son, for example, the young hedonist had a lot of fun while spending his father's inheritance. "But when he had spent all . . . he began to be in want" (Lk. 15:14). Memories of a free-spirited past could not relieve the misery of his pig-pen existence—and the path to pleasure was now permanently closed.

Second, devotion to pleasure is also *unsatisfying*. When we squander our talents on frivolous pastimes, we injure our sense of purpose. A life spent in the pursuit of pleasure consumes much and gives little; it is not concerned with the betterment of self or others, only with gratifying the carnal senses. In the end, it has nothing to show for its profligacy. Solomon sought fulfillment in carnal pleasures, but that path left his soul empty: "Surely this also was vanity." Emptiness will plague the souls of all who have no higher goal in life than self-gratification.

Finally, when pleasure-worship takes over our lives, it becomes *destructive*. Paul warned Timothy that the love of pleasure is a gateway drug to a host of damaging social evils: "disobedient to parents, unthankful, unholy, unloving, unforgiving, slanderers, without self-control, brutal, despisers of good, traitors, headstrong, haughty" (2 Tim. 3:2-4). These malevolent behaviors are easy to justify when pleasuring myself becomes my chief aim in life.

The love of pleasure and the love of God cannot co-exist in the same heart. Setting aside occasional moments to enjoy the leisure side of life is a wholesome thing, but we must take care never to allow pleasure to become our god.

Managing Our Money

Money is a fact of life, but how we use it often gets us into trouble. Proverbs provides simple guidelines for achieving financial wisdom.

The rich and the poor have this in common, the LORD is the maker of them all. . . . By humility and the fear of the LORD are riches and honor and life (Prov. 22:2, 4).

For riches are not forever, nor does a crown endure to all generations (Prov. 27:24).

Much of our life is defined by our *money*—our jobs, our lifestyle, even our character. These verses reveal the complexity with which Proverbs treats the topic of money. On the one hand, there is no difference between rich and poor in God's sight. On the other hand, riches are a reward of a godly life. On a third hand, riches are irrelevant in the end. It's no wonder people are confused about what the Bible says on the subject.

Study the rest of the book of Proverbs, however, and we can at least learn some practical lessons about how to manage the money with which the Lord blesses us.

Develop your earning potential. "Prepare your outside work, make it fit for yourself in the field; and afterward build your house" (24:27). You cannot buy a house until you have established the means to pay for it. That requires a marketable skill that will assure a steady income. Before you start buying things, first learn a trade, gain expertise in a craft, develop a base of knowledge. This will require a lot of hard work at the beginning, but the payoff will be worth it.

Monitor your financial condition. "Be diligent to know the state of your flocks, and attend to your herds. . . . The lambs will provide your clothing, and the goats the price of a field" (27:23-27). How much are you worth? How much do you owe? What major expenses are coming up in your life? You cannot manage what you do not know. Having a good understanding of where you are financially will allow you to plan ahead and maintain a reasonable level of security.

Save for a rainy day. "Go to the ant, you sluggard! Consider her ways and be wise, which, having no captain, overseer or ruler, provides her supplies in the summer, and gathers her food in the harvest" (6:6-8). Just like the seasons, economic fortunes are cyclical, and the wise wage-earner will prepare for the bad times during the good times. Investing a little out of every paycheck is not difficult once the habit is established, and will serve the saver well in the future.

Avoid credit. "The rich rules over the poor, and the borrower is servant to the lender" (22:7). Every credit purchase involves "enslaving" oneself to a financial master. Some credit buying is unavoidable (big ticket items like a home or car). But the credit buying that gets most people in trouble involves discretionary spending that gets out of control (as with credit cards). Discipline yourself to live within your means, and you will be a lot happier.

Share your wealth. "The generous soul will be made rich, and he who waters will also be watered himself" (11:25). Ironically, the greatest happiness in managing your money comes when you give it away. The money you give to those who are less fortunate provides the satisfaction of seeing your bounty help another human being. The money you give to the Lord helps spread the gospel and makes the world a better place for all.

Managing your money does not require financial genius—just practical godliness.

Foresight

The ability to recognize trouble ahead and take a detour around it is an important life skill. But it is a skill that must be nurtured in a wise heart.

A prudent man foresees evil and hides himself, but the simple pass on and are punished (Prov. 22:3; 27:12).

֍

Most of us learn early in life that "hindsight is better than foresight"; which is to say, it is easier to look back on our mistakes and see what we should have done, than it is to look forward to the future and know what we ought to do. Unfortunately, hindsight usually comes too late to be of any value. All the second-guessing in the world cannot erase the disastrous results of a bad decision made in the past. We could save ourselves a lot of grief if we could see the problems before they develop and take steps to avoid them.

Such foresight is not a product of blind luck or psychic powers. It is the possession of the "prudent" man, literally, one who is "shrewd" or "crafty"—in a good sense, of course. He carefully calculates the long-range impact of everything he says and does, and has a fairly good idea of the direction he is heading. He is a student of human nature, and can spot potential troublemakers before he becomes entangled with them. He has a keen understanding of cause-and-effect relationships, and dodges bad effects by avoiding bad causes. If he seems to have a knack for staying out of trouble, it's because he is alert to the danger signals that usually precede trouble.

In contrast to the prudent man is the "simple" man. Taken from the Hebrew root *pathah* ("to be open"), "the fundamental idea . . . seems to be open to influence, *i.e.,* easily influenced" (McPheeters, *International Standard Bible Encyclopedia*). The simpleton leaves himself open for trouble because he pays no heed to the danger signals. He follows the impulses of his heart, giving little thought to where those impulses might take him. His foolish mistakes are not the result of mental deficiency or defiant rebellion, but of careless indifference. He is so busy chasing butterflies that he pays no attention to the stumbling blocks before his feet. His falls are painful, but usually avoidable, if he would only open his eyes to the path before him.

Even the simpleton can become prudent, if he learns from his mistakes as he goes along. But we do not have to rely solely on experience to gain the foresight we need. God has provided a valuable aid in the form of His revelation: "Your word is a lamp to my feet and a light to my path" (Psa. 119:105). The Bible can guide us safely around many of the obstacles that litter the path before us—but only if we take the trouble to become prudent in using it.

Lazy Men and Lions

Many of the excuses we offer for not stepping up to the challenges before us are merely alibis that cover up the real reason: Our own lethargy.

The lazy man says, "There is a lion outside! I shall be slain in the streets!" (Prov. 22:13).

ಲ್ಯ

Every endeavor in life involves a certain degree of risk. Getting married, starting a new business, driving across the country, building a house, and so on—all of these projects will pose problems for the individual who takes them on. But if he avoids these endeavors for fear of the dangers involved, he will never know the joy of marital companionship, become prosperous, see the sights, or have a house of his own. The successful man is the one who is not afraid to tackle the "lions" that stand in his way.

Sometimes, however, we use these challenges as an excuse to hide the real problem: We just don't want to bother with it. We're too lazy to step up to the plate.

Few lazy people will openly admit to their laziness. Instead, they try to justify their lack of ambition by pointing to the obstacles that, in their mind, would surely prevent them from achieving their goal. In most cases, however, the dangers are either non-existent or terribly exaggerated. The "lions" are really just kitty cats that could be overcome with a little courage and perseverance.

Noah's ark was no week-end project. He could have avoided this gigantic task by pointing to the many obstacles he surely would face (the lack of qualified help, the drain on his pocketbook, the lack of adequate testing of the design, the unpredictable results of stuffing all those animals in the same box for year, and so forth). The order was a tall one, and God had to wait quite a while to see the finished product. But Noah was not a lazy man. He took on the risks and finished the job. By his hard work and perseverance, Noah "condemned the world" (Heb. 11:7).

Why do some young people avoid marriage and parenthood? Usually they convince themselves that, given all the catastrophes they've seen in other relationships, they would fail in that challenge also. "I can't handle the conflicts and disappointments that might arise"; or, "The sacrifices are not worth it." *Lions in the street!* They decline the opportunity to even try.

Why do Christians neglect the souls of their fellowmen? It's never "Because I'm lazy," but always, "Because it won't do any good," or "I'll say the wrong thing," or "It will drive them away." *Lions in the street!*

Why do churches hoard their money and fail to explore different methods of spreading the gospel to the world around them? It's usually because "We'll be throwing away our money," or "Nobody will listen." *More lions!*

Nothing good in life is ever accomplished without pushing ourselves to step outside our comfort zone. The greatest threat to success in our lives is not the lions in the streets, but the lion that prowls within our hearts, seeking to destroy us (1 Pet. 5:8)—and passivity is as good a weapon as any in accomplishing Satan's goal. As soon as we muster the courage to stand up to him, we will see the other challenges for the kitty cats they are.

On Raising Children

Of all the challenges we take on in life, the greatest is raising our children to be responsible adults. A few simple guidelines can ease the task.

Foolishness is bound up in the heart of a child; the rod of correction will drive it far from him (Prov. 22:15).

The rod and rebuke give wisdom, but a child left to himself brings shame to his mother (Prov. 29:15).

Comedian Jim Gaffigan—the father of five children—once observed, "I don't know what's more exhausting about parenting: the getting up early, or acting like you know what you're doing." Every parent can relate to that sentiment. We know that how our kids turn out in adulthood will be determined largely by what kind of parents we are now; yet we are painfully aware of our struggle to do the job well.

After raising my own children and watching other parents raise theirs, I've come to the conclusion that child-rearing can be boiled down to one simple principle: *Children need boundaries that are enforced consistently with love.* Let's examine the four key elements in this formula.

First, *children require boundaries.* "Foolishness is bound up in the heart of a child" is another way of saying that kids, especially younger ones, are ignorant of how life works. They are a bundle of appetites and passions, but lack the wisdom to know how to channel those impulses appropriately. They're not evil; they just don't know any better. It's the role of parents to set limits that will teach the kids the difference between right and wrong behavior. Kids who grow up in the absence of restrictions or rules usually end up as out-of-control adults—much more dangerous, and not nearly as cute. The child who is "left to himself" will someday shame the parents who were too busy or too tired to bother.

But setting boundaries is worthless if those boundaries are not *enforced*. "The rod of correction" is much more than a swat on the bottom. It is a network of predictable consequences built into a child's life by parents who strive to make the rules stick. Reacting to misbehavior with a weak comment like "that's not nice," with no further consequence, teaches a child that the rules really don't exist and can be ignored with impunity. (As a side note, efforts to enforce the rules on children are negated by parents who do not follow the rules themselves. Parental hypocrisy is enormously destructive in teaching kids respect for authority.)

Taking this a step further, a child will learn that the boundaries are meaningful only when they are enforced *consistently*. If there is one area where most parents stumble, it is on this point. Uttering rash threats in a moment of frustration—threats that we have no real intention of carrying out—or throwing up our hands and giving up after repeated acts of defiance, teaches the kids that the system can be manipulated to their advantage. And trust me, children are quite good at spotting those weaknesses.

Finally, discipline must be administered *in a spirit of love*. Everything said above about discipline does not give parents a license to become control freaks. Children need to know that their parents love them intensely, even when they are being disciplined. Parents should actively encourage their kids to explore their world—within reasonable limits—and to express their interests in ways that will allow them to grow and become confident. Smothering our kids under a mountain of stifling regulations designed to "show them who's boss" crushes their spirit and sets them up for depression or rebellion in adulthood.

Raising children is a challenge, but it need not be a nightmare. Trust God, hold your kids close, and enjoy the journey!

Of Chasing Sparrows

The allure of prosperity pulls us into a lifestyle of endless work and drudgery. But someday we will realize how short-sighted our values were.

Do not overwork to be rich; because of your own understanding, cease! Will you set your eyes on that which is not? For riches certainly make themselves wings; they fly away like an eagle toward heaven (Prov. 23:4-5).

~

According to Derek Kidner, the ancient Sumerians had their own version of this proverb: "Possessions are sparrows in flight which can find no place to alight." Both of these nuggets of wisdom reflect one of humanity's greatest challenges: to distinguish between the eternal and the temporal. Our attention is easily captured by the things of this world, the tangible objects we can see and hold. Yet these material things blind us to the intangible ideals that better define a life well-lived. That's why God must constantly remind us of the folly of chasing earthly possessions as though they were the *summum bonum* of life.

Despite our best efforts to hold on to our riches, Solomon says they "certainly" make wings and fly away. One way or the other, they are going to leave us, robbing us of the happiness and security we thought they would provide. They can be destroyed by accidents or natural disasters; stolen by thieves; lost through economic reversals or carelessness; or worn out through time and use. Even if we can avoid all these dangers, the day will eventually arrive when we must go, leaving our wealth behind for someone else to worry about.

On and on it goes through endless generations, riches being gained and lost, held briefly then passed on to others. The fleeting nature of wealth is obvious to anyone who is willing to open his eyes and see the whole picture.

Yet like a child vainly chasing after a sparrow to catch it, people will "overwork to be rich"—literally, "wear themselves out" (NIV). Never content with what they have, they push themselves harder and harder, eager to get more and more. In their drive to achieve the good life, family duties are neglected and spiritual interests are weakened. Nerves become frazzled, and tempers short. Yet on they toil, looking for that elusive satisfaction they believe lies just around the next corner. But someday, when they least expect it, they will watch helplessly as all their accumulated wealth sprouts wings and flies away. And for what did they wear themselves out? Nothing!

Contrary to conventional wisdom, "one's life does not consist in the abundance of the things he possesses" (Lk. 12:15). Our real treasure lies in another realm, and until we can redirect our attention to that distant grail, we will never find the contentment that our soul seeks.

Why I Do Not Drink

The debate over whether a Christian can consume alcohol in any amount misses deeper principles that should guide our decisions on this matter.

Do not look on the wine when it is red, when it sparkles in the cup, when it swirls around smoothly; at the last it bites like a serpent, and stings like a viper. Your eyes will see strange things, and your heart will utter perverse things" (Prov. 23:31-33).

I do not drink alcoholic beverages. It's a personal conviction that I have lived by all my life. I am aware of the discussion over whether or not the Bible absolutely prohibits the drinking of alcohol, given that safe drinking water was a rare commodity in ancient cultures (see 1 Tim. 5:23). But whatever the merits of that dispute, there are two principles, both rooted in Scripture, that inform this personal stance.

The first principle is admittedly selfish. The drinking of alcohol in any amount is the first step toward becoming drunk. So by choosing not to drink, I eliminate any risk of becoming an alcoholic and suffering the miseries associated with that condition. No alcoholic ever started drinking with the intention of becoming an alcoholic. Yet in all too many cases, that is what happens, and the consequences are catastrophic. Thousands die every year in alcohol-related auto accidents; spouses and children are abused and/or impoverished; marriages are destroyed; careers are ruined; crimes are committed—all because of alcohol. My life has enough challenges without adding alcohol-related problems to it. By choosing not to drink, that's one set of problems I will never have to deal with.

The wise man in this proverb gave good advice on how to avoid the problems associated with drunkenness: "Do not look on the wine when it is red." The only way to guarantee that alcohol will never make a fool of me is to never drink it. That policy has worked out well for me thus far, and I can highly recommend it to others.

Beyond my own selfish concerns, there is a second reason I do not drink: I do not want my behavior to influence others to become alcoholics. If I choose to drink, others will know it, and will be emboldened to drink alcohol themselves. Whether or not I can hold my liquor, I cannot control whether others can hold theirs. If my example leads a brother to pursue a path that eventually results in his ruin, I am complicit in his downfall. "It is good neither to eat meat *nor drink wine* nor do anything by which your brother stumbles or is offended or is made weak" (Rom. 14:21). In a culture where alcohol abuse affects the lives of millions, how can I lend my influence to the carnage? By choosing not to drink, I am taking a strong and consistent stand against the suffering brought on by alcohol—and that example may influence others to stand against it, too.

The debate over whether or not the Scriptures prohibit all alcohol consumption misses a greater issue: In our current time and culture, *which behavior better displays my love for God and for my fellow man* (Matt. 22:37-40)? With so many healthy alternatives available, there is no reason why I need to drink it; and looking around at the problems caused by alcohol, there are many reasons why I should not.

This choice is a no-brainer: It's safe, scriptural, and contributes to a happy life.

Adversity and Faith

The true quality of our faith is not measured by how many religious activities we cram into our life. One simple test reveals all we need to know.

If you faint in the day of adversity, your strength is small (Prov. 24:10).

For years I puzzled over this verse. On the surface, it appears to be one of those "well, duh!" observations on life: When you stumble, it's your fault. That's a big help, huh?

Then it occurred to me that I was looking at this verse from the wrong angle. It's not a commentary on a simple cause-and-effect relationship, but a nudge calling for a serious self-examination of the foundation of our faith.

Let's start with your current spiritual condition. How would you characterize your faith? More importantly, what factors would you point to as measures of your faith? Would you list things like your level of Bible knowledge? Your involvement in church activities? The number of brotherhood papers you subscribe to? The number of times you attend church? The amount of time spent in personal Bible reading? Do a quick inventory on all the things that contribute to your current spiritual condition. Then from that inventory, rate yourself on a scale of one to ten. How do you rate?

Now answer one more question: *How well do you hold up under stress?*

You see, it really doesn't matter how you answer the first questions. If you buckle whenever Satan turns the screws, then your faith is shallow. All the religious busy-work you cataloged in the first exercise obviously isn't getting the job done. You need to conduct a major overhaul of the foundation of your faith.

Whatever else we may be doing in our spiritual lives, the best test of our faith is how we handle adversity. Our response to hardship reveals what we really think about God, life, and eternity. If Satan can intimidate us into a life of passive resignation, he really doesn't care if we're religious. He has already achieved his primary objective with us.

Step back and do a quick survey of all the Bible heroes you can think of. What made these people great? It wasn't their knowledge, or speaking skills, or charming personalities, or driving ambitions. In fact, in many cases, they were heroes *in spite of* weaknesses in these areas. Rather, what made them heroes was their willingness to look evil in the eye and stubbornly push on. In their hearts, they knew that God was in control, that this life was only a temporary journey to a far better home, and that no matter what happened, everything was going to turn out alright in the end. Sure, they felt the pain and cried; but their lives were securely tied to a hope that anchored their existence. They did not faint in the day of adversity, because their strength—their faith—was great.

Going to church, reading the Bible, and getting involved in other religious activities can be helpful tools in building your faith. But the real change must come from within. Somewhere in the deepest recesses of your heart, you have to make a fundamental decision about what your life is all about. Only then will you find the strength to stand firm in the day of adversity.

When Your Enemy Falls

> Loving our enemy involves much more than just not hurting him. In fact, it goes to the very heart of what it means to be a child of God.

Do not rejoice when your enemy falls, and do not let your heart be glad when he stumbles; lest the LORD see it, and it displease Him, and He turn away His wrath from him (Prov. 24:17-18).

༺☙

From a purely human standpoint, there is nothing more satisfying than watching an enemy suffer, especially if we had nothing to do with his downfall. At no cost to ourselves or our honor, we can revel in the fact that our enemy got what he deserved. Ah, sweet justice!

That sense of justice may be sweet, but it's still wrong. Not only should we refrain from actively seeking our enemy's hurt, we should not even wish it, or rejoice when it happens. As with so much in life, it is not just the behavior, but the *attitude* behind the behavior that will condemn us.

Jesus taught that the true measure of a man's religion is seen in how he deals with his enemies (Matt.5:43-48; Lk. 6:27-28). Treating our friends with respect is no challenge; even pagans can do that. Jesus' command to "love your enemies" may be more difficult to obey, but it's a truer indicator of the genuineness of our connection with God.

Love seeks what is best for another (Rom. 13:10; Gal. 5:13; Matt. 7:12). Applied to an enemy, that means we want him to share the happiness and blessings we enjoy as forgiven creatures. We may hate his evil ways, but we can never hate the man. We pity him and work for his repentance and reconciliation. We do not retaliate when he mistreats us, because we love him, not because God says "don't." We do good to him out of a genuine desire to help, not to showcase our patience. Likewise when his evil deeds return upon his own head and he is afflicted, we will not laugh and jump for joy; we love him too much to enjoy his pain.

A good example of this noble spirit is David. For years he suffered miserably at the hands of Saul. He was hunted like a criminal through the caves and deserts of Judea. Twice David had opportunity to slay Saul and end his troubles, but both times he let his enemy go. Saul finally lost his life in a battle with the Philistines. Did David cheer? Not at all! He wrote a beautiful eulogy to the fallen king: "Saul and Jonathan, beloved and pleasant in their life, and in their death they were not parted; they were swifter than eagles, they were stronger than lions. O daughters of Israel, weep over Saul" (2 Sam. 1:23-24). It was that kind of unselfish love that made David a man after God's own heart.

Love for a fallen enemy is, after all, a characteristic of God. "I take no pleasure in the death of the wicked, but rather that the wicked turn from his way and live" (Eze. 33:11). He gave His Son for us while we were enemies (Rom. 5:10). We cannot call ourselves children of God unless we imitate the characteristics of our Father.

Learning how to love our enemies—including not rubbing it in when our enemy stumbles—can have a profound impact on human relations. Troubled marriages can be salvaged, strained friendships can be strengthened, and estranged brethren can be reconciled, if everyone one would take the time to re-examine their hearts: Do I really love my enemy, or do I secretly wish for harm to come upon him?

Priorities

Life moves in stages, and it's important for young people learn what's truly important in each stage, before rushing into the next.

Prepare your outside work, make it fit for yourself in the field; and afterward build your house (Prov. 24:27).

In an agricultural society like ancient Israel, tending to the crops is more important than building a house. Any crude dwelling will suffice until the harvest comes in; afterward a man can turn his attention to improving his living quarters. Jewish rabbis and some modern commentators take a different view, understanding "house" as referring to one's family. By this interpretation, a young man should concentrate on establishing himself financially before he takes on the responsibility of supporting a wife and children. Both views are valid, of course, and underscore a broader principle that defines success: *A balanced life requires that we set correct priorities.*

Some people, especially young ones, have a hard time learning that they cannot have everything in life they want, at least not all at once. Resources and abilities are limited, so they must learn to concentrate them on those things that are most important, and not spread themselves too thin. Of course, in order to do that they must first determine what is "important" and what is not.

That's not always easy. Some of their more exciting dreams (bigger house, new boat, Hawaiian vacation, and so on) may have to be postponed in order to take care of more mundane responsibilities (braces for the kids, retirement savings, taxes, home maintenance). The sacrifices aren't fun, but the reward—when it comes—is well worth the price.

Unfortunately, some people cannot or will not discipline themselves to make these hard choices. They think that somehow they can have their cake and eat it too, so they obligate themselves beyond what they can safely handle. Young people desire the same standard of living they enjoyed under their parents' roof (fine home, new car, nice restaurants), and get themselves into financial trouble by rushing into that lifestyle before they're ready. Those problems would be avoided if they would learn to live in a cracker-box house and eat baloney sandwiches for a few years, while working hard to build a solid foundation for the fulfillment of their dreams. Such a life may not be glamorous, but it is certainly happier.

The farmer who concentrates on building an elegant house while his crops are rotting in the field will lose everything and be thought a fool by his neighbors. What are our priorities saying about us?

Don't Be a Toothache

Like the members of a body, our role in a broader social network requires consistent performance. When we fail, others notice—and form opinions.

Confidence in an unfaithful man in time of trouble is like a bad tooth and a foot out of joint (Prov. 25:19).

Everyone who has had a severe toothache or who has tried to walk on a foot that has "gone to sleep" can appreciate the lesson in this proverb. We depend heavily on our teeth to chew the food that keeps us alive, and on our feet to get us around. When they fail to perform as they should, our whole body suffers.

A "faithless" man is like the bad tooth or the weak foot. He assures others of his willingness to help out if needed, but somehow is never able to deliver on his promise when the time comes, usually after others have already linked their plans to his promise. It doesn't take many such performances for a man to get a reputation as one whose promises can't be trusted. People don't like bad teeth, and they don't like undependable friends. Unforeseen impediments can disrupt the best of intentions, of course. But the occasional glitch cannot excuse habitual negligence, which is the subject of this proverb.

When Paul and Barnabas departed on their first missionary journey, Luke records that "they also had John as their helper" (Ac. 13:5). Shortly thereafter, in Pamphylia, John Mark left them and returned to his home (v. 13). Commentators point out that the route the missionaries were taking was rugged and dangerous. The "helper" apparently got cold feet and withdrew his help. Later, when Paul and Barnabas were making plans for a second journey, Paul refused to take John Mark along, because he "had deserted them . . . and had not gone with them to the work" (Ac. 15:37-40). It was many years later before Paul's confidence in Mark would be restored (2 Tim. 4:11).

In contrast, Timothy had Paul's confidence because of his "proven worth" in past service (Phil. 2:19-22). Philemon was a man whose obedience Paul could depend upon (Phe. 21). Paul himself knew that others leaned heavily on him for leadership and support, and he tried hard not to betray that confidence (Phil. 1:25-26). These individuals did their best to live up to their obligations, and others respected them for their fidelity.

Every one of us, no matter what our role in life, is a "tooth" or a "foot" to someone else. Our family, our friends, our neighbors, the local church of which we are a member—all of these depend on us to some extent, and we must take care not to let them down.

Meanwhile, we will trust in God, whose promises will *never* fail.

How to Defeat an Enemy

Cries for revenge and justice in a world wracked by conflict ignore the only strategy that has a proven track record. We should try it more often.

If your enemy is hungry, give him bread to eat; and if he is thirsty, give him water to drink; for so you will heap coals of fire on his head, and the LORD will reward you (Prov. 25:21-22).

◈

Centuries before Jesus shocked His audiences with His radical mandate to "love your enemy," Solomon defined it. Contrary to human intuition, the best way to deal with an enemy is to *be kind to him*.

Our initial reaction to this advice is incredulity. This is my *enemy* we're talking about—someone who actively seeks to do me harm. And I'm supposed to ignore the mistreatment and give him aid and sustenance? This violates the very definition of justice. I can't do that! I *won't!*

But Solomon and Jesus had a deeper insight into human nature than we do. There is something deep within the human psyche—a spark of the divine, perhaps—that responds to unconditional kindness. When we witness someone performing an act of good will entirely for the recipient's sake, with no strings attached, we admire it. When that good will is extended to an enemy, we stand in awe. On occasion, even the enemy himself is softened by love's gentle touch. How is that possible?

There is a power in kindness that no evil can withstand. When we respond to ill-treatment with active grace, we occupy the moral high ground. Bystanders who witness our kindness will applaud our magnanimity and see our enemy's cruelty for what it is. Even our enemy will be shamed by the stark contrast in behaviors; our benevolent—and quite unexpected—response will "heap coals of fire on his head." To use Paul's language, we will have accomplished something that we never thought possible: We will "overcome evil with good" (Rom. 12:21).

That is the language of *conquest*. In the larger framework of social relations, our altruism will tower above the pettiness of our tormentors. Paul himself was well aware of how this phenomenon worked. As an active participant in the stoning of Stephen, he heard the young martyr cry, "Lord, do not charge them with this sin" (Ac. 8:16). Many years later, as Paul faced his own martyrdom, he echoed Stephen's language regarding those who had abandoned him: "May it not be charged against them" (2 Tim. 4:16). If the forgiveness of Stephen in his death throes could melt the heart of an enemy like Saul of Tarsus, what other victories might it achieve?

Of course, this outcome is not an absolute guarantee. Jesus loved His enemies to the end, yet they murdered Him anyway. In that case, the triumph lay in the aftershock, the ripples of which are still bearing fruit among God's enemies today. Whatever the immediate result, we can take comfort in the knowledge that in the end, "the Lord will reward you."

Justice is a laudable goal in human society, but making justice an end within itself usually sets up a destructive cycle of resentment and revenge. There is a better way, and God looks to His people to show the world how it's done.

Standing Up to Evil

As a dark cloud of depravity settles over our land, God's people are faced with hard decisions in response. Much is riding on the choices we make.

A righteous man who falters before the wicked is like a murky spring and a polluted well (Prov. 25:26).

In the arid Middle East in ancient times, life depended on a reliable source of water. Whether it came from a flowing spring or a deep well, potable water was not a luxury—it was critical to survival. But if the water coming from a spring or well was polluted, the life-sustaining liquid was worse than no water at all; it killed those who drank from it.

This metaphor is an apt description of the good man who fails to stand firm in the face of evil. By training and experience, his character should serve his community as a bulwark against the encroaching tentacles of sin. But if, to save his own skin or to preserve his social status, he backs down before the wicked who are aggressively pushing their agenda, his compromised reputation will do more damage to the cause of truth than if he never existed at all.

Consider the example of Aaron, whom Moses left in charge of the people when he went up on Mt. Sinai to receive the Law (Ex. 32). The people took advantage of Moses' absence to pressure his brother to build a golden calf. Aaron folded under their demands and built the idol, resulting in an orgy of debauchery. One good man who was in a position to hold firm, instead yielded to the mob, and the character of the nation spiraled out of control.

In our lifetimes, the principle behind this metaphor has been little more than an academic topic. But increasingly Christians are finding themselves in positions where the most basic elements of their belief system are being challenged, even threatened. This parable is becoming a reality in our own experience.

When corporate diversity training sessions require that participants celebrate gay marriage and transgenderism as acceptable alternative lifestyles, will we voice our convictions, or meekly go along with the perversion? Put another way, will a loyal Christian renounce these ungodly behaviors, or support them? The world is watching our response.

When Christian business executives are pressured to sign on to radical programs that elevate one race or group over another, will they remain faithful to Biblical standards of true equality and fairness for all, or buckle to the woke mob?

The righteous man who refuses to capitulate in the face of evil will probably pay a price for his convictions. Such is the way of the world. But whatever his losses, he will retain the most important thing of all: his *integrity.*

In the end, that's all that matters.

The Folly of Self-Praise

We have clever ways of bragging on ourselves without being too obvious about it. But why do we want to promote ourselves at all?

It is not good to eat much honey; so to seek one's own glory is not glory (Prov. 25:27).

Let another man praise you, and not your own mouth; a stranger, and not your own lips (Prov. 27:2).

As surely as God made man with a stomach, He also made him with an ego. And egos, like stomachs, desire to be satisfied. The food that egos thrive on, of course, is praise. But the temptation to overindulge this emotional need is just as great as the physical, and some people pig out on a form of adulation that is almost inexhaustible: *praise of self*.

In its crudest form, self-praise manifests itself in open bragging. Most of us realize the tactlessness of such behavior, so we seek glory in more subtle ways. We might fish for compliments using loaded questions; or deftly steer conversations toward our accomplishments; or secretly lobby for positions of prominence where our talents can be displayed for all to see. We might be surprised to know the full extent to which this craving for attention corrupts our behavior.

Whatever device we use, such self-glorification hurts the perpetrator. Sooner or later, the self-promoter will over-extend himself and end up looking foolish. Peter's loud boast of faithfulness came back to haunt him following his denial of the Lord (Matt. 26:35, 69-75). Jesus taught His disciples not to seek the best seat at a feast, lest they be bumped down to a lower seat, "then you begin with shame to take the lowest place" (Lk. 14:7-11). If we are as great as we think we are, others will be able to see it without any advertising from us. And if we are *not* as great as we think we are—which is a real possibility—we do ourselves a favor by staying quiet and laying low.

Self-glorification also damages one's influence with others. A characteristic of love is that it "does not parade itself" (1 Cor. 13:4). The implication in this definition is that one who brags on himself is not considerate of the feelings of others. By definition, trying to make oneself look big is just another way of making others look small. That is why no one likes a braggart. Whether he intends to or not, he is in the business of running down other people. If we truly have the interests of others at heart, humility demands that we seek to lower ourselves and exalt others (Rom. 12:16; Phil. 2:3-4).

We must learn to do our jobs quietly to the best of our ability, whether or not others applaud our efforts. Instead, we can look forward to that day when "each one's praise will come from God" (1 Cor. 4:5). Then we will have all the praise our hearts desire, from the only One whose praise matters.

Inspected Your Walls Lately?

An impatient spirit leaves us open to external vexations that can wreak havoc in our lives. We need a solid emotional barrier to protect us.

Whoever has no rule over his own spirit is like a city broken down, without walls (Prov. 25:28).

In the ancient art of warfare, a city's most important defensive weapon was a massive wall ringing its outer perimeter. Properly prepared, a city with a good wall could hold off a large army almost indefinitely. Because their walls were so vital to security, cities usually spared no expense to insure they were properly maintained. When Nehemiah became governor of Judah, for example, his first priority was a crash program of wall-building for Jerusalem, "that we may no longer be a reproach" (Neh. 2:17-18). Without walls, a city was easy prey for every third-rate army that passed by. Because enemies could so easily impose their will upon it, such a city had little control over its own destiny.

That is a fitting illustration of the plight of the man who has no control over his spirit, one who is impulsive, quick-tempered. A person who is given to flashes of anger does not display strength, but weakness. He is a prisoner of every frustration, insult, or misunderstanding that comes his way. He does not control these outward forces; they control him, and provoke behavior that is not in his best interest. Without a "wall" of self-restraint to control his passions, he is exposed to a multitude of temptations that can wreck his life.

This principle is seen in the career of Alexander the Great, probably the greatest military genius the world has known. In twelve short years his armies created an empire that stretched from Greece to India. Cities that for centuries had defied capture, fell in a few months in the face of brilliant tactics that still amaze military strategists. But Alexander had an unpredictable temper. Sometimes he flew into violent rages, doing things that he later regretted. During one such outburst, he killed his best friend. He died of a fever brought on by a drunken orgy when only 33 years old. The man whom no city wall could stop, had no walls to protect himself, and that defect destroyed him.

"He who is slow to anger is better than the mighty, and he who rules his spirit than he who takes a city" (Prov. 16:32). We may never conquer an empire or a city, but if we can learn to maintain firm control of our passions throughout life, we will have won a far greater victory.

The Wile E. Coyote Syndrome

The traps we set for others have a nasty habit of ensnaring ourselves. At some point you would think we would learn our lesson.

Whoever digs a pit will fall into it, and he who rolls a stone will have it roll back on him (Prov. 26:27).

There is no finer demonstration of this proverb than Wile E. Coyote, the cartoon canine whose futile efforts to capture the Roadrunner was portrayed on television every Saturday morning for many years. That poor coyote was run over, blown up, thrown down, and squashed flat more than any other cartoon character around. (Now *there* is a lesson in perseverance!) The consistent theme in every episode was his failure to learn from his nefarious schemes: The disasters that befell him were almost entirely of his own creation. The traps that he set for his victim had a way of entrapping himself.

If you prefer a more serious illustration, read the stories of Haman, who was hung on the gallows that he had built for Mordecai (Esth. 3-7); or the Persian officials who plotted to have Daniel thrown in the lions' den, and ended up as lion food themselves (Dan. 6). Wile E. has had lots of company among us humans.

In the context (v. 18-28), this proverb is dealing primarily with a misuse of the *tongue*. Few of us ever plot to bring physical harm on people, but it is a rare individual who has never used his tongue to hurt another (Jas. 3:2-8). Such verbal ambushes can easily boomerang on us.

Gossip is one such pit that we dig for ourselves. When we habitually spread unkind information about others behind their backs, we may tarnish their reputations a little, but we will probably destroy our own in the process. A gossip is despised by everyone.

Crafty questions designed to self-incriminate an opponent can backfire. These were often used by the scribes and Pharisees who sought to destroy Jesus. He was a master logician, however, and they always came away from such encounters with red faces, crushed by their own "stones." Truth does not need such devices to meet error.

Misrepresentation of facts is likewise self-defeating. We can place someone in a bad light by simply withholding key information, or slightly exaggerating the real story. But when the full truth is discovered, our credibility will be damaged.

The root problem underlying all such schemes, of course, is an evil heart that desires to harm another person. Someone who has the love of God in his heart has no need of digging pits or rolling stones in the first place.

Tomorrow

We have no guarantee of what will happen tomorrow. It is in our best interest, therefore, not to pin all our hopes on an uncertain future.

Do not boast about tomorrow for you do not know what a day may bring forth (Prov. 27:1).

Every day the news offers stories about people dying suddenly. Whether in car wrecks, plane crashes, heart attacks, industrial accidents, murders, or natural disasters, thousands of people every day are plunged into eternity without warning. Most of these unfortunate people are cut down in the middle of active, busy lives. They have families, friends, homes, and investments. They have schedules to keep and dreams to chase. Yet in one brief moment their whole future is abruptly erased. Whatever plans they had for tomorrow are now meaningless, because for them, tomorrow will never come.

For many other people, tomorrow will come but bringing surprises that will drastically alter their lives. It may be an accident inflicting horrible injuries, or an unexpected inheritance involving millions of dollars (and headaches). They may get laid off from their job, or meet their future mate. For better or worse, their lives will never be the same, thanks to what "tomorrow" brings.

If life teaches us anything, it is that nothing in the future can be guaranteed. We can make plans, calculate probabilities, and even prepare for contingencies, but the fact remains that when we wake up in the morning, we simply don't know what the new day may bring forth. It's a risky business, therefore, to brag about what we will do tomorrow. Life may have other plans for us.

James gives us an expanded version of this proverb in his epistle: "Come now, you who say, 'Today or tomorrow we will go to such and such a city, spend a year there, buy and sell, and make a profit'; whereas you do not know what will happen tomorrow. For what is your life? It is a even a vapor that appears for a little time and then vanishes away. Instead you ought to say, 'If the Lord wills, we shall live and do this or that.' But now you boast in your arrogance. All such boasting is evil" (Jas. 4:13-16).

James is not condemning advance planning in our personal affairs. He is warning against a self-centered attitude toward life that makes no allowances for the over-ruling hand of Providence. "If the Lord wills" is more than a pious cliché; it is a sobering reminder to ourselves of how fragile and uncertain our lives are. It is good to make plans, but it is better not to build all our hopes on those plans coming to pass. So much can happen to disrupt the future that we have planned for ourselves.

When tomorrow brings these surprises into our lives, it is generally the person who has developed this respect for life's uncertainty who is best prepared to respond to them. Rather than lashing out at the unfairness of it all, this person accepts the new reality, adjusts his plans accordingly, and moves on. His planning includes an allowance for the unforeseen surprises that tomorrow may bring.

Only by trusting in God, not in a tomorrow that may never come, can we find the happiness that makes *today* worth living.

The Wounds of a Friend

Like a strong antiseptic, criticism stings. But sometimes that's exactly what we need, and we would do well to listen with an open mind.

Open rebuke is better than love carefully concealed. Faithful are the wounds of a friend, but the kisses of an enemy are deceitful (Prov. 27:5-6).

※

According to modern standards of etiquette, a true friend always compliments and never criticizes. Such a policy may succeed in building a circle of flattering admirers, but that's a far cry from true friendship. Friendship is based on love. (Interestingly, "friend" comes from an Old English word for "love.") Love seeks what is best for another, and sometimes "what is best" may not be pleasant. The best favor we can extend to a friend may be to pierce him with a verbal thrust that will hurt in the moment, but provide long term healing. Which is to say, true friends appreciate the value of *constructive criticism*.

It is understandable why we are reluctant to criticize a friend's conduct. A rebuke may throw cold water on the warm companionship we enjoy. But what is the alternative? Silence allows a friend's error to go uncorrected, possibly leading to greater mistakes in the future. If the one we love then becomes mired in troubles because we remained silent, what kind of friend have we proven to be? We have concealed our love, and our friend pays the price.

Of course, this proverb does not advocate a faultfinding disposition that pounces on every minor infraction and demands penance. Love first seeks to "cover" transgressions where possible (Prov. 10:12; 17:9; 1 Pet. 4:8). Criticism is rendered as a last resort, and always in the kindest possible way.

This proverb offers a lesson for the one criticized as well as the critic. No one likes to be reprimanded, especially if we think the criticism is unwarranted. While some of the censure that comes our way may be motivated by malice and can be ignored, we err badly if we dismiss *all* criticism as unworthy of consideration. It is a fact of human nature that others can often see more clearly the faults that we cannot see in ourselves. The one who is admonishing us may have something to say that we need to hear.

When someone approaches us with a suggestion for improvement, especially if spoken in a spirit of love and concern, we would do well to swallow our pride and listen. He may be the best friend we have. "He who heeds rebuke gets understanding" (Prov. 15:32).

But what if a friend is offended by our criticism, and refuses to speak to us anymore? Then perhaps the "friendship" needs to be reevaluated. The true test of friendship is the openness with which two people can talk to each other about their concerns.

The Satisfied Soul

The greatest danger with prosperity is that we become indifferent to the value of what we have, especially the small blessings in our life.

A satisfied soul loathes the honeycomb, but to a hungry soul every bitter thing is sweet (Prov. 27:7).

ଏକ

How we value the things we have often depends on how many things we have. For example, when the prodigal son received his father's inheritance, he did not appreciate the value of what he had, and quickly blew the entire sum on fun and frolic. Out of luck and out of money, he ended up working in a pig pen, where "he would gladly have filled his stomach with the pods that the swine ate" (Lk. 15:16). His value system was now dramatically altered by his change in circumstances.

Growing up, I heard stories from the Depression-era generation before me who in their childhood would get nothing but a few oranges or apples for a Christmas present—and were thrilled to get that. They treasured what they had so little of.

The message in this proverb, however, does not concern the poor who have no other alternatives, but "the one who is full" (NIV); that is, the rich person who has an abundance and doesn't appreciate any of it.

Many years ago, I held a gospel meeting in a town in Texas. One morning, a well-to-do couple in the church invited me and the local preacher to breakfast at the local country club. The wife's order included fried bacon. When her food arrived, she was incensed at what she saw. The bacon had not been flattened as it was being fried, so it was twisted and curled—horrors! She complained to the waitress, demanding that it be replaced with bacon that had been fried correctly. Perfectly edible bacon was thrown away because this good sister didn't like the way it looked. Then and there, I made a commitment to myself: If this is what being rich does to a person, then Lord, please keep me poor. What ingratitude!

The satisfied soul "loathes the honeycomb" because he can afford to. If he does not like what he has, for whatever reason, he can spend whatever it takes to get a replacement that suits him. This ability to get what he wants soon becomes a habit that poisons his appreciation for everything in his life. Why cherish anything, when he can always get something bigger, better, bolder any time he wants?

This mindset also corrupts his relationship with the people in his life. Rather than work with others to achieve a mutually beneficial objective, the rich man becomes self-centered and petty, demanding that everyone bow down to his wishes. Those who work in the service industry generally agree that their most difficult clients are the rich—always demanding, never satisfied.

"Rich" is a relative term, of course, and in our prosperous society, this disease of ingratitude afflicts many of us middle-class folks, too. How often do we complain about things that the rest of the world would gladly accept as precious gifts from heaven?

The solution to this problem is not to take a vow of poverty, but to train our hearts to be grateful for *everything* God has given us, whatever our status in life. A soul that is not only satisfied but also contented, will eat the honeycomb with thanksgiving and gladness.

Keeper of the Fig Tree

Reaping the harvest of hard work requires... hard work. It's a lesson that is hard to appreciate at the outset of a project or a career.

Whoever keeps the fig tree will eat its fruit; so he who waits on his master will be honored (Prov. 27:18).

In ancient Israel, the fig tree was symbolic of peace and prosperity. The fig tree provided an abundance of convenient and tasty food, and its broad leaves furnished a welcome shade during hot days. But these benefits did not come free. Fig trees required several years of patient labor before they begin bearing fruit profitably. Even after reaching maturity, they required constant care to remain healthy and productive. Jesus once referred to this investment of labor in one of His parables (Lk. 13:6-9). The work was boring and tedious, but a tree's owner never complained. He knew that someday his sacrifices would be rewarded.

That's what Solomon would have us to know about any honorable career. The work may be menial, but the sacrifices will usually pay off in time, if we do not get discouraged and quit. Often the only thing that separates the young gofer on the bottom rung of the company ladder from the president at the top, is about thirty years of loyal, steady service. If a young man will work hard, accept sacrifices, and shrug off discouragements, he will find himself gradually moving up the ladder. While his co-workers are grumbling about their lousy jobs, mean bosses, or low pay, he is busy "keeping his fig tree"—and reaping the rewards.

It's a lesson that so many young people have a hard time learning in their early job experiences. They hire on with a company, thinking only of the benefits. But after the boss yells at them a few times, or they are required to perform some degrading task, they quit in frustration. Their next employment is no better, so on and on they go, looking for that "perfect" job that offers great rewards with no hassles. Of course, they never find it. The neglected fig tree bears no fruit.

The proverb can be given an application in the Lord's church as well. Service in the kingdom usually involves duties that are not glamorous. That's why it's so hard to get brethren to do them. But there are a few good souls who don't mind the toil and trouble, and willingly commit themselves to the work. It is they who "keep the fig trees" in the Lord's vineyard, and will someday be honored by their Master for their labor.

What is your fig tree? And how much attention are you giving it?

Why Government Grows

In every election season, attention is focused on our politicians and their qualifications. Perhaps we're looking at the wrong people.

Because of the transgression of a land, many are its princes; but by a man of understanding and knowledge right will be prolonged (Prov. 28:2).

౸

When the delegates to the Continental Congress of 1776 signed the Declaration of Independence, they listed a number of complaints that, in their view, warranted the creation of a new government. One of the charges they leveled against King George III was that "he has erected a multitude of New Offices, and sent hither swarms of Officers to harass our people, and eat out their substance." They saw the growth of government bureaucracy as a curse upon the colonies, an unnecessary burden that rendered their King "unfit to be the ruler of a free people." So they severed their ties with that government and established another, based upon their conviction that good people do not require the heavy hand of government to rule themselves.

Over two thousand years before the American colonies rebelled against their British overlords, Solomon observed a connection between the character of a nation and its government. Moffatt translates this proverb, "Many a mishap crime brings on a country; good order is maintained by honest men." In other words, the expansion of an oppressive government is inversely proportional to the moral fiber of the population. If people cannot regulate their own passions to maintain an orderly society, someone (the government) will have to impose the regulations for them.

A modern version of this proverb is captured in the maxim, "every country has the government it deserves." This saying (attributed to Joseph de Maistre, a French diplomat and writer, 1753-1821), turns attention away from the government to *the people* being governed. Citizens who display honesty, hard work, and compassion in their lives do not need a government telling them how to run their affairs—and resent the intrusion when it does. On the other hand, people who are greedy, irresponsible, and lazy cannot maintain good order on their own, and require someone else to do it for them. They deserve the government they get.

In our own nation, the Founding Fathers created a form of government designed for a moral people, with a bare minimum of governmental oversight. But over a hundred Congresses and a civil war later, today we have the very thing our forefathers once rebelled against: "a multitude of new offices, and . . . swarms of officers to harass our people, and eat out their substance." Solomon tells us that we cannot blame our politicians for this development. The real story here is that *the character of our people has changed.* Over the last several generations, we have turned into a nation of self-indulgent sheep who are more than willing to let our government make the tough decisions for us. We deserve the government we've created.

This development is not surprising. In fact, Thomas Jefferson—the author of the Declaration of Independence—believed that "the natural progress of things is for liberty to yield, and government to gain ground" (letter to Edward Carrington, May 27, 1788). That it should be thus is a reflection on the people, not their politicians.

Dealing with Our Sin

Our world is a wreck, corrupted by the power of sin. We can't fix the world, but personal healing is available to each of us, if we are willing to seek it.

He who covers his sins will not prosper, but whoever confesses and forsakes them will have mercy (Prov. 28:13).

In this simple couplet, the book of Proverbs summarizes two competing approaches to dealing with sin in our lives. Understanding these two approaches explains much of the brokenness we see in the world around us and within us—and a way out of it.

First, the author describes the man who chooses to "cover" his sins. Other translations read "conceal" (ESV), "hide" (GNT) or "whitewash" (Message). The image is that of a man who, instead of addressing his sin problem directly, seeks to camouflage the defects that are undermining his life. We humans have devised a number of ways to cover our sins: We deflect the blame onto others; or we redefine our sin as a mere "misstep" or "mistake in judgment" that can be shrugged off; or we justify our sin as a legitimate response to the wrongdoing of others. Whatever the details, the goal is always the same: to avoid the hard fact that we have done wrong. Our pride will not allow us to admit failure.

Regardless of the strategy, the concealment never works to our advantage—we "will not prosper." Sin is a cancer on our character, and denying its presence only allows it to metastasize and spread. The disease in our soul sets us up for greater failures, and in time will eventually destroy us.

But it doesn't have to be that way. The preferred alternative involves two responses: *confessing* and *forsaking* our sins. Both are necessary to fix what's broken.

Confessing our sin is the antithesis of covering it. We confess our sin when we openly admit it—no excuses, no subterfuge, no equivocations, just an honest admission that "I have sinned" (2 Sam. 12:13; Psa. 41:4; Lk. 15:21). That confession first must be directed to God, the chief victim in every sin; then to others who may have been affected by our failure (Jas. 5:16; Matt. 5:23-24). Confession of sin is not a magic formula that confers benefits, but a realignment of our heart with the truth of who we are and what we have done. We cannot deal with sin in our lives if we harbor a lie in our heart.

But confession alone is meaningless if we do not also "forsake" the sin. That's a synonym for *repentance*, a change of heart that resolves on a new direction in our life. Pharaoh, King Saul, Judas, and many others were willing to admit "I have sinned" (Ex. 10:16; 1 Sam. 15:30; Matt. 27:4), but their confessions were not coupled with true repentance, so their lives descended deeper into chaos and destruction. The same fate awaits us if we do not commit to radical change.

Finally, notice the outcome of a policy of confession and repentance. We would expect the outcome to be "shall prosper"—the opposite of "not prosper" in the first part of the verse. Instead, the result is "will have mercy." By building confession and repentance into our lives as a habitual response to our failings, we are promised God's forgiveness. The burden of guilt is gone, and that psychological freedom allows us to move on with our life. There is no room here for moral preening. Remember, we have confessed to *failure*—we have earned nothing but have been given so much.

This world is a broken mess, and each one of us contributes our fair share to the problem by wearing masks, playing games, and pretending to be something we are not—and the dishonesty is killing us. The path to healing begins with learning to confess and forsake my sin. Do I have the integrity and courage to do so?

Navigating Relationships

The process by which a young man and young woman bond together must respect some basic ground rules, if their relationship is to endure.

There are three things which are too wonderful for me, yes, four which I do not understand: The way of an eagle in the air, the way of a serpent on a rock, the way of a ship in the midst of the sea, and the way of a man with a virgin (Prov. 30:18-19).

This proverb is puzzling at first reading, but with a little thinking the hidden meaning emerges—and provides much-needed guidance for young people in navigating gender relations in our modern age.

The first three items describe natural phenomena consisting of an *object* (eagle, serpent, ship) making its way through a given *environment* (air, rock, sea). The pairings make sense, because the objects are designed to function only in their respective environments. There are laws that govern how these objects and environments interact. But mix up the pairings and disaster ensues: A serpent flying in the air? An eagle sailing in the sea? A ship slithering along on a rock? These pairings don't fit, because they were not designed to fit. The laws of nature will not allow it.

These examples, says the wise man, illustrate "the way of a man with a virgin." There is a natural order ("laws") that define how a man finds his way into the heart of a woman. If a man and woman respect those laws and behave accordingly, a beautiful relationship can be realized. Their companionship will be as graceful as an eagle soaring in the sky, as smooth as a snake gliding along a rock, as powerful as a ship plowing through the waves—*but only if the rules are honored.*

In our modern Western culture, the rules governing male/female relationships have been trashed. Traditional gender roles have been muddled. Sex is no longer considered sacred. Covenant marriage has been replaced by casual hookups. Relationships are no longer permanent and enduring, but transactional and fleeting. Ships are trying to fly like eagles, and it's not working. Young people by the millions are suffering from an epidemic of loneliness, depression, and guilt.

The cure for the problem is simple, but it requires a surrender to age-old principles that define the innate relationship between men and women:

- Men and women are distinct genders with naturally defined roles.
- Healthy companionship is based on more—a *lot* more—than just sex.
- Emotional and spiritual compatibility is far more important than physical compatibility, and must be negotiated up front.
- Mutual happiness is forged in a commitment to lifelong permanence—"till death do us part."

Young people, don't be discouraged by all the relational wreckage around you. Respect the rules, and seek the one your heart desires. You'll be glad you did.

The Virtuous Wife—
and Her Husband

A curious detail in the well-known description of a virtuous wife highlights her role in her husband's success. The wise husband will honor her for it.

Who can find a virtuous wife? For her worth is far above rubies. . . Her husband is known in the gates, when he sits among the elders of the land" (Prov. 31:10, 23).

Solomon's description of the virtuous wife in Proverbs 31 has been the foundation of many sermons on the qualities of a good wife. Her hard work, generosity, devotion to her family, kindness to others—all of these traits are lauded as the attributes of a woman who will be highly esteemed by her family and her community.

But there is a oddity in this text that bears a closer look. The entire section of v. 12-27 is devoted to a description of the wife—except for v. 23. Right in the middle of extolling her many fine qualities, the author inserts a comment about her husband's reputation in the community. I suppose it's possible to draw a connection from his reputation back to her character, but the comment seems out of place. What is it doing there?

The answer is found in a common literary device often found in the Hebrew Scriptures known as *chiasm*. A chiasm is a structural arrangement that links thoughts in an *ascending* order up to a key pivot point, or central concept, then repeats the same thoughts in a reverse *descending* order. In Proverbs 31, for example, "She works with her hands" (v. 13) is mirrored by "she does not eat the bread of idleness" (v. 27).

Likewise, "she makes tapestry for herself" (v. 22) links to "she makes linen garments and sells them" (v. 24). It's a fun exercise to go through this passage and find the parallels going up to, and down from, the central verse.

So what is the central verse in this chiasm? It's v. 23—"Her husband is known in the gates, when he sits among the elders of the land." This is not a random observation thrown in to break the monotony. His place in the community is the whole point of this paean to feminine virtue: *A good wife makes a successful husband.* Note that the entire passage begins with "her husband trusts in her" (v. 11) and ends with "her husband praises her" (v. 28)—more evidence of the chiasm. Thus, the beginning, middle, and end of the text stresses her primary objective in life as empowering her husband to be successful in society.

Naturally, modern feminists go nuts with this. The very idea of a woman's worth being tied to a man is considered demeaning. But that criticism fails to see the beauty of this arrangement. Yes, her contributions at home enable her husband to go out into the world and make a name for himself. But here is the key message in this chapter: *She shares the honor with her husband.* This passage emphasizes the symbiotic relationship of a husband and wife in a healthy marriage. She helps him get ahead in his career by maintaining a happy and productive home; and she enjoys all the perks of being the life companion of a successful man. Everybody wins (including, by the way, the children who are fortunate to be raised in such a balanced family).

A wise woman recognizes the unique role in which God has placed her, and stays busy fulfilling it. A wise husband recognizes the value of such a wife, and goes out of his way to praise, honor, and dignify her for her sacrifices. God's design for marriage works, if we will only give it a chance.

Women and Children

By ditching the traditional model of father, mother, and children, radical feminism has unleashed a wave of destruction on family life.

Who can find a virtuous wife? For her worth is far above rubies. The heart of her husband safely trusts her; . . . She watches over the ways of her household, and does not eat the bread of idleness. Her children rise up and call her blessed; her husband also, and he praises her (Prov. 31:10-11, 27-28).

"A woman needs a man like a fish needs a bicycle."

That feminist proverb, first coined by Australian Irina Dunn and popularized by Gloria Steinem in the 1970s, became the rallying cry for millions of young women in the decades that followed. Eager to cast off the patriarchal shackles that (they believed) stifled their freedom, women launched themselves into education, business, politics, and even the military, determined to prove that they could do just fine without men, thank you.

This spirit of independence impacted their view of family life as well. Aided by looser divorce laws, women ditched their husbands at much higher rates than before. Many women bypassed marriage altogether, choosing to have babies by men who had no intention of sharing in the raising of their offspring. Inspired by female celebrities whose fatherless kids enjoyed lives of glamour, ordinary young women also had babies without marrying the fathers. Of course, in the absence of a staff of nannies, cooks, and housekeepers, single motherhood for these girls turned out to be not so glamorous.

Half a century into this revolution, the results are appalling. Several generations of children have grown up without a father in their lives. The boys raised in this environment are restless, rootless, and undisciplined. The girls are struggling with self-image and relationship issues. Rates of depression, mental illness, and suicide among the young are skyrocketing. Meanwhile, the older women who proudly chose to live their lives solo are approaching their later years lonely and sad.

When God created the nuclear family with a husband/father and wife/mother working as a team to raise their own children, He knew what He was doing. Moderns can mock this traditional arrangement all they want, but history has demonstrated that it is by far the most efficient and effective way to prepare little humans for the rigors of the life that lies before them. We tamper with this design to civilization's peril.

If a woman chooses to live her life without a man, she is free to do so. But the old feminist motto has a corollary that is often overlooked: "A child needs a father like a fish needs water." Young women, if you choose to bring a little baby into this world, then for the child's sake, don't even think of doing so without a good man by your side.

Liberated ... and Lonely

Decades of feminist dogma have achieved remarkable gains for women—but at a steep price. The Bible offers a sensible alternative.

Strength and honor are her clothing; she shall rejoice in time to come. . . . A woman who fears the Lord, she shall be praised. Give her of the fruit of her hands, and let her own works praise her in the gates (Prov. 31:25, 30-31).

This description of the virtuous wife has been the model to which young women have aspired for ages. This ideal involved a lot of hard work, but the payoff came in the form of the gratitude heaped upon women by their families and by society. The praise that women received "in the gates"—that is, in the highest echelons of cultural power—was the reward for their hard work.

All that changed in the 1960s, at least in Western cultures. Women began to be exposed to a drumbeat of discontent, being told that as wives and mothers they were being victimized and taken advantage of. Women were encouraged to "liberate" themselves from the chains of their traditional roles and to "fulfill their potential" outside the home. The watchword was "equality," and women were led to believe that they ought to compete with men as absolute equals, recognizing no distinctions between the sexes. So today women can work like men, drink like men, curse like men, and have unrestricted sex like men (except on college campuses, where women reserve the right to be treated as delicate little snowflakes who can be traumatized by a single inappropriate glance from a male. Go figure.).

Half a century later, how is that project working out? The latest evidence suggests: not too well.

Sociologists are now worried about a looming crisis in women's mental health. A report published by UK's NHS Digital revealed that one in five women have CMD [common mental disorder] symptoms, compared to one in eight men. Among young women (age 16 to 24), CMD symptoms are almost three times that of young men. CMD symptoms include various forms of depression and anxiety (*The Adult Psychiatric Morbidity Survey—Survey of Mental Health and Wellbeing, England*, 2014).

This trend is personalized in a recent book by journalist Andrea Tantaros, *Tied Up in Knots* (subtitled: *How Getting What We Wanted Made Women Miserable*) (2016). She wrote: "My generation felt the deluge of motivational messages that encouraged us to capitalize on our newfound female power. While I'm truly thankful for this array of choices, nobody told us there would be consequences. It almost seems like we were duped, or unconsciously misled at best."

In her review of Tantaros' book, author Suzanne Venker noted, "In the name of equality, women have renounced their femininity and are now regretting it. . . . A woman's true value lies in the way she was made. She doesn't need to change anything or to prove anything in order to be worthy or happy. She only needs to embrace it" ("The Unhappy Female, Brought to You by Feminism," *PJ Media* online, June 6, 2016).

Feminism was doomed to fail for one obvious reason: Men and women are not equal. Biologically, psychologically, emotionally, and temperamentally they are different, and no amount of social engineering can change that fact. They were designed by God to occupy distinct but complementary roles in society, and we disregard that design to our harm—as a generation of young women is now learning.

Feminine Women

Men and women are different . . . for a perfectly valid reason. We tinker with that distinction to the detriment of everybody involved.

Charm is deceitful and beauty is passing, but a woman who fears the LORD, she shall be praised (Prov. 31:30).

In an effort to understand the stubborn pay gap between men and women that exists in the workplace, researchers at Harvard University recently conducted a long-term study to isolate the reasons for the disparity. They took pains to study men and women who worked the *same* jobs at the *same* place under the *same* work rules. Even in those conditions, they found a small pay gap. As the researchers dug deeper into the details, they discovered the culprit: When overtime opportunities arose, the women were less likely than men to seize those opportunities. Men wanted the extra money to support their families, while women wanted the extra time to spend with their kids. The researchers concluded that "the gap . . . can be explained entirely by the fact that, while having the same choice sets in the workplace, women and men make different choices" (John Phelan, "Harvard Study: 'Gender Wage Gap' Explained Entirely by Work Choices of Men and Women," *FEE Stories* online, December 10, 2018).

Men and women make different life choices because on the whole, they have different interests, different priorities, different goals. Contrary to what radical feminists assert, women have a nurturing instinct that makes them ideally suited for caring for children. They have an innate level of tenderness, patience, and unselfish devotion that men struggle to grasp. That explains the universal phenomenon of mothers giving up the last piece of pie for the kids to eat, or little ones running to mom rather than dad to treat a skinned knee, or judges in divorce cases overwhelmingly awarding custody of kids to the mother.

The description of "the virtuous wife" in Proverbs 31 is saturated with this kind of domestic language. Her primary role is to "watch over the ways of her household" (v. 27), and she accomplishes that mission with dignity and honor. This does not preclude her from earning an income on her own (v. 13-14, 18, 24); but that is secondary to her primary role as homemaker. In contrast to the feminist dogma that denigrates homemakers, this woman is praised for the work she does for her family (v. 28-30).

If men build civilization, it is women who preserve it. When women try to compete with men as absolute equals, they not only lose, they undermine that which makes them special. Young women, your femininity contributes a unique benefit to humanity. Take pride in that role, and you will find all the fulfillment your heart desires.

Ecclesiastes: Making Sense of Life

Ecclesiastes can be perplexing to the casual reader, but a few keys reveal it to be the most relevant book in the Bible for modern man.

"Vanity of vanities," says the Preacher; "Vanity of vanities, all is vanity" (Eccl. 1:2).

ତ∞ଧ

The word "vanity" in this opening line—meaning futility, emptiness, or meaninglessness—sets the tone for much of the book of Ecclesiastes. The author (Hebrew: *Qoheleth*, the Preacher, or the Assembler) struggles to find some purpose in life, but at least initially that purpose escapes him: "All is vanity and grasping for the wind" (1:14); that is, everything about life is empty, useless, pointless. To the casual reader, Ecclesiastes can be the most depressing book in the Bible.

But God put this book in the Bible for a reason, and the pessimism that pervades its pages is there for a reason. As difficult as the quest might be, we can profit from exploring the Preacher's painful view of life.

Three keys unlock the book's message for the modern reader. Read with these keys in mind, and it makes sense.

First, unlike other Biblical writers, the author of Ecclesiastes writes largely from the standpoint of *personal experience*, not divine guidance. Nowhere in this book do we read, "thus says the Lord." Instead, the author tells us again and again, "I have seen" (1:14; 5:13; 6:1; 10:5). He is describing an attempt to figure out the purpose of life on his own, without any direction from an outside authority. Like every skeptic before and after him, the author is on a quest to figure out life on his own terms. But this approach restricts his evaluation of life to a narrow range of vision. The scope of his observations is vast, but it is still limited to what is done "under the sun"—a phrase that is used 29 times in the book. With that self-imposed limitation, his brooding observations may or may not be valid.

Second, the author is obsessed, not with the general rules by which life should be lived, but with the *exceptions* to those rules. In this respect, Ecclesiastes is the antithesis of its predecessor, Proverbs. Proverbs catalogs general maxims which will lead to a happy, successful life; Ecclesiastes is preoccupied with those occasions where the maxims break down.

Finally, in sharp contrast to modern skeptics, the author *has an open mind*, a willingness to learn from his quest. While he starts from a position of skepticism, his investigation teaches him truths that believers take for granted. That's why, despite all the gloom and pessimism that pervades the book, God makes frequent appearances throughout (2:24; 3:13-18; 5:18-20; and more). The author comes to realize that only by acknowledging the overarching hand of Providence can life on this earth make any sense.

If we study Ecclesiastes with these three keys in hand, the book reveals itself to be perfectly suited to a skeptical age such as our own. It acknowledges that life can be unfair, full of contradictions and pain, having no apparent purpose. But it also points us to our Creator, who gives meaning and purpose to our lives, despite the disorientation.

The author began his search with a despairing premise, "all is vanity." But his search finally revealed that, in fact, nothing in this life is vain; even the smallest details have meaning, if performed under the watchful eyes of God: "Let us hear the conclusion of the whole matter: Fear God and keep His commandments, for this is man's all. For God will bring every work into judgment, including every secret thing, whether good or evil" (12:13-14).

The Empty Life

> A life spent accumulating for ourselves will leave us feeling empty, as though something is missing. In fact, something *is* missing.

*All things are full of labor; man cannot express it. The eye is **not satisfied** with seeing, nor the ear filled with hearing (Eccl. 1:8).*

*There is one alone, without companion: He has neither son nor brother. Yet there is no end to all his labors, **nor is his eye satisfied** with riches (Eccl. 4:8).*

*He who loves silver will **not be satisfied** with silver; nor he who loves abundance, with increase. This also is vanity (Eccl. 5:10).*

*All the labor of man is for his mouth, and yet the soul is **not satisfied** (Eccl. 6:7).*

⚜

The repeated refrain in these verses of someone being "not satisfied" with life contributes to the grim portrait of human existence found in the book of Ecclesiastes. The author complains that life under the sun is not only not fair, it is often pointless. Despite all our hard work, we remain disillusioned with what we have accomplished. We push ourselves to work more, accumulate more, experience more—but it's never enough. A perpetual emptiness hangs over our days like a crotchety old school teacher, reminding us of the insignificance of our efforts. It's not that we make mistakes—at least we can grow through those—but that even our accomplishments do not provide a lasting sense of purpose in our lives.

This dissatisfaction poisons every aspect of our lives, including how we relate to others. As social critic Eric Hoffer observed, "Our greatest pretenses are built up not to hide the evil and the ugly in us, but our emptiness. The hardest thing to hide is something that is not there" (*The Passionate State of Mind*, 1955). We want desperately for others to see us as important, while deep inside we ache for the smallest scrap of self-worth. So we posture and strut to convince others—and ourselves—that we really are special. Only it never works, and we come off looking foolish.

It is this "nothing there" feeling that Qoheleth is addressing in Ecclesiastes. We cram our lives with so much activity that we can't find time for it all, yet struggle with a gnawing sense that what we're doing is not enough—or worse, is not all that important. There's something still missing from our lives. What is it?

Go back and read these verses again, and notice a clue that the author gives us. The dissatisfaction he describes is tied directly to *work* and *money*. If our lives feel empty, it's because we're trying to fill them with the wrong treasure. Work and money have a legitimate place in our lives, but it's a mistake to expect them to define our self-worth. They can't.

Jesus picked up where Qoheleth left off, and went straight to the core of the matter: "One's life does not consist in the abundance of things he possesses" (Lk. 12:15). Contrary to the popular maxim, clothes do not make the man—and neither do houses, cars, careers, investments, and so on. If we're going to find fulfillment, we'll have to look elsewhere. Jesus points the way: "Seek the kingdom of God . . . sell what you have and give alms; provide yourselves money bags which do not grow old, a treasure in the heavens that does not fail" (v. 31, 33). Our souls will find satisfaction, in other words, when we put God first and use our lives to serve others.

The empty life is not a problem of busy-ness; it's a problem of priorities. Get your priorities straight, and your life will be rich with meaning.

The Search for Meaning

Working may provide momentary satisfaction, but someday we will look back on our toil with regret. What are we knocking ourselves out for?

Then I looked on all the works that my hands had done and on the labor in which I had toiled; and indeed all was vanity and grasping for the wind. There was no profit under the sun. . . . Therefore I hated life because the work that was done under the sun was distressing to me, for all is vanity and grasping for the wind (Eccl. 2:11, 17).

※

In his autobiography, John Stuart Mill tells of an unsettling insight he experienced as a young man. As an exercise in self-reflection, he posed the following question to himself: "Suppose that all your objects in life were realized; that all the changes in institutions and opinions which you are looking forward to, could be completely effected at this very instant: Would this be a great joy and happiness to you?"

After pondering the question for a while, he finally came to the conclusion that the most honest answer was, "No." He realized that even if he succeeded in transforming this world into everything he thought it should be, something would still be missing. That epiphany had a profound influence in charting the direction of his life.

Mill had stumbled upon the same truth that the author of Ecclesiastes had discovered thousands of years before: *External circumstances are not the door to inner peace.* We long for a place of contentment and happiness in life, where all our needs are satisfied and the world poses no threat to our security. We have different avenues of pursuing that Nirvana: through hard work and thrift; through social activism; through carnal pleasure and excitement; through plumbing the depths of thousands of years of human knowledge and wisdom. Yet whichever path we choose, the end result is always the same: "vanity and grasping for the wind." We fill our lives with activities, but our souls remain starved of any meaningful reason for existence. The existential angst that is consuming our current generation—the most prosperous and privileged that has ever lived—proves that the paradigm hasn't changed. *Something is still missing*, and we can't seem to put our finger on it.

The author of this book resolved his search for meaning in life when he put God back into the equation: "Let us hear the conclusion of the whole matter: Fear God and keep His commandments, for this is man's all. For God will bring every work into judgment, including every secret thing, whether good or evil" (Eccl. 12:13-14). He came to realize that this world and its affairs are not the ultimate reality. There is a judgment and an eternity beyond this life, and it is *that* life that gives this one meaning. Only when our work is performed for God's glory, not ours, will we be pleased with it.

If your major goals in life are confined to this realm, you're aiming too low. Cast your gaze upon a more distant haven, and discover a deeper contentment you did not know was possible.

Is That All There Is?

If it seems like your life is missing something, despite all your work and leisure activities, maybe it's because you're looking in the wrong place.

Therefore I hated life because the work that was done under the sun was distressing to me, for all is vanity and grasping for the wind (Eccl. 2:17).

Those of my generation will recall the following lines from the 1969 Peggy Lee song, "Is That All There Is?":

Is that all there is?
Is that all there is?
If that's all there is, my friends
Then let's keep dancing
Let's break out the booze and have a ball
If that's all there is.

The song reflects the struggles of a young woman who, having experienced a series of tragedies in her life, fails to see any purpose in her existence. The best she can do is just keep dancing and drinking, waiting for the final disappointment in a death that will be as meaningless as her life.

These words captured the *zeitgeist* of the Sixties, and continue to define the unhappiness of a deeply secular culture today. We long for contentment, peace, and fulfillment in a variety of worldly pursuits, but our goal remains elusive. Like this young woman, we end up disillusioned, resigned to a life of drudge labor and cheap pleasures, haunted by a nagging fear of emptiness: *Is that all there is?*

The book of Ecclesiastes informs us that this sense of lostness is not a new development in human history. Three thousand years ago, a wise man recognized the same spirit of futility in his life. Like him, we chase our dreams furiously, determined to find our purpose in industry, the arts, wealth, education, or whatever. Yet no matter what we accomplish, we always come back to the same forlorn doubt: *Is that all there is?* There is a reason the suicide rate is highest in the most prosperous societies on earth . . . among those who have drifted farthest from God.

It never occurs to us that the despair we feel in this world is because we were designed for life in another. If what we experience here seems so fleeting, so ephemeral, that's because it is. What we do in this life has meaning only in the context of a far greater existence that lies beyond the grave.

The author of Ecclesiastes did not find the answer to life's riddle in booze and partying. He finally found it in a more expansive view of life: "Fear God and keep His commandments, for this is man's all. For God will bring every work into judgment, including every secret thing, whether good or evil" (12:13-14).

Yes, everything we do in this life matters. But we won't see the real value until we reach the other side. Choose your lifestyle accordingly.

The Builders

God did not put us on this earth merely to take up space, but to make things of value. For Christians, that duty has a special significance.

A time to break down, and a time to build up (Eccl. 3:3).
I will build My church, and the gates of Hades shall not prevail against it (Matt. 16:18).

Have you noticed how often the Bible describes people building things? Consider some examples:

- Noah built the ark to save his family from the flood, using instructions God gave him.
- Moses and the Israelites built the tabernacle and its furnishings in the wilderness, to serve as God's meeting place for His people.
- Centuries later, Solomon built his magnificent temple to replace the tabernacle. It became a monument to the glory of God, not only to the Jews but also among the Gentiles.
- Following the return from Babylonian captivity, Nehemiah led the people in rebuilding the walls of Jerusalem, so essential to the city's long-term security.
- The apostle Paul, so famous for building local churches, was also a tent-maker. He found dignity in building things with his hands.

There is something about human nature that drives us to build things. All of human history can be summarized as one long building enterprise. We have learned to master the physical world around us to build houses, monuments, tools, machines, works of art, clothing, farms, ships, vehicles, computers, systems, cities, corporations, empires, civilizations. We are so clever we can even build devices that can take us to the moon and beyond. Whether for functionality or beauty—or sometimes both—humans love to build things. Even in the aftermath of terrible wars, earthquakes, and other disasters that demolish our works, we immediately set about to build anew.

It should not surprise us, therefore, to read of Jesus the carpenter "building" His church. This is a figure of speech, of course; He has no interest in temples of wood and stone. The metaphor describes *a special group of people* who honor and follow Him. These people have an outlook on life that sets them apart from others. Like Jesus, they use their time and talents to serve others, not themselves. They have a remarkable resiliency that allows them to weather the storms of life with dignity. As a whole, this group of people is a wonder to behold. Like a magnificent cathedral that displays the genius of its architect, they were built for that very purpose.

And guess what? A major component of these people's work is also building. They "build up" (edify) one another by their teaching, encouraging, and exhorting each other (1 Cor. 14:12; Eph. 4:12). It's what God created them to do, and He has equipped them with the resources to do it well.

Friend, God put you on this earth to build. Whatever your talents and inclinations, get busy using them to fulfill God's purpose for your life. When your time on earth is done, the world will be a better place for your having been here.

Eternity in the Heart

Human beings are unique in the animal kingdom, but one particular feature puts us closer to God than anything else: our awareness of the infinite.

He has put eternity in their hearts, except that no one can find out the work that God does from beginning to end (Eccl. 3:11).

For since the creation of the world His invisible attributes are clearly seen, being understood by the things that are made, even His eternal power and Godhead, so that they are without excuse (Rom. 1:20).

༺༻

The Hebrew word translated "eternity" in Ecclesiastes literally means "that which is hidden," particularly in respect of time. Elsewhere in the Old Testament it is used to describe the infinite, the everlasting, a long span of time, neither the beginning nor ending of which is visible to us.

Our bodies are captive to the concept of time, having distinct boundaries at conception and death. We measure our time upon this earth in days, months, and years, knowing that it won't last forever. We are transient creatures painfully aware of our limits.

However, unlike the lower animals, whose consciousness is largely focused on the present moment, humans have the ability to think of time as a continuum that stretches far beyond what we experience in this mortal life. This awareness of the infinite, stretching behind and before us, is a gift that God has placed in our hearts. It's a unique quality that positions us to contemplate reality far outside the bounds of our brief lives.

Alexander MacLaren describes this awareness as "a repressed but immortal consciousness that [one] belongs to another order of things, which knows no vicissitude and fears no decay." It is "a spark of eternity" that has enormous implications for how we think about life.

This conception of the infinite, for example, allows us to ponder the vastness of the universe. When we look up into the heavens on a clear moonless night, our minds are drawn to wonder at the seemingly endless expanse of space and time it displays. As science presses deeper into the far reaches of space, we have an understanding of the magnitude of the cosmos that the ancients could scarcely imagine. To our more enlightened ears, this "spark of eternity" screams even louder.

Our awareness of eternity also reinforces an intuition of personal immortality. That intuition, in turn, affects how we use the life we've been given. Even those who dismiss the idea of life after death must struggle with the bigger questions: Why am I here? What purpose does my brief passage through this life have? Or does it even have a purpose? These questions are hard-wired deep inside all of us—because we were created for eternity.

Finally, this eternity in the heart drives us to embrace the concept of God. It is no coincidence that virtually every branch of the human race has some kind of belief in a higher power. As Paul argues in Romans, all humanity can "clearly see" the eternal power of deity through what has been made. We have to suppress part of our humanness to deny Him.

But for all that, it remains that "no one can find out the work that God does from beginning to end." Our knowledge of the past and the future is shrouded in a fog we cannot penetrate. Our only recourse is to look to the revelation of the One who equipped us for Himself, the God who can see what we cannot.

Quietness in the House of God

When we come together to worship God, it's not about us—it's about Him. Our conduct in that moment should reflect our awe of Him.

Walk prudently when you go to the house of God; and draw near to hear rather than to give the sacrifice of fools, for they do not know that they do evil. Do not be rash with your mouth, and let not your heart utter anything hastily before God. For God is in heaven, and you on earth; therefore let your words be few (Eccl. 5:1-2).

When this book was written, "the house of God" referred to the temple, the grand edifice in Jerusalem where God's people came to worship Him. Today, Christians do not recognize any building as the dwelling place of God. Instead, God's "temple" is His people assembled in His name, whatever physical space they might occupy (1 Cor. 3:16; Eph. 2:20-21; Matt. 18:20).

With that distinction in mind, the advice here regarding going to the house of God still holds an important lesson today when we come together to worship God. When we gather in God's presence, we must take care to "walk prudently." Other versions read "watch your step" or "be careful." He is not telling us to avoid tripping in the foyer or to stay away from back-stabbing brethren (although either might be an issue in some churches). Rather, he is reminding us that we are coming into the presence of the almighty Creator, and must not treat the occasion lightly.

This principle is particularly appropriate in the words we speak. When we draw near to God, it should be "to hear." We are in the presence of the One who is in heaven; therefore, "let your words be few."

Too often, however, instead of listening, our worship consists of "the sacrifice of fools"—words spoken rashly or in haste (v. 2). For example, if we come before God to tell Him about *our* desires, *our* needs, *our* troubles, *our* concerns, we're missing the point. God already knows all that. Maybe our problems wouldn't be so burdensome if we would just be quiet and let God tell us how to respond to them with greater patience.

Or even worse, if we approach God to thank Him for making us so righteous that we are not like other men, then our pious prayers will rise no higher than the ceiling. Like the proud Pharisee, we've lost sight of our proper place; "we do not know that we do evil."

When we come together to worship God, our goal should be *to hear God speak* rather than to inform Him. We should listen to His word read and expounded; hear songs of encouragement; follow prayers of praise and adoration; be reminded again and again of the indescribable love of God displayed in His Son. *We are in the presence of God*—be quiet and listen!

But doesn't worship require words? Certainly, but listening must still be the primary emphasis. The preacher must deliver words that prick honest hearts; the prayer leader must speak words to which all can say "amen"; and when we join our voices in song, shouldn't we be listening to the words we are singing?

In any human relationship it's hard to learn anything if we are the ones doing all the talking. Effective communication requires careful listening; how much more so in our relationship with God! There is so much we could learn from Him, but we can't learn unless we close our mouths, open our ears, and listen quietly with reverent hearts.

The Misery of the Rich

> We set our hearts on getting rich, thinking that wealth is the path to contentment. But eventually we learn that money cannot buy happiness.

He who loves silver will not be satisfied with silver; nor he who loves abundance, with increase. This also is vanity (Eccl. 5:10).

Martin Sheen is an accomplished actor whose career has richly rewarded him, but it wasn't always that way. He grew up in a poor family, and had to support himself through his teen years, serving as a caddy for rich people at a nearby golf course. The experience taught him a valuable lesson: "The rich were my best teachers: I saw their inhumanity, selfishness, dishonesty, but I never saw a satisfied rich man. They were never happy with themselves. They always wanted more" (*Parade Magazine*, December 2, 2001).

Sheen's observation of the wealthy echoes that of Solomon thousands of years ago. Those who love money are never satisfied with what they have. The misery of the rich is not a product of our modern American culture; it is a common human weakness that can be found in every society throughout history.

What is it about wealth that makes people so unhappy? There are two principles at work here that explain this phenomenon.

First, *riches come with a whole set of unexpected troubles.* "When goods increase, they increase who eat them; so what profit have the owners except to see them with their eyes? The sleep of a laboring man is sweet, whether he eats little or much; but the abundance of the rich will not permit him to sleep" (Eccl. 5:11-12). The rich man has to worry about higher taxes, security, market collapses, maintenance costs, accounting fees, chiseling friends and relatives, and a host of other hassles that his more humble neighbors don't have to deal with. It is this hidden cost of wealth that makes many rich people so miserable.

But the greater problem is less tangible: *The abundance of the rich man cannot satisfy the deepest needs of his soul.* Qoheleth noted that "all the labor of man is for his mouth, and yet the soul is not satisfied" (Eccl. 6:7). Jesus expressed it a different way: "Take heed and beware of covetousness, for one's life does not consist in the abundance of the things he possesses" (Lk. 12:15). Material wealth can only buy material things; it cannot touch the soul of man. So when we seek to "buy" happiness, we will always end up disappointed, for we are using the wrong currency. Genuine happiness is the product of giving ourselves in service to others. God created human beings to give, not get; so a life devoted primarily to getting will always be shallow and empty.

The misery of the rich should teach all of us a lesson: "Godliness with contentment is great gain. For we brought nothing into this world, and it is certain we can carry nothing out. And having food and clothing, with these we shall be content" (1 Tim. 6:6-8).

The Tyranny of Stuff

Our consumeristic culture convinces us that we "need" more and more stuff. But accumulating more usually only leads to more headaches.

He who loves silver will not be satisfied with silver; nor he who loves abundance, with increase. This also is vanity. When goods increase, they increase who eat them; so what profit have the owners except to see them with their eyes? The sleep of a laboring man is sweet, whether he eats little or much; but the abundance of the rich will not permit him to sleep (Eccl. 5:10-12).

꘎

In this simple commentary on wealth, the author offers three reasons why prosperity is not all it's cracked up to be.

First, *the more we have, the less satisfied we are with what we have* (v. 10). Like any addiction, the accumulation of material wealth only feeds an insatiable lust for more. Once "getting more" becomes our goal, we've become hooked on a behavior that is as destructive as any drug.

Second, *the more we have, the more we must spend*—not "get" to spend, but "must" spend (v. 11). Think of taxes, security, maintenance, insurance, repairs, and so on—not to mention the time that must be devoted to all these activities. And then there are all the hangers-on who now see us as a good "friend," especially when they need a loan.

Finally, *the more we have, the more we worry.* Our anxiety over all the threats to our assets keeps us awake at night (v. 12). The pressures that come with maintaining a lifestyle of abundance make it difficult to enjoy it. Derek Kidner comments on this verse by pointing to our modern obsession with health clubs and exercise equipment: "It is one of our human absurdities to pour out money and effort just to undo the damage of money and ease" (*A Time to Mourn and a Time to Dance*, 1976).

Many years after this commentary on wealth was written, Jesus summarized the message even more succinctly: "One's life does not consist in the abundance of the things he possesses" (Lk. 12:15). No matter how much we may wish it so—or how hard we work to make it so—our possessions will never define who we are. In fact, in many cases, our possessions will feed behaviors that harm our character, not help it. We become slaves to the tyranny of our stuff, no longer in control of our own destiny.

Recognizing this danger, some argue for a lifestyle of minimalism, getting by with only the barest essentials in life. God does not require such a drastic response. What He wants is a fundamental *shift in thinking* about our possessions, an attitude of detachment that views our possessions not as an end unto themselves, but as tools for serving others. "Command those who are rich in this present age not to be haughty, nor to trust in uncertain riches but in the living God, who gives us richly all things to enjoy. Let them do good, that they be rich in good works, ready to give, willing to share" (1 Tim. 6:17-18).

Adopting such an attitude will result in decisions that likely will simplify our lives. More importantly, it will free us from our bondage to all the junk we have allowed to dominate our time. The lighter burden we carry will allow us to see the world—and ourselves—in a clearer light.

Winning and Losing

In a world that measures winning in material terms, it takes a radical mindset to view success using an entirely different set of criteria.

There is an evil which I have seen under the sun, and it is common among men: A man to whom God has given riches and wealth and honor, so that he lacks nothing for himself of all he desires; yet God does not give him power to eat of it, but a foreigner consumes it. This is vanity, and it is an evil affliction (Eccl. 6:1-2).

Donald Savastano, a construction worker in Sydney, New York, recently won a million dollar scratch lottery. Naturally, this windfall transformed his outlook on his future. "I'm probably going to go get a new truck and . . . probably go on vacation," he said when he collected his check. His new wealth also allowed him to pay a visit to the doctor, since he was not feeling too well.

Less than three weeks later, Mr. Savastano was dead from advanced brain and lung cancer.

I don't know who will inherit this man's fortune. But at this point, does it really matter? He won the lottery, but lost his life, and now the money means absolutely nothing to him.

Life is unfair, and stories like this reinforce that bitter truth. We work hard to accumulate more and more of this world's goods, with no guarantee that we will live to enjoy it. Even if we live a long life, death will eventually overtake us and separate us from everything we've gathered. In the end, no matter what else happens, we will lose it all.

Why does the pursuit of wealth blind us to this stark truth? Jesus identified the problem when a man requested that He intervene in an inheritance dispute with his brother (Lk. 12:13-21). This man had his eyes set on gaining control of the family fortune—and was even willing to blow up his family, if necessary, to get it. Jesus declined to get involved, and issued a stern warning to him and anyone else who would listen: "Take heed and beware of covetousness, for one's life does not consist in the abundance of the things he possesses" (v. 15). This man's problem was not a recalcitrant brother, but covetousness in his own heart. He was obsessed with something that someday he would have to leave behind for someone else to fight over.

Covetousness always warps our ability to see reality. It leads us to view success strictly in terms of monetary gain. More altruistic values, like generosity, service, compassion, hospitality, and so forth, get sacrificed on the altar of mammon. By concentrating our attention on worldly goods, we convince ourselves that we're on our way to winning the jackpot in life.

Except life doesn't work that way. Wealth is an illusion, an insidious con artist that draws our attention in one direction while robbing us of what's truly important in another. Only too late do we realize we've been swindled. Solomon pegged it correctly: "This is vanity . . . an evil affliction."

Whether we win or lose in life is not measured by our physical holdings. That's a losing hand, guaranteed. Life's purpose lies elsewhere, in using whatever resources we've been given to serve others. There's nothing glamorous about this lifestyle, but in the end, we'll appreciate the investment we made in this heavenly treasure. That is a winning strategy worth pursuing.

All the Work of God

The complexity of human life—indeed, of the whole universe—can overwhelm us with despair. But there is One who can help us make sense of it.

When I applied my heart to know wisdom and to see the business that is done on earth, even though one sees no sleep day or night, then I saw all the work of God, that a man cannot find out the work that is done under the sun. For though a man labors to discover it, yet he will not find it; moreover, though a wise man attempts to know it, he will not be able to find it. For I considered all this in my heart, so that I could declare it all: that the righteous and the wise and their works are in the hand of God (Eccl. 8:16 - 9:1).

As a wise and learned man, the author of Ecclesiastes sought to "see the business that is done on earth . . . the work that is done under the sun." Like many philosophers since, he wanted to understand it all—every detail of every activity of the entire human race. All the projects, all the achievements, all the labor, every piece of the magnificent puzzle that we call life.

But his grand mission failed. He came to realize that the scope of this project was so vast and complex that "a man will not be able to find" the full extent of this enterprise. The footprint of the human race is infinitely large, too large for us to comprehend, much less control. Those who look to centralized government planning for a solution to all our problems would do well to ponder this inescapable reality.

On a personal level, each one of us grapples with this same sense of helplessness as well. We struggle to understand the complexities of our own inner motives and behaviors. How could we hope to grasp even a tiny sliver of the rest of what's going on out there in the world? What meaning can my life have in the maelstrom of a chaotic universe? We feel so powerless, so weak, so lost.

The Preacher found the answer to his quest in one simple truth: "The righteous and the wise and their works are in the hand of God." We cannot understand everything that is going on around us—*but God can!* If we draw close to Him, if we place ourselves in the warm embrace of His love, we will find the solace our soul desires. Life has significance, but only in the context of a relationship with the One who created us and who alone understands all His work. That should be the focus of our life's endeavors.

Is it yours?

A God of Surprises

Historically, how God fulfills His promises has often caught people off-guard. How He fulfills His promises to us may also surprise us.

Then I saw all the work of God, that a man cannot find out the work that is done under the sun. For though a man labors to discover it, yet he will not find it; moreover, though a wise man attempts to know it, he will not be able to find it (Eccl. 8:17).

God promised Abraham that he would become the father of a great nation, a nation through which "all the families of the earth shall be blessed" (Gen. 12:2-3). The old patriarch lived just long enough to see the first sprouts of that tree come forth, but he died having no idea how it would play out.

When his descendants became a great nation, God sent prophets to them promising the arrival of a mysterious Messiah—"the anointed one"—who would judge the nations and bring righteousness to His people. For over a thousand years, Israel pined for their Savior to come. In the meantime, they endured afflictions externally from neighboring adversaries, and internally from wicked rulers and self-serving oligarchs. How long would they have to wait? And how would this Messiah make His entrance on the world stage? The Jews developed ideas about how it would all play out, but they really didn't know. The prophecies were not too specific.

When the Messiah did come, He surprised everyone. Instead of swooping down out of heaven on a white charger, smiting godless pagans in mass numbers, He came as a lowly carpenter. His teaching was unlike anything the people had ever heard, emphasizing personal character rather than political reform. He exposed the hypocrisy of the ruling classes, which got Him in serious trouble with them. The few disciples who stuck with Him to the bitter end were crushed to see Him crucified like a common criminal. Only after His resurrection did it all begin to make sense.

Now it's our turn. After His ascension into heaven, His apostles spoke of a Second Coming and a great judgment and eternal life in glorious bliss, far beyond the toils of this life. For two thousand years now, God's people are once again waiting, waiting, waiting . . . .

A cynic would say that God keeps moving the goal posts. He gets our hopes up, only to dash them on the rocks of reality, followed by more promises of future glory—someday. Yet after all this drama, here we are, still stuck in a world dominated by evil and suffering. What gives?

This quick overview of sacred history teaches us two important lessons:

First, *God keeps His promises.* The fulfillment may not be what we expected, but that's due to our myopic perspective, not His incompetence. If we are still awaiting the next stage in His master plan, we can be confident that He will deliver.

Second, *God's promises are enigmatic.* He shrouds them in cryptic language, revealing only the barest details in a manner that gives hope to the faithful while misleading the faithless. Only in retrospect can we make sense of the perplexing meanings in the earlier texts.

These two facts should temper my faith as I go through life. I can trust that God is working out a plan, and that someday I will see its final realization. In the meantime, I must be humble about my expectations, knowing that God may have surprises in store that I cannot now comprehend.

It's all about Him, not me. And that is enough.

Your Vain Life

Leave God out of the picture, and we have every reason to see our lives as meaningless. But put God back in the picture, and everything changes.

Live joyfully with the wife whom you love all the days of your vain life which He has given you under the sun, all your days of vanity; for that is your portion in life, and in the labor which you perform under the sun (Eccl. 9:9).

༄

Ecclesiastes has earned a reputation as one of the strangest books in the Bible. While it has none of the bizarre imagery of Daniel or Revelation, the gloomy theme of "vanity" (futility, meaninglessness) that dominates its pages leaves people shaking their heads. Unlike Proverbs, which highlights the clean cause-and-effect orderliness of this world, the author of Ecclesiastes is obsessed with its brokenness—the injustices, the tragedies, the inexplicable twists and turns that cause us to question if anyone is in charge.

Death plays a major role in this book. No matter what we may accomplish or how good we try to be, we all end up in the same place: dead (3:18-21; 6:3-6; 9:2-6). The author tries to put a positive spin on this dreary reality, but it comes across almost as an "eat, drink, and be merry" kind of fatalism (2:24-26; 3:22; 5:18; 8:15). What is the point of life anyway?

The pessimistic message of Ecclesiastes leaves the casual reader cold. Why is this book even in the Bible?

First, Ecclesiastes speaks directly to the hopelessness of a deeply secular culture. Ours is not the first culture to lose its reason for existence. As belief in God and religion declines in our society, the growing rates of mental illness and suicide that replace it validate the book's depressing message. When we try to live our life without God, we lose any ground for enjoying it. Ecclesiastes is a book for our time, a fitting starting point for someone grasping for meaning in their lives.

But the book does not leave us dangling in midair. In the closing chapter, the author ties all the loose ends together in a single burst of intellectual clarity: "Remember your Creator" (12:1). This life under the sun, with all its messiness and joylessness, is not all there is. "God will bring every work into judgment, including every secret thing, whether good or evil" (12:14). Everything I say and do in this life—*everything!*—echoes in eternity. I have a compelling reason, therefore, to make every moment count.

My life matters. It is not vain, so long as I keep my sight fixed on the eternal destiny that awaits me in the afterlife, and cling to the God who gives me that hope.

The Providence of God

God indeed works in mysterious ways. That He does so should cause us to treat His providence with a generous dose of humility.

As you do not know what is the way of the wind, or how the bones grow in the womb of her who is with child, so you do not know the works of God who makes all things (Eccl. 11:5).

A king has a torrid love affair with a neighbor's wife, and murders the neighbor to cover up the sin. Overcome with remorse, the king eventually makes things right with God; but the infant that is born from this illicit relationship is smitten with a serious illness. The king cries out to God for mercy on the innocent little life. Will God answer his fervent prayer? The king can say only, "Who can tell?" (2 Sam. 12:22).

To nurse a bruised ego, a corrupt government official plots to destroy all the Jews in the land. But his master the king has just married, and out of all the available women in the land, his bride happens to be a Jewess. The new queen discovers the plot and intercedes for her people. The corrupt official is hanged. Was the young woman's timely rise to royalty an act of God? Her cousin and counselor will say only, "Who knows?" (Esth. 4:14).

A slave becomes frustrated at his hopeless lot in life, and takes advantage of an opportunity to escape. He traverses hundreds of miles over land and sea to a foreign city where he hopes to find a new life. Out of the thousands of people who surround him in his new home, he happens to befriend a preacher who is personally acquainted with his old master. The preacher helps him find a new life in Christ, and sends him back to his Christian master, with a plea to receive him back as a brother. Was God responsible for the remarkable chain of events that led to the happy ending of this story? The inspired preacher will say only, "Perhaps" (Philemon 15).

Reading these stories thousands of years later, the outcomes seem so obvious, so inevitable. But to the original actors in these dramas, the last acts were agonizingly uncertain. They had no idea how everything would play out. "Who can tell?" "Who knows?" "Perhaps."

The Bible clearly teaches the active role of God in the affairs of men, or what we like to call "the providence of God." Every divine promise to answer prayer or provide assistance argues for it. But this does not give us a license to declare His hand in every detail of life. God does indeed work in mysterious ways, and it is impossible for us to accurately read every subtle influence that He exerts in our lives. Some things that seem to be favorable signs from God may really be delusions designed to test our faith (2 Thess. 2:11-12). And some things that seem to be sorrowful may actually be blessings in disguise (such as the sufferings of Joseph, Gen. 50:20).

How can we tell the difference between a providential act of God and an ordinary act of nature uninfluenced by divine will? We can't! For that reason, we should always address the subject with a heavy dose of humility, using phrases like "who can tell?" or "perhaps" or "who knows?" Dogmatic claims of divine favor ("the Lord gave me a sign") smack of arrogance, and can be self-deceiving. Better to receive God's favor unknowingly, than to be lulled into a false sense of security by assumptions based on uncertain evidence.

Our duty in life is not to read God's mind, but to obey what He has revealed in His word. Let us be content with that, and trust God to do what is best regarding everything else.

Why Young People Are Depressed

American youth live in the freest, most prosperous nation on earth—yet are the most anxious and depressed. There is a solution to this problem.

Rejoice, O young man, in your youth, and let your heart cheer you in the days of your youth; walk in the ways of your heart, and in the sight of your eyes; but know that for all these God will bring you into judgment. Therefore remove sorrow from your heart, and put away evil from your flesh, for childhood and youth are vanity (Eccl. 11:9-10).

ೞೀಲ

These words echo the counsel of old timers to the young throughout the ages: Enjoy your youth! Be happy! Have fun! Childhood should be a time of playful enthusiasm, of preparing to take on the world with boundless energy. Make the most of these exciting years!

But for many American young people, there is nothing to be excited about. Authorities are alarmed at the growing rates of anxiety, depression, drug abuse, and even suicide that are taking a toll among the young. Why is this happening?

There are several factors contributing to this generational meltdown. *The educational institutions* in which our kids spend much of their early lives have abandoned a commitment to truth and are engaged in a program to indoctrinate children in a secular worldview that leaves no room for God or traditional morality. Convince young people that they are merely an advanced species of ape, and they'll eventually start questioning life's purpose. If human existence has no meaning, why should their individual lives have meaning?

The news media in recent years has ginned up mass hysteria on issues relating to politics, gender, and apocalyptic scaremongering. Constant exposure to this kind of negativity leaves kids terrified of their adult futures. If the world is this awful, why should I want to live my whole lifetime in it?

These threats are magnified by the role that *social media* now plays in young people's lives. Several academic studies have noted that the sharp rise in these mental health issues coincided with the creation of Facebook and similar apps in the late 2000s. Young people in every generation have always struggled with peer pressure, but this generation's exposure to a vast network of instantaneous and unfiltered opinions and gossip has amplified that problem exponentially.

These are the influences that are converging to crush the spirits of our young people. But there is one other factor that looms larger than all others: *Poor parenting.* It is the role of parents not just to feed, clothe, and house their kids, but to prepare them for life emotionally, psychologically, and spiritually. Regrettably, the current generation of American parents is doing a dismal job of that. Far too many children are being raised as little more than family pets, with little or no guidance from the adults in their lives.

When children grow up in the embrace of a father and mother who love God, love each other, and love their offspring, they will thrive, regardless of what the surrounding culture is doing. The propaganda of a godless education system cannot offset the influence of parents who are teaching and modeling respect for God at home. Kids can brush off the fatalism of a negative media if they see parents who take on the challenges of life with hopeful enthusiasm. And social media cannot mess with kids' minds if parents are monitoring its use and enforcing restrictions as necessary.

Parents, be forewarned! Our culture has sinister designs on your children's future. You are the only thing standing between your kids and Satan's minions. You have one chance to do this job right, and precious little time. Make it count!

Young People, Remember God

The carefree exuberance of youth is a good thing, but only if it is tempered by an awareness that life has a higher purpose than fun.

Remember now your Creator in the days of your youth, before the difficult days come, and the years draw near when you say, "I have no pleasure in them" (Eccl. 12:1).

Youth is an awkward time of life. Young people are eager to grow up and find their purpose in life, but they must stumble over countless obstacles to reach that goal. Some young people learn humility and wisdom through these experiences; others learn nothing, and end up as embittered old people. Whichever direction a young person takes in making this transition, the simple truth is that the decisions she makes in her younger days will largely determine the kind of person she will be throughout the remainder of her life.

Having learned this truth the hard way, many of us older folks tend to lecture our young people to be serious, study hard, be responsible—in other words, act like grown-ups. The problem, of course, is that our young people are *not* grown-ups, and we err in trying to force them into that mold before they are ready. The author's advice to young people here is more reasonable: Be happy in your youth; enjoy all that life has to offer; explore the different paths before you; don't grow up before you have to.

But there is one caveat to this life lesson: "Know that for all these God will bring you into judgment" (Eccl. 11:9). The Preacher is not throwing cold water on a young person's fun here. He is reminding young people that the decisions they make now have consequences in later life. Have fun, yes; but keep one eye on the future, knowing that you are laying a foundation for the rest of your life. And once youth is spent, it cannot be recalled to live over again.

How does a young person maintain this balanced approach? The author summarizes it in a few words: "Remember now your Creator." This doesn't mean a young person must become a Bible-thumper, constantly reading the Bible and spouting scripture. Rather, it is describing a fundamental mindset that recognizes God, rather than self, as the center of one's life. If a young person can pass through these early years with an awareness that God is watching everything, her youthful exuberance will be tempered by a desire to do it right. She will make mistakes, of course; but they will not be fatal, and she will become a better person for them.

The Greek philosopher Euripides observed that "whoever neglects learning in his youth, loses the past and is dead for the future" (*Phrixus*). The greatest truth a young person can learn is that she is on this earth to glorify the God who created her. Once she learns this, she can really begin to enjoy life.

Tend Your Garden

Marriages, like gardens, require work to keep them healthy. The couple that reaps the fruit of that labor will be grateful they invested the effort.

"A garden enclosed is my sister, my spouse, a spring shut up, a fountain sealed. Your plants are an orchard of pomegranates with pleasant fruits, fragrant henna with spikenard, spikenard and saffron, calamus and cinnamon, with all trees of frankincense, myrrh and aloes, with all the chief spices. . . ." (Song of Solomon 4:12-13).

"Awake, O north wind, and come, O south! Blow upon my garden, that its spices may flow out. Let my beloved come to his garden and eat its pleasant fruits" (Song of Solomon 4:15).

The Song of Solomon is written as a dialogue between two lovers (with occasional commentary thrown in from the "daughters of Jerusalem," a sort of choral accompaniment). In this passage, the bridegroom addresses his bride as a garden full of all manner of delightful fruits and spices. The bride responds with an invitation to her lover to "come to his garden and eat its pleasant fruits."

If you want an erotic thrill, read 5:1 to see how this exchange turns out. Our concern here, however, is not with the conjugal nature of this couple's relationship, but with the metaphor that is used to describe that relationship, that of a garden full of fruits and spices.

That metaphor holds a lesson for couples today who are seeking to build a strong and stable marriage. Fruitful gardens do not grow on their own. They are the result of a lot of hard work. Tilling, fertilizing, weeding, pruning, pest control, watering—all of these activities must be attended to regularly in order for the garden to remain healthy and productive. Without this maintenance, a garden will degenerate into a weed patch and eventually die. The same thing will happen to a marriage if a couple does not work hard to prevent it.

Having made that point, however, I ask you to go back and read the opening text carefully. You will notice that the garden metaphor is specifically applied to the *bride*, not to the marriage in general. Husbands need to get a clue here. If a man desires to have a wife who is happy, supportive, and loving, then he must invest the time and effort to ensure that his "garden" is thriving. This interpretation is supported by Paul's admonition to husbands to "nourish and cherish" their wives (Eph. 5:29), language that reinforces the idea of tending and feeding a growing organism. (Think also of Adam's role in the Garden of Eden to "tend and keep it" [Gen. 2:15]. So when Eve came along, he had *two* gardens to care for—lucky guy!)

This does not mean that a successful marriage is entirely the husband's responsibility; nor does it imply that if the marriage fails, it is automatically the husband's fault. The wife also has a duty to make her husband's stewardship over the family as pleasant and easy as possible (Eph. 5:22-24; Tit. 2:3-5; 1 Pet. 3:1-6). The garden must respond to the tender care it is being given.

Couples, especially husbands, would do well to keep this garden metaphor in front of them constantly. They must work hard to keep their romance alive, to root out the little weeds that frequently pop up and threaten to choke their love for each other. There is nothing glamorous about this work; it's hard, annoying, and sometimes frustrating. But a strong and happy marriage is worth every bit of that work.

Scripture Index

Items highlighted in **bold text** are primary passages upon which the related articles are based. Items that are not bolded receive some level of additional treatment in articles. Incidental scripture references are not included here.

Reference	Page
Gen. 1	39
Gen. 1:26-27	**25**
Gen. 2:18	125, **289**
Gen. 2:15	400
Gen. 3:9	28
Gen. 3:22	26
Gen. 4:9	28
Gen. 11:7	26
Gen. 12:2-3	389
Gen. 18:17-19	197
Gen. 28:20-22	307
Gen. 50:20	182, 394
Ex. 4:14	33
Ex. 8:2	185
Ex. 10:16	356
Ex. 16:20	33
Ex. 20:1-17	197
Ex. 20:3	53
Lev. 5:17	61
Lev. 18:25	163
Num. 11	157
Num. 16:15	33
Num. 30:2	307
Deut. 4:9	197
Deut. 8:16	45
Deut. 12:31	163
Deut. 23:21-23	307
Deut. 24:19-21	198
Deut. 28:20, 28-29	**225**
Josh. 3:1	185
Josh. 23:16	33
Judg. 3:7	**159**
Judg. 11:30-40	307
1 Sam. 2:12-17	137
1 Sam. 13:8-14	282
1 Sam. 15:30	356
1 Sam. 20:41	115, 117
1 Sam. 21:10-15	117

Reference	Page
1 Sam. 30:4	115
1 Sam. 30:6	32
2 Sam. 1:11-12	115
2 Sam. 1:23-24	330
2 Sam. 3:32, 38	115
2 Sam. 12:13	356
2 Sam. 12:14	208
2 Sam. 12:16-21	116
2 Sam. 12:22	393
2 Sam. 14:25-26	248
2 Sam. 16:4	295
2 Sam. 18:33–19:4	116
2 Sam. 19:24-30	295
1 Kgs. 19:4	305
1 Chron. 16:27	**145**
1 Chron. 6:33	137
1 Chron. 15:16-17	137
2 Chron. 28:19	**149**
2 Chron. 30:18-20	62
2 Chron. 34:27	**143**
Neh. 2:17-18	341
Esth. 4:14	393
Job 1:1	5, 167
Job 1:5	185
Job 1:9-11	**1**
Job 1:21	**2, 3**
Job 1:22	1
Job 2:11, 13	19
Job 4:7-8	**5**
Job 4:17-19	**7**
Job 7:3-4	**9**
Job 7:15-16	**11**
Job 7:20	27
Job 9:2	27
Job 9:15	16
Job 9:27-28	**13**
Job 13:15	**65**
Job 13:15-16	**15**
Job 13:24	27
Job 13:26	**17**
Job 16:1-2	**19**
Job 23:4	27
Job 23:10	182
Job 27:8-9	**15**
Job 30:20	**207**
Job 31:1	**21**
Job 31:9-12	197
Job 31:14	27
Job 31:17-18	126
Job 35:14	**23**
Job 36:26	**25**
Job 38:3	**27**
Job 38:31-33	60
Psa. 2:2-4	**29**
Psa. 3:2	**31**
Psa. 4:4-5	**33**
Psa. 4:6	**31**
Psa. 4:23	144
Psa. 6:2	**35**
Psa. 6:6	181
Psa. 7:1	38
Psa. 7:14-16	**37**
Psa. 8:3-4	**39**, 60
Psa. 10:13	**41**
Psa. 11	43
Psa. 11:3	**43**, 45
Psa. 11:4	46
Psa. 11:5	**45**
Psa. 14:1	**47, 49**
Psa. 15:1-2	**51**
Psa. 16:4	**53**
Psa. 16:5-6	**55**
Psa. 18:2	71
Psa. 19:1	**57, 59**

Psa. 19:12-13	**61**, 306	**Psa. 51:12**	**109**
Psa. 22:10	108	**Psa. 53:1**	**47, 49**
Psa. 24:3-4	**63**	Psa. 55	111
Psa. 25:2	**65**	**Psa. 55:6-8**	**111**
Psa. 25:7	**17**, 309	**Psa. 55:12-14**	**113**, 285
Psa. 27:14	**67**	Psa. 56:2	117
Psa. 28:5	**69**	**Psa. 56:8**	**115**, 117
Psa. 31	71	**Psa. 56:9**	**117**
Psa. 31:2-3	**71**	Psa. 58:3	108
Psa. 32:5	**73**	**Psa. 61:1-3**	**119**
Psa. 32:9	**75**	Psa. 62	121
Psa. 34:11-14	**77**	**Psa. 62:5-6**	**121**
Psa. 34:19	**79**	**Psa. 63:2**	**123**
Psa. 37	81, 83, 87	**Psa. 68:6**	**125, 127**
Psa. 37:1, 3, 7, 8	**81**	**Psa. 69:30**	**129**
Psa. 37:7	**67**	Psa. 71:3	71
Psa. 37:9, 11, 22, 29	**87**	Psa. 73	133
Psa. 37:11	**83**	**Psa. 73:3-5**	**131**
Psa. 37:13	**29**, 82	**Psa. 73:24-25**	**133**
Psa. 37:25, 28	**85**	**Psa. 73:25-26**	**135**
Psa. 39:4-5	**89**	Psa. 88	137
Psa. 39:7	90, 181	**Psa. 88, 6, 18**	**137**
Psa. 41:1-2	92	**Psa. 90:9, 10, 12**	**139**
Psa. 41:4	356	**Psa. 94:17-19**	**141**
Psa. 41:3, 12	**91**	**Psa. 95:8-9**	**143**
Psa. 42:9-10	**93**	**Psa. 96:6**	**145**
Psa. 44:21	**95**	**Psa. 97:6**	**59**
Psa. 46:1-2, 10-11	**97**	**Psa. 100:3**	**147**
Psa. 46:10	**99**	Psa. 101	149
Psa. 49	101, 105	**Psa. 101:7**	**149**
Psa. 49:1-2	**101**	Psa. 102	151
Psa. 49:5, 15	**103**	**Psa. 102:2**	**151**
Psa. 49:11-12	**105**	**Psa. 103:2-5**	**153**
Psa. 49:14-15	104	Psa. 103:17-18	154
Psa. 51:3	305	Psa. 104	155
Psa. 51:5	**107**	**Psa. 104:5-9**	**155**
Psa. 51:6	52	**Psa. 106:13-15**	**157**

Psa. 106:13,14, 21	**159**	**Prov. 1:7**	**213, 215**
Psa. 106:24-25	**161**, 178	**Prov. 1:8**	**217**
Psa. 106:37-38, 40	**163**	Prov. 1:20-21	219
Psa. 107	165	**Prov. 1:30-33**	**219**
Psa. 107:1, 8	**165**	Prov. 1:32	216
Psa. 107:17	**167**	Prov. 3:1-10	221
Psa. 107:43	166	**Prov. 3:11-12**	**221**
Psa. 110:1-3	**169**	**Prov. 3:35**	**215**, 216
Psa. 118:5	**171**	Prov. 4:3-4	217
Psa. 118:6	**173**	**Prov. 4:18-19**	**223**
Psa. 118:9	**175**	**Prov. 4:19**	**225**
Psa. 118:14	176	**Prov. 4:20**	**227**
Psa. 118:24	**177**	**Prov. 4:20, 22**	**229**
Psa. 119:9	**179**	Prov. 4:23	63, 144, **231**
Psa. 119:71	**167, 181**	Prov. 5:8	242
Psa. 119:105	318	**Prov. 5:18-19**	125, **233**
Psa. 119:127-128	**183**, 282	**Prov. 5:18-20**	**235, 237,** 242
Psa. 119:147	**185**	**Prov. 5:22**	**239**
Psa. 119:160	**187**	Prov. 6:6-8	318
Psa. 119:162	**189**	**Prov. 6:25**	21, 242, 244
Psa. 121:3-4	**9**	Prov. 6:26	242
Psa. 127:3	**193**	**Prov. 6:32**	**241**
Psa. 127:4-5	**211**	**Prov. 7:10**	**243**
Psa. 128:1-2	**191**	**Prov. 9:10**	**213**
Psa. 128:1-4	125, **195**	**Prov. 9:12**	**245**
Psa. 128:3-5	**197**	Prov. 9:16	242
Psa. 130:5	**67**	**Prov. 10:7**	**247**
Psa. 131:1	**199**	Prov. 10:12	348
Psa. 139:13-14	**201**	**Prov. 10:19**	**249**
Psa. 139:23	**95**	Prov. 10:23	271
Psa. 142:4	**203, 205**	**Prov. 11:12**	**251**
Psa. 143	209	**Prov. 11:13**	**253**
Psa. 143:1	**207**	**Prov. 11:16, 22**	**255**
Psa. 143:4, 7	**209**	**Prov. 11:24**	**257**
Psa. 144:15	**211**	Prov. 11:25	318
Psa. 146:3	**175**	Prov. 11:29	216
Psa. 146:5	176		

Prov. 12:15	215, **259**	Prov. 19:12	62
Prov. 12:25	**261**	**Prov. 19:22**	**301**
Prov. 13:10	**263**	Prov. 19:26	218
Prov. 13:12	**293**	Prov. 19:29	215
Prov. 13:15	**265**	Prov. 20:3	216, **303**
Prov. 13:19	216	**Prov. 20:9**	**305**
Prov. 13:20	216	**Prov. 20:25**	**307**
Prov. 13:21, 23	267	**Prov. 20:29**	**309**
Prov. 14:7	216	**Prov. 21:2**	**295**
Prov. 14:8	216, **269**	**Prov. 21:9**	**277**
Prov. 14:9	**271**	**Prov. 21:15**	**311**
Prov. 14:16	215	**Prov. 21:17**	**313**
Prov. 14:34	**273**	Prov. 21:20	216
Prov. 15:1	**275**	**Prov. 22:2, 4**	**315**
Prov. 15:2	216	**Prov. 22:3**	**317**
Prov. 15:5	215	Prov. 22:6	217
Prov. 15:18	**277**	Prov. 22:7	318
Prov. 15:22	**259**	**Prov. 22:13**	**319**
Prov. 15:32	348	**Prov. 22:15**	**321**
Prov. 16:19	**279**	**Prov. 23:4-5**	**323**
Prov. 16:25	**281**	Prov. 23:9	215
Prov. 16:32	342	Prov. 23:18	24
Prov. 17:6	**283, 287**	Prov. 23:24-25	218
Prov. 17:9	348	**Prov. 23:31-33**	**325**
Prov. 17:10	215	**Prov. 24:6**	**259**
Prov. 17:17	**285**	**Prov. 24:10**	**327**
Prov. 17:24	216	**Prov. 24:17-18**	**329**
Prov. 17:25	218, **287**	Prov. 24:27	317, **331**
Prov. 17:27	**275**	**Prov. 25:15**	**275**
Prov. 17:28	216	**Prov. 25:19**	**333**
Prov. 18:1	**289**	**Prov. 25:21-22**	**335**
Prov. 18:2	216, **249**	**Prov. 25:26**	**337**
Prov. 18:10-11	**291**	**Prov. 25:27**	**339**
Prov. 18:14	**293**	**Prov. 25:28**	**341**
Prov. 18:17	**295**	Prov. 26:3	215
Prov. 18:22	**297, 299**	Prov. 26:6	216
Prov. 18:24	**285**	Prov. 26:11	216

Prov. 26:27	**343**	Eccl. 3:18-22	391
Prov. 27:1	**345**	**Eccl. 4:8**	**369**
Prov. 27:2	**339**	**Eccl. 5:1-2**	**379**
Prov. 27:5-6	**347**	Eccl. 5:5	308
Prov. 27:7	**349**	**Eccl. 5:10**	**369, 381**
Prov. 27:12	315	**Eccl. 5:10-12**	**383**
Prov. 27:18	**351**	Eccl. 5:11-12	382
Prov. 27:22	216	Eccl. 5:18	391
Prov. 27:23-27	316	**Eccl. 6:1-2**	**385**
Prov. 27:24	**317**	Eccl. 6:3-6	391
Prov. 28:2	**353**	**Eccl. 6:7**	**369**, 382
Prov. 28:13	**355**	Eccl. 7:20	107, 305
Prov. 28:26	215	**Eccl. 7:29**	**107**
Prov. 29:11	216	Eccl. 8:15	391
Prov. 29:15	**321**	**Eccl. 8:16 - 9:1**	**387**
Prov. 29:18	192	**Eccl. 8:17**	**389**
Prov. 29:20	**249**	Eccl. 9:2-6	391
Prov. 30:18-19	**357**	**Eccl. 9:9**	125, **391**
Prov. 31:10-31	359, 366	**Eccl. 11:5**	**393**
Prov. 31:10, 23	125, **359**	**Eccl. 11:9-10**	**395**, 397
Prov. 31:10-11, 27-28	**361**	Eccl. 12:1	392, **397**
Prov. 31:11-12	278	Eccl. 12:13-14	41, 368, 372, 374, 392
Prov. 31:25, 30-31	**363**	Song of Solomon	236
Prov. 31:26	301	**S. of S. 4:12, 13, 15**	**399**
Prov. 31:27	366	Isa. 5:20	188
Prov. 31:28-29	278, 366	Isa. 6:5	305
Prov. 31:30	**365**	**Isa. 29:19**	**279**
Eccl. 1:2	**367**	Isa. 40:14	26
Eccl. 1:8	**369**	**Isa. 40:26**	**59**
Eccl. 1:14	367	**Isa. 59:9-10**	**225**
Eccl. 2:1	**313**	Isa. 59:9-15	188
Eccl. 2:11, 17	**371**	**Jer. 3:21**	**159**
Eccl. 2:17	**373**	**Jer. 5:4**	**69**
Eccl. 2:24-26	391	Jer. 10:23	192
Eccl. 3:3	**375**	Jer. 17:9	270
Eccl. 3:11	**377**	**Lam. 1:21**	**203**
Eccl. 3:13	313		

Eze. 33:11	330	Lk. 6:27-28	329
Hos. 13:6	160	Lk. 6:37-38	252
Mic. 6:3	28	Lk. 6:38	257
Mal. 2:14-15	**233**	Lk. 12:15	324, 370, 382, 384, 386
Matt. 5:5	**83,** 87	Lk. 12:31, 33	370
Matt. 5:13-16	274	Lk. 14:7-11	340
Matt. 5:22	252	Lk. 15:11-24	51
Matt. 5:23-24	356	Lk. 15:14	314
Matt. 5:28	**21,** 198, 242, 244	Lk. 15:16	349
Matt. 5:43-48	329	Lk. 15:21	356
Matt. 5:44	120	**Lk. 16:15**	**95**
Matt. 6:19-20	**189**	Lk. 18:9-12	305
Matt. 6:25, 34	261	**Lk. 18:11**	**131**
Matt. 7:7-11	207	Lk. 18:13-14	306
Matt. 7:12	329	Lk. 22:44	142
Matt. 7:15	183	Lk. 22:48	28
Matt. 7:21-23	282	Lk. 22:34	120
Matt. 12:36-37	249	Jn. 1:1	26
Matt. 16:13-16	32	Jn. 8:9	18
Matt. 16:18	**375**	**Jn. 9:1**	**5**
Matt. 18:6-7	244	Jn. 9:3	6
Matt. 18:20	379	**Jn. 9:4**	**139**
Matt. 19:1-15	198	Jn. 9:38	26
Matt. 19:24	101	**Jn. 11:40**	**123**
Matt. 22:37-40	326	Jn. 14:6	183
Matt. 23:27	188	Jn. 15:15	285
Matt. 24:24	183	Jn. 18:37-38	188
Matt. 26:35, 69-75	339	Jn. 20:28	26
Matt. 27:4	356	Ac. 2:34-36	169
Matt. 27:46	94, 204	Ac. 8:8, 39	110
Mk. 1:35	185	Ac. 8:16	336
Mk. 3:5	33	Ac. 9:36, 39	247
Mk. 6:31	99	Ac. 13:5, 13	333
Mk. 14:35-36	208	Ac. 15:37-40	334
Mk. 16:2, 9	185	Ac. 16:34	110
Lk. 5:8	305	Ac. 17:21	199

Ac. 17:31	41
Ac. 20:35	**257**
Ac. 26:5-11	282
Rom. 1:20	**57, 377**
Rom. 1:28-30	**253**
Rom. 3:23	107
Rom. 5:2	110
Rom. 5:10	330
Rom. 5:12	108
Rom. 7:24	306
Rom. 8:31	**117, 142**
Rom. 8:36	80
Rom. 10:17	32
Rom. 12:12	110
Rom. 12:16	340
Rom. 12:19	38
Rom. 12:21	336
Rom. 13:1-4	103
Rom. 13:10	38, 78, 329
Rom. 14:13, 21	244, 326
1 Cor. 3:16	379
1 Cor. 3:21	88
1 Cor. 4:5	340
1 Cor. 7:1-5	236, 238
1 Cor. 10:10	161
1 Cor. 13:4	340
1 Cor. 13:6	**253**
1 Cor. 14:12	376
1 Cor. 15:53	**7**
2 Cor. 4:8	293
2 Cor. 4:17-18	124, 294
2 Cor. 7:5	142
2 Cor. 8:12	170
2 Cor. 9:5, 7	170
2 Cor. 11:13	183
2 Cor. 11:27	142
2 Cor. 12:7-9	208
2 Cor. 12:20	33, 263
2 Cor. 13:5	51, 270
Gal. 2:4	184
Gal. 2:20	132
Gal. 5:13	329
Gal. 5:20	33, 263
Gal. 6:7-8	246
Eph. 2:8	268
Eph. 2:19	126
Eph. 2:20-21	379
Eph. 4:12	376
Eph. 4:26-27	33
Eph. 4:32	**301**
Eph. 5:22ff	198
Eph. 5:29	400
Eph. 6:2-3	**127**
Phil. 1:25-26	334
Phil. 2:14	**161**
Phil. 2:3-4	340
Phil. 2:19-22	334
Phil. 3:12	306
Phil. 4:4	110
Phil. 4:6	**129**
Phil. 4:6-7	262
Phil. 4:10-11	158
Col. 1:24	182
Col. 1:28	274
Col. 3:18-21	198
Col. 4:6	**275**
1 Thess. 5:16	110
2 Thess. 2:11-12	394
1 Tim. 2:9	**243**
1 Tim. 4:8	230
1 Tim. 5:1-2	126
1 Tim. 6:7-8	106, 382
1 Tim. 6:18-19	257, 384
2 Tim. 2:22	309

Reference	Page(s)
2 Tim. 3:2-4	**313,** 314
2 Tim. 4:11	334
2 Tim. 4:16	336
2 Tim. 4:18	**79**
Tit. 2:13	26
Tit. 3:8	226
Phe. 14	170
Phe. 15	394
Phe. 21	334
Heb. 1:8	26
Heb. 1:13	169
Heb. 3:12	144, 178
Heb. 5:7	182, 208
Heb. 6:19	294
Heb. 9:7	62
Heb. 11:7	320
Heb. 12:3-11	221
Jas. 1:19	250, 264
Jas. 1:27	198
Jas. 2:13	252
Jas. 3:2	77, 275, 343
Jas. 4:8	**63**
Jas. 4:13-16	346
Jas. 5:16	**73,** 356
1 Pet. 1:6-8	110
1 Pet. 3:8	126
1 Pet. 3:10-12	77
1 Pet. 4:8	348
1 Pet. 5:6-7	**205**
1 Pet. 5:8	320
2 Pet. 1:5-9	160
2 Pet. 2:1	184
2 Pet. 3:10	88
2 Pet. 3:18	62
1 Jn. 1:7	**223**
1 Jn. 1:8	52, 306
1 Jn. 2:14	18
1 Jn. 3:20	**95**
1 Jn. 4:1	184
1 Jn. 4:8, 16	26
Rev. 3:16	184
Rev. 21:1	88
Rev. 21:4	116

Subject Index

Aaron, 337
Abner, 115
Abortion, 163, 201
Abraham, 389
Absalom, 113, 116, 248
Addiction, 21, 239
Adultery, 198, 233, 237, 241
    How to avoid, 238, 242
Ahaz (king), 150
Ahithophel, 12, 112, 113
Alcohol, 325, 374
Aldrin, Buzz (astronaut), 40
Alexander the Great, 342
Anders, Bill (astronaut), 39
Anger
    Addictive habit, 239, 341
    How to manage, 34, 172
    In marriage, 277
    Legitimate versus sinful, 33
    Response to frustration, 16, 168, 224, 275
Antiochus Epiphanes, 30
Anxiety, 65, 68, 81, 103, 141, 261, 364, 383, 395
Apollo (space program), 8, 39
April Fool's Day, 215
Armstrong, Neil (astronaut), 40
Asaph, 133
Asherah, 53

Atheism
- *"Don'ts,"* 69
- *Morality and,* 96, 165
- *Obstacles to,* 49
- *Rise of militant,* 47

Baal, 53
Baldwin, Alec, 227
Barna, George, 69
Barnes, Albert, 185
Beatitudes, 84, 87

Beauty
- *A function of personality,* 145

"Be Careful Little Eyes" (song), 231
Betrayal, 113

Bible, the
- *As God's word,* 65, 99, 187
- *Source of encouragement,* 121, 192, 210, 262
- *Source of self-discipline,* 76
- *Source of wisdom,* 183, 214, 245, 270, 276, 282
- *Value of,* 190

Bildad, 19, 23
Borman, Frank (astronaut), 38
Brooks, David, 127
Brumley, Albert, 133
Caiaphas (high priest), 30
Calvinism, 1, 107
Canaanites, 163

Character
- *As a bulwark against evil,* 337
- *Damaged by addictions,* 239
- *Defined,* 248
- *Discernment as a function of,* 223
- *Hardship and,* 16, 24, 181
- *Honesty as a function of,* 73, 78, 168, 308, 355
- *In choosing a mate,* 256
- *In identifying false teachers,* 304
- *In the teachings of Jesus,* 390
- *Money and,* 315, 384
- *National,* 274, 353

    Optimism as a function of, 146
    Pride and, 263
Chemosh, 53
Chiasm, 359
Child sacrifice, 163
Children, 193, 217, 227, 284, 321, 360
Choices
    Consequences of, 76, 245, 265, 269, 273
    Linked to view of God, 72, 82
    Unique attribute of humans, 75
Church, the
    Definition, 376
    Councils, 25
    False, 184
    Healthy, 258
    Involvement in, 352
    Leadership, 180
    Source of companionship, 262, 334
Clinton, Bill, 241
Clothing, 243
Cohabitation, 226
Complacency, 160
Complaining, 203
    Root cause of, 162, 177
Confession (of sin), 73, 356
Conscience, the, 14, 95
Contentment, 106, 157, 230, 280, 324, 350, 371, 373, 382, 383
Counselors, 259, 264
Courtship, 357
Covetousness, 296, 386
Coyote, Wile E., 343
Creation
    As evidence for God, 39, 48, 49, 58, 59, 210
    Orderly nature of, 60, 156
Critical Race Theory, 201
Criticism, 250, 251, 347
Culture
    Influence on faith, 68, 69, 108, 127, 179, 235, 358, 373, 383, 391, 395
Cynicism, 42, 114, 150, 188, 221, 310

Daniel, 343
David
    Bathsheba and, 109, 116, 207, 265
    Faith of, 32, 37, 56, 67, 71, 79, 82, 92, 116, 118, 119, 121, 123, 181, 205, 209
    Hasty judgment of, 295
    Honest heart of, 51, 74, 96
    Leadership principles of, 149
    Magnanimous spirit of, 330
    Moral code of, 63, 77
    Persecuted by others, 31, 71, 79, 81, 91, 93, 111, 115, 117, 205, 285
    Positive attitude of, 55, 72, 81, 112, 118, 145
    Repentance of, 109
    Sins in youth, 17
    Sorrow in the life of, 31, 45, 79, 91, 93, 111, 113, 115, 117, 181, 207, 209
    Weakness of, 35, 72, 107
Dawkins, Richard, 47
de Maistre, Joseph, 354
Death, 7, 11, 80, 89, 91, 102, 139, 151, 212, 247, 292, 345, 373, 377, 385, 391
Declaration of Independence, 353
Demas, 113
Dependability, 78, 333
Depression, 14, 72, 137, 203, 205, 261, 322, 358, 360, 362, 364, 395
Depression, The Great, 349
Discouragement, 120, 178, 204, 209, 358
Divorce, 42, 198, 226, 233, 237, 271, 361
Dorcas (Tabitha), 247
Douthat, Ross, 57
Dunn, Irina, 361
Edification, 376
Edwards, John, 241
Elihu, 26
Elijah, 203
Eliphaz, 5, 19, 23
Enlightenment, the, 58
Ensign, John, 241

Economic inequality, 101, 267
Eternity, 377
Ethiopian eunuch, 110
Ethnicity, 202
Euripides, 398
Eve, 281, 400
Faith
- *How to identify a strong,* 327
- *How to strengthen a weak,* 209
- *In response to hardship,* 44, 46, 87, 90, 92, 94, 98, 104, 112, 118, 123, 182, 206

False religion, 183
Family
- *As primary support group,* 125, 197, 211, 287
- *Biblical teaching on,* 197, 284, 359
- *Grandparents in,* 283, 288
- *Limitations of,* 173
- *Social decay and,* 226, 274, 360
- *Sources of dysfunction in,* 127, 179, 198, 324, 361
- *Traditions,* 195

Fear (see *Anxiety*)
Feminism, 164, 256, 361, 360, 363, 365
Flood, the Great, 155
Fool, the
- *Description of, in Proverbs,* 215
- *Lack of self-awareness in,* 270
- *Poor decision-making of,* 168, 219, 318

Foresight, 317
Frankl, Viktor, 171, 294
Free will, 78, 170, 178, 245, 273
Friends and friendship, 262
- *Bad,* 19, 71, 111, 113, 254, 333
- *Benefits of,* 290
- *Constructive criticism in,* 347
- *Foundation of,* 136, 285

Gaffigan, Jim, 321
Gallagher, Maggie, 226
Gender, 202, 255, 277, 357, 365, 396
Generosity, 170, 230, 247, 257, 268, 316, 359, 386
Glenn, John (astronaut), 40

God
- *Anger of,* 33
- *As foundation of life,* 176, 211
- *As supreme authority,* 43, 98, 147, 171, 174, 176, 245
- *Evidence for seen in creation,* 39, 48, 49, 58, 59, 95
- *False,* 53
- *Fear of,* 1, 214, 372
- *Foolishness of denying,* 47
- *Forgetting,* 159
- *Godly life as evidence for,* 48
- *Justice of,* 24, 38, 41, 44, 104, 166, 172
- *Laughter of,* 29, 82
- *Love of, for humanity,* 117, 204, 206
- *Mercy of,* 356
- *Motive in serving,* 2
- *Not subject to fatigue,* 10
- *Omniscience of,* 95, 231
- *Providence of,* 65, 79, 119, 206, 346, 393
- *Questioning humanity,* 27
- *Trinitarian nature of,* 25
- *Trusting (or waiting on),* 65, 67, 71, 79, 82, 87, 94, 98, 100, 104, 112, 116, 122, 123, 134, 136, 138, 142, 152, 172, 174, 206, 222, 346, 388, 390
- *Worshiping,* 379

Gossip, 251, 253, 296, 344
Gottman, John, 301
Government
- *Foundation of good,* 150
- *Growth of,* 353
- *Limitations of,* 42, 103, 173, 175, 268, 353, 387

Grandparents, 197, 212, 283
Greek philosophy, 199, 269
Growth, spiritual, 52, 62, 74, 114, 144, 160, 224, 310
Guilt
- *Cause for anxiety,* 13, 72, 73
- *Consequence of sin,* 74, 109, 358

Habits, personal, 22, 74, 140, 185, 195, 239, 316
Haman, 38, 343
Hands, clean, 64

Happiness
- *As a choice,* 4, 14, 146, 152, 158, 177, 293
- *Fake,* 13
- *In families,* 126, 195, 211, 360
- *Not the ultimate goal in life,* 191
- *Secret to,* 77, 178, 211, 266, 293, 312, 382

Harris, Sam, 47
Harvey (hurricane), 155
Hate, 96, 251, 330
Health, physical
- *Affected by lifestyle choices,* 229, 246

Heart
- *Biblical definition of,* 143
- *Deceitfulness of,* 270
- *Eternity in,* 377
- *Grateful,* 350
- *Hard,* 143
- *Honestly mistaken,* 62
- *Proud,* 160
- *Pure,* 63, 305
- *Seen by God,* 95
- *Source of behavior,* 95, 144, 231, 242, 261, 266, 268, 282, 344
- *Tender,* 143
- *Truth in the,* 51
- *Unbelieving,* 162, 178
- *Willing,* 170

Hedonism, 188
Heman the Ezrahite, 137
History
- *Controlled by God,* 85, 88, 152, 166, 390
- *Pattern of,* 43, 69, 82, 87, 274

Hoffer, Eric, 370
Holt, Jim, 48
Homosexuality and gay marriage, 42, 198, 226, 235, 338
Honesty, 51, 78, 307, 356
Hope
- *As a source of encouragement,* 56, 80, 82, 90, 92, 116, 181, 212, 292, 294
- *Bolstered by prayer,* 120

Hopelessness, 12, 138, 391

Hospitality, 126
Humility, 18, 58, 74, 91, 168, 199, 221, 264, 279, 305, 340, 393
Hypocrisy
    Defined, 15, 188
    False hope of, 15
Idolatry, 53, 337
Ignorance
    Sins of, 61, 108
    Willful, 62
    Youthful, 17, 108, 321
Inherit the earth, 83, 87
Integrity, 70, 91, 149, 338, 356
Intentions, good
    Inadequacy of, 19
Introverts, 289
Irwin, James (astronaut), 40
Islam, 169
Israel,
    In Canaan, 163
    Wilderness experience, 143, 157, 159, 161, 177
"Is That All There Is?" (song), 373
Jefferson, Thomas, 354
Jesus
    Advocate of traditional family, 197
    Anger of, 33
    As the basis of a healthy self-identity, 132
    Deity of, 26
    Messianic promises of, 389
    Prayer in the life of, 120
    Resurrection of, 8, 30
    Suffering of, 94, 167, 182, 204, 208
    Urgency in the work of, 140
    Voluntary nature of our service to, 169
Job
    Faith of, 1, 16, 182
    Questions of, 27, 166
    Sins of, in youth, 17
    Sufferings of, 1, 5, 11, 13, 167, 182
    Theology of, 5, 15, 20, 23, 167
Jonathan (David's friend), 115, 117

Joseph, suffering of, 93, 182, 394
Joseph, brothers of, 38
Josiah (king), 143
Joy
- *As a personal choice,* 178
- *Effect on personality,* 145
- *Examples of, in New Testament,* 110
- *Justice and,* 311
- *Product of forgiveness,* 109, 142, 329
- *Product of healthy family,* 126, 195, 218, 233, 236, 283, 288
- *Product of serving God,* 192, 272, 279

Judas, 113
Judgment
- *As incentive to righteousness,* 41, 95, 372, 392, 397
- *Of the wicked,* 29, 38, 44, 85, 88

Justice
- *Characteristic of stable societies,* 268, 296
- *Duty of rulers,* 149
- *God and,* 23, 37, 83, 85
- *Injustice eventually answered by,* 101, 103, 133
- *Joy in doing,* 311
- *Mercy greater than,* 335

Kidner, Derek, 272, 323, 383
Korah, Sons of, 93
Kuhn, Thomas, 58
LaHaye, Tim & Beverly, 236
Lazarus, 124
Laziness, 62, 106, 239, 267, 319, 354
Leadership
- *Habits of effective,* 185
- *Impact on national character,* 149

Lee, Peggy, 373
Lifestyle
- *Effect on mental health,* 99, 279
- *Godly,* 77, 82, 195
- *Influenced by one's view of God,* 144, 374
- *Money and,* 146, 315, 323, 383, 386
- *Simple,* 199, 279

Loneliness, 125, 203, 205, 362, 358

Love,
- *Definition of,* 26, 329, 340, 347
- *For God,* 114, 282, 326
- *Familial,* 125, 128, 194, 195, 212, 228, 233, 236, 237, 301, 321, 396, 399
- *Humility and,* 340
- *Of enemies,* 44, 65, 329, 335
- *Of God,* 6, 109, 118, 132, 221, 380, 388
- *Of money,* 383, 381
- *Of neighbor,* 38, 78, 174, 253, 285, 347
- *Of pleasure,* 313

MacLaren, Alexander, 378
Mark, John, 333
Marriage
- *Character as the foundation of,* 256, 299, 358
- *Complementary roles in,* 364, 365
- *Conflict in,* 277
- *Gay,* 43
- *Husbands and,* 233, 277, 360, 400
- *Kindness in,* 301
- *Patience in,* 278
- *Sexual pleasure and,* 236, 237, 399
- *Shared experiences essential in,* 286, 297
- *Social decay and,* 226, 361
- *Wives and,* 233, 277, 359, 365

Martha, 124
McMillen, Dr. S. I., 229
Meditation, 124, 210, 262
Meekness
- *Defined,* 83, 88

Meister, Chad, 213
Mephibosheth, 295
Meyer, Stephen, 58
Mill, John Stuart, 371
Molech, 53
Mordecai, 38
Morality,
- A*s evidence for God,* 50

Moses
> *Anger of,* 33
> *Leadership of,* 203
> *View of death,* 139

Nabal, 258
Nash, Ronald, 213
Nebuchadnezzar, 30
Nehemiah, 341
O'Conner, Bryan (astronaut), 40
Older people
> *Sins of,* 310
> *Wisdom of,* 18

Onesimus, 170
Original sin, 107
Parenting
> *Challenges of,* 217, 287, 320
> *Poor,* 179, 227, 396
> *Rewards of,* 198, 284, 288
> *Role of discipline in,* 221, 321
> *Successful,* 193, 195, 217, 227, 321

Parker, Theodore, 85
Patience, 81, 83, 87, 168, 194, 278, 351
Paul
> *Misguided zeal of,* 282
> *Sufferings of,* 142, 182, 208

Peace
> *Consequence of a godly life,* 14, 82, 84, 99, 246, 279
> *Product of trusting God,* 43, 66, 176, 262
> *Seeking,* 78, 99, 264, 371, 373

Pessimism, 31, 367, 391
Pharaoh of the Exodus, 30
Pharisees, 305
Philemon, 170, 334
Philippian jailor, 110
Pleasure, love of, 313
Politics, 97, 149, 175, 241, 274, 353
Polygamy, 198
Pompeii, 21
Pontius Pilate, 30
Pornography, 21, 96, 235, 239, 244

Poverty (see also *Riches*), 102, 267, 314
Prager, Dennis, 127
Prayer
    Family, 196
    For enemies, 78, 120
    Of confession, 73
    Of thanksgiving, 129
    Power of, 119
    Source of encouragement, 119, 121, 123, 138, 174, 209, 262
    Unanswered, 207, 393
Pride, 52, 74, 200, 245, 253, 263, 279, 303, 305, 355
Priorities, 331, 370
Prodigal Son, the, 51, 314, 349
Proverbs
    Choices and consequences as the theme of, 5, 219, 245
Public opinion, 32
Qoheleth, 367
Racism, 201
Relationships
    Broken, 113, 131, 135, 205, 246, 255, 265, 273
    Enhanced by one's relationship with God, 136, 144, 211, 226
    Healthy, 51, 74, 264, 302, 357
    Necessity of, 290
    Role of honesty in, 74
Remnant, godly, 70
Repentance, 168, 240, 266, 356
Reputation, 247
Responsibility, Personal, 76, 108, 152, 178, 180, 219, 223, 232, 245, 265, 267, 269, 317, 331, 397
Revenge, 24, 38, 329, 336
Riches (see also *Poverty*)
    Contentment and, 106, 279, 349, 381
    Deceitfulness of, 101, 106, 122, 174, 291, 323, 370, 381, 383, 386
    Displayed in housing, 105
    Equal with poverty at death, 102, 190, 385
    Proper use of, 315
Samaria, 110
Sanford, Mark, 241

Satan
    Cynical nature of, 1
    Deceitfulness of, 183
    Defeated in the resurrection, 30
    Role in suffering, 1, 20, 327
Saul, King, 12, 282
Savastano, Donald, 385
Science
    Compatible with religion, 57
Self-deception, 52, 216, 281
Self-discipline, 22, 76, 246, 266, 267, 276, 341
Self-knowledge, 269
Self-pity, 206
Self-praise, 339
Selfishness, 12, 63, 96, 164, 246, 257, 264, 290, 350, 381
Sex and sexuality
    Biblical view of, 235, 238, 242, 358, 399
    Clothing and, 243
Sexual revolution, 128, 164, 361, 363
Sheen, Martin, 381
Sheol, 102
Shimei, 252
Sickness, 91, 229, 265
Simpleton, the, 318
Simplicity (lifestyle), 199, 279
Sin
    Confession of, 73, 356
    Effect on character, 355
    Generational, 309
    Mental health and, 73, 164, 261, 362, 364, 392
    Nature of man and, 107, 269, 281
    Of ignorance, 61, 108
    Physical health and, 229
    Social impacts of, 225, 265, 271, 274
Skepticism, 368
Sleep, 9, 176, 185
Smith, Emily Esfahani, 301
Social collapse
    As a consequence of rejecting God, 42, 69, 274
    How to deal with, 43

Social media, 179, 396
Socialization, value of, 290
Sophistry, 187
Sorrow, 115, 181
Spitzer, Eliot, 241
Steinem, Gloria, 361
Stenger, Victor, 47
Suffering
- *Answered in the resurrection,* 30, 102, 134
- *As a consequence of sin,* 5, 79, 165, 168, 207, 274
- *As a fact of life,* 97, 165, 167
- *As a means of strengthening faith,* 91, 114, 124, 168, 181, 208
- *As a test of faith,* 44, 45, 327
- *As an opportunity to serve others,* 6
- *Attitude in response to,* 158, 161, 168, 182
- *Hidden benefits of,* 45, 181, 394
- *Inexplicable nature of,* 27, 93, 141, 166, 390
- *Inflicted by the wicked,* 87, 103, 133, 135, 173
- *Natural,* 155, 165
- *Not always a consequence of sin,* 6, 13, 15, 20, 23, 80, 167, 221, 246
- *Wrong approach to comforting,* 19

Suicide, 11, 164, 362, 374, 392, 395
Tantaros, Andrea, 364
Thankfulness, a spirit of, 129, 166, 350
Thanksgiving (holiday), 129
"This World Is Not My Home" (song), 133
Timidity, 337
Timothy, 334
Tomorrow, 261, 345
Tongue, the, 77, 249, 275, 303, 307, 343, 380
Trust (*see* Faith)
Truth
- *About self,* 51, 356
- *Character and,* 78, 295
- *Definition of,* 99, 187
- *Obscured,* 32, 183
- *Rejected for a lie,* 53, 184, 188, 273, 395

Tyrants
- *Laughed at by God,* 29, 82
- *Oppressing the weak,* 103

Venker, Suzanne, 364

Washington, George, 129

Weakness
- *As part of life,* 35, 74, 208, 328

Welch, Edward, 239

Wesley, John, 25

Wisdom
- *Antithesis of foolishness,* 215, 245, 272
- *Defined,* 245
- *God's word as source of,* 121, 190, 210, 214, 270
- *Growth in,* 223, 269
- *Learned by counselors,* 259, 263, 290
- *Learned by experience,* 17, 276, 397
- *Personified,* 219

Work, 54, 106, 158, 246, 260, 313, 315, 323, 331, 351, 363, 365, 370, 372, 375, 385, 399

Worldview, 98, 147, 152, 168, 178, 179
- *Defined,* 213

Worry (*see* Anxiety)

Youth
- *Enthusiasm of,* 18, 397
- *Loss of faith among,* 179, 395
- *Sins of,* 17, 309

Ziba, 295

Zimri, 12

Zophar, 19, 23

www.ingramcontent.com/pod-product-compliance
Lightning Source LLC
Chambersburg PA
CBHW060048190426
43201CB00034B/441